UNDERSTANDING WILLIAM GIBSON

UNDERSTANDING CONTEMPORARY AMERICAN LITERATURE

Matthew J. Bruccoli, Founding Editor

Linda Wagner-Martin, Series Editor

Volumes on

Edward Albee | Sherman Alexie | Nelson Algren | Paul Auster
Nicholson Baker | John Barth | Donald Barthelme | The Beats
Thomas Berger | The Black Mountain Poets | Robert Bly | T. C. Boyle
Truman Capote | Raymond Carver | Michael Chabon | Fred Chappell
Chicano Literature | Contemporary American Drama
Contemporary American Horror Fiction
Contemporary American Literary Theory
Contemporary American Science Fiction, 1926–1970
Contemporary American Science Fiction, 1970–2000
Contemporary Chicana Literature | Robert Coover | Philip K. Dick | James Dickey
E. L. Doctorow | Rita Dove | Don DeLillo | Dave Eggers | John Gardner
George Garrett | Tim Gautreaux | William Gibson | John Hawkes | Joseph Heller
Lillian Hellman | Beth Henley | James Leo Herlihy | David Henry Hwang
John Irving | Randall Jarrell | Charles Johnson | Diane Johnson | Adrienne Kennedy
William Kennedy | Jack Kerouac | Jamaica Kincaid | Etheridge Knight
Tony Kushner | Ursula K. Le Guin | Jonathan Letham | Denise Levertov
Bernard Malamud | David Mamet | Bobbie Ann Mason | Colum McCann
Cormac McCarthy | Jill McCorkle | Carson McCullers | W. S. Merwin
Arthur Miller | Steven Millhauser | Lorrie Moore | Toni Morrison's Fiction
Vladimir Nabokov | Gloria Naylor | Joyce Carol Oates | Tim O'Brien
Flannery O'Connor | Cynthia Ozick | Suzan-Lori Parks | Walker Percy
Katherine Anne Porter | Richard Powers | Reynolds Price | Annie Proulx
Thomas Pynchon | Theodore Roethke | Philip Roth | Richard Russo | May Sarton
Hubert Selby, Jr. | Mary Lee Settle | Sam Shepard | Neil Simon | Isaac Bashevis Singer
Jane Smiley | Gary Snyder | William Stafford | Robert Stone | Anne Tyler
Gerald Vizenor | Kurt Vonnegut | David Foster Wallace | Robert Penn Warren
James Welch | Eudora Welty | Colson Whitehead | Tennessee Williams
August Wilson | Charles Wright

UNDERSTANDING

WILLIAM GIBSON

Gerald Alva Miller, Jr.

The University of South Carolina Press

Published by the University of South Carolina Press
Columbia, South Carolina 29208

www.sc.edu/uscpress

Manufactured in the United States of America

25 24 23 22 21 20 19 18 17 16
10 9 8 7 6 5 4 3 2 1

Library of Congress Cataloging-in-Publication Data
can be found at http://catalog.loc.gov/.

ISBN 978-1-61117-633-9 (cloth)
ISBN 978-1-61117-634-6 (ebook)

This book was printed on recycled paper with
30 percent postconsumer waste content.

To the memory of my father, Jerry Miller,
Who taught me to love science fiction.
For my mother, Debbie Miller,
Who has always supported me no matter what.
For Jane, my daughter,
Who has brought new inspiration into my life.
And, finally, for Leigh,
Without whom none of this would have been possible.

CONTENTS

SERIES EDITOR'S PREFACE

The Understanding Contemporary American Literature series was founded by the estimable Matthew J. Bruccoli (1931–2008), who envisioned these volumes as guides or companions for students as well as good nonacademic readers, a legacy that will continue as new volumes are developed to fill in gaps among the nearly one hundred series volumes published to date and to embrace a host of new writers only now making their marks on our literature.

As Professor Bruccoli explained in his preface to the volumes he edited, because much influential contemporary literature makes special demands, "the word understanding in the titles was chosen deliberately. Many willing readers lack an adequate understanding of how contemporary literature works; that is, of what the author is attempting to express and the means by which it is conveyed." Aimed at fostering this understanding of good literature and good writers, the criticism and analysis in the series provide instruction in how to read certain contemporary writers—explicating their material, language, structures, themes, and perspectives— and facilitate a more profitable experience of the works under discussion.

In the twenty-first century Professor Bruccoli's prescience gives us an avenue to publish expert critiques of significant contemporary American writing. The series continues to map the literary landscape and to provide both instruction and enjoyment. Future volumes will seek to introduce new voices alongside canonized favorites, to chronicle the changing literature of our times, and to remain, as Professor Bruccoli conceived, contemporary in the best sense of the word.

Linda Wagner-Martin, Series Editor

ABBREVIATIONS

Works by William Gibson

BC	*Burning Chrome*
CZ	*Count Zero*
DTPF	*Distrust That Particular Flavor*
N	*Neuromancer*
PR	*Pattern Recognition*

Other Frequently Cited Works

WGLC	Tom Henthorne's *William Gibson: A Literary Companion*
WGO	Lance Olsen's *William Gibson*
WGW	Gary Westfahl's *William Gibson*

CHAPTER 1

Understanding William Gibson

Born on March 17, 1948, William Ford Gibson is often given the moniker "father of cyberpunk," the subgenre of science fiction (or sci-fi or SF) that focuses on computer information systems, corporate control, and hyperurbanized spaces. Ironically, Gibson's early years were not spent in an urban environment or in an area known for technological advancement. Born in the coastal town of Conway, South Carolina, he spent the bulk of his childhood in Wytheville, a small Virginia town in the Appalachian Mountains (Dellinger 1). As Andrew Ross and Scott Bukatman discuss, many of the major cyberpunk authors also hailed unexpectedly from southern locales instead of from the major northern cities one might expect. Bruce Sterling, John Shirley, and Rudy Rucker, for example, were born in Brownsville, Texas; Houston, Texas; and Louisville, Kentucky, respectively.[1] Despite his rural upbringing, Gibson became a dual citizen of Canada and the United States and a critic and visionary of the digital age.

From the Rural to the Virtual: A Brief Chronology of Gibson's Life

Gibson spent his first eight years in various parts of the South. His father, William Ford Gibson, Jr., managed a construction company that did plumbing work at Oak Ridge, where "the first atomic bomb was built" (Feller). Gibson's father died when the boy was eight, after which he and his mother, Elizabeth Otey, moved back to her hometown of Wytheville, Virginia (Feller). Because his mother was the town librarian, Gibson developed an early passion for books, and his writing style was influenced equally by sources as diverse as hard-boiled crime authors such as Raymond Chandler and postmodern novelists such as Thomas Pynchon (Dellinger 1). But it was the Classics Illustrated comic book version of *The Time Machine* that led Gibson to H. G. Wells's original novel and the genre of science fiction (Feller). At this time in the 1950s and 1960s, Gibson was inundated by science fiction from all sides. Gibson developed a "voracious reading" habit that included Philip K. Dick's classic *The Man in the High Castle* (1962), as well as "other major science fiction writers of the 1950s, including Alfred Bester, [Robert A.] Heinlein, and Theodor Sturgeon" (*WGW* 11). Television also bombarded him with sci-fi in the form of shows such as *Tom Corbett, Space Cadet* (1950–55), *The Mysterious Dr. Satan* (1940), and *The Twilight Zone* (1959-64), and he found even more sci-fi in genre magazines such as *Galaxy* (*WGW* 10-11). However, Gibson soon discovered an author who would forever transform his outlook not just on science fiction but also on the potential of literature more generally—William S. Burroughs.

Gibson's discovery of Burroughs came at an opportune time—right before his departure from Wytheville. When he was fifteen years old, his mother sent him to a school in Tucson, Arizona, called the Southern Arizona School for Boys (*WGLC* 7). As Gibson explains in his biographical essay "Since 1948" on his website, he made an important discovery before leaving Wytheville: "I had stumbled, in my ceaseless quest for more and/or better science fiction, on a writer named Burroughs—not Edgar Rice but William S., and with him had come his colleagues Kerouac and Ginsberg. . . . The effect, over the next few years, was to make me, at least in terms of my Virginia home, Patient Zero of what would later be called the counterculture" (*DTPF* 22–23). Burroughs showed Gibson the possibilities of combining science-fictional plots with experimental aesthetics, and he also introduced the teenager to a world of hustlers, con artists, and drug addicts that helped shape the plots of Gibson's early works.

When he arrived at the Arizona school, Gibson recounts that he "began the forced invention of a less Lovecraftian persona" (*DTPF* 22–23). Gibson suggests that his acquaintance with the Beat Generation helped him experiment with one identity after another in an attempt to find himself. Then, another tragedy occurred that shaped Gibson's life: his mother died suddenly when he was only eighteen. During this time at school, Gibson began smoking marijuana and frequenting countercultural locations, such as coffeehouses and folk music venues. He was consequently expelled from school and sent back home to Wytheville to live with relatives. Another turning point came when he was called before the local draft board, causing Gibson to leave Wytheville and journey, like so many other young American men during this time period, to Canada to avoid being drafted to fight in the Vietnam War (*WGW* 15–16). In "Since 1948," Gibson characterizes this period of his life by saying that he "joined up with the rest of the Children's Crusade of the day and shortly found myself in Canada, a country I knew almost nothing about. I concentrated on avoiding the draft and staying alive, while trying to make sure that I looked like I was enjoying the Summer of Love" (*DTPF* 23). He "was at once drawn to hippie culture and repelled by it, and he was certainly no idealist or revolutionary," yet the Summer of Love proved to be auspicious for him nonetheless (*WGLC* 36).

Generally considered the high point of the hippie era, the Summer of Love occurred in 1967, a year that witnessed the release of many of the most influential works of psychedelic rock: the self-titled debuts of the Doors, the Grateful Dead, and David Bowie; the Beatles' pair of LSD-fueled albums, *Sgt. Pepper's Lonely Hearts Club Band* and *Magical Mystery Tour;* Jefferson Airplane's *Surrealistic Pillow;* Pink Floyd's first album, *Pipers at the Gates of Dawn;* the Velvet Underground's genre-shattering *The Velvet Underground & Nico;* and the Jimi Hendrix Experience's *Are You Experienced.* This music provided a background that was simultaneously poetic, revolutionary, surrealistic, and consistently obsessed with the ideas of space and mind exploration. During this period, Gibson lived in a hippie neighborhood of Toronto called Yorkville and even appeared as a guide and narrator in a documentary called *Yorkville: Hippie Haven* (1967) for the Canadian Broadcasting Company. He returned to the United States for two years, participated in protests in Washington, D.C., and attended the Woodstock music festival in 1969, an experience that he appears to have found thoroughly repellent. Gibson was even in northern California during the ill-fated Altamont Free Concert (*WGLC* 8).[2] While Gibson came of age during the hippie era, he remained skeptical and pessimistic about it, and another musical generation would provide a much more profound influence on him.

Gibson's period of youthful experimentation began to wane when he returned to Toronto and met his future wife, Deborah Thompson. The couple spent a year traveling in Europe together before returning to Canada where she could resume her university studies. They wed in 1972 and began living in Vancouver, where Deborah completed her B.A. and M.A. degrees at the University of British Columbia (*WGLC* 8). Gibson also became an English major at the University of British Columbia, and Professor Susan Wood's science fiction course directly impacted his career as a writer. Wood prompted Gibson to submit a short story as his final class project instead of a final term paper. With her support, in 1977, Gibson published his first story, "Fragments of a Hologram Rose," in the short-lived science fiction magazine *Unearth,* a periodical that also featured the first publication of fellow cyberpunk Rudy Rucker (*WGO* 5). In 1977 Gibson completed his collegiate studies, and Deborah gave birth to their first son, Graeme (*WGLC* 9). Despite publishing a story, Gibson lacked confidence in himself as a writer until he met Bruce Sterling, a fellow devotee of William S. Burroughs, punk music, and sci-fi. Sterling had already published a novel called *Involution Ocean* (1977), and his promptings helped persuade Gibson to try writing as a full-time profession (*WGO* 5; *WGLC* 9).

Gibson was mostly a stay-at-home father, which allowed him to experiment with his writing, leading to a banner year in 1981. That year witnessed the publication of four stories, two of them in *Omni* magazine, one of the premiere venues for cutting-edge sci-fi. "The Gernsback Continuum" and "Johnny Mnemonic," in particular, began to truly build his reputation. In 1982 he published "Burning Chrome" (also in *Omni*), which more fully developed the Sprawl from "Johnny Mnemonic" and featured the first use of the word "cyberspace." During 1981 and 1982, Gibson also began writing his first novel, having already secured a contract with the legendary sci-fi editor Terry Carr of Ace Books. Gibson continued publishing stories while writing his novel: "Hippie Hat Brain Parasite" and "Red Star, Winter Orbit," his first collaboration with Bruce Sterling, both appeared in 1983 (*WGW* 19).

Another crucial moment in the history of cyberpunk occurred in 1983 at a science fiction convention in Amarillo, Texas, where a panel titled "Behind the Mirrorshades: A Look at Punk SF" featured Gibson, John Shirley, Bruce Sterling, and Lewis Shiner (*WGLC* 10). This panel set the stage for Gibson's future success; however, it was the year 1984, already tinged with sci-fi resonance because of George Orwell's classic dystopian novel *Nineteen Eighty-Four* (1949), that forever changed Gibson's career. July 1984 saw the publication of his short story "New Rose Hotel" and the publication of his first novel, *Neuromancer,* which landed with a resounding bang, garnering all three of the major science fiction awards for the year: the Hugo, the Nebula, and the Philip K. Dick award. It was the first novel to receive this trifecta of accolades. Gibson published two more short stories in 1985 before temporarily abandoning the medium to focus on his novels. Coauthored with Michael Swanwick, "Dogfight" first appeared in *Omni,* and Gibson's final '80s short story, "The Winter Market," appeared in the November 1985 issue of *Vancouver Magazine.* Gibson would not publish another story until 1990 because the bulk of his energy went toward publishing two sequels to *Neuromancer.*

As evidenced by the last line of *Neuromancer,* Gibson never intended for *Neuromancer* to develop into a trilogy, but *Neuromancer*'s popularity and critical success and the various bids for a film adaptation (none of which ever materialized) convinced Gibson to write a sequel, resulting in 1986's *Count Zero* (*WGO* 85). The novel further developed the universe of the Sprawl by introducing almost entirely new characters. In the novel, Gibson experimented with a new narrative structure featuring alternating chapters that focused on different characters whose story lines would later converge toward the climax. He has continued to experiment with this form throughout the rest of his career. Gibson rounded out the "Sprawl Trilogy" with *Mona Lisa Overdrive* (1988) before beginning to pursue alternate interests, particularly in Hollywood.

In this interstice between Gibson's "Sprawl Trilogy" and his "Bridge Trilogy," he worked on a variety of projects: Hollywood screenplays, digital poetry, and a collaborative novel with Bruce Sterling. This period represented a stage of experimentation for Gibson before he returned to his predominant mode—writing novels. His next major work was the collaborative steampunk novel *The Difference Engine* (1990), which he coauthored with fellow cyberpunk Bruce Sterling. An alternative history or counterfactual novel, *The Difference Engine* reimagines Victorian England and such major historical figures as Ada Lovelace and Charles Babbage and remains a highly respected example of the steampunk genre. Gibson also tried to produce various unrealized adaptations of his story "Burning Chrome" and was briefly attached to a film called *Neuro-Hotel,* with Katherine Bigelow slated to direct. He completed a script for *Alien³*, which would have been the follow-up to Ridley Scott's classic *Alien* (1979) and James Cameron's action-packed sequel *Aliens* (1986), but almost nothing remained from Gibson's script when David Fincher's *Alien³* (1992) finally appeared. Gibson's *Alien³* script has never been officially released but can easily be found online (*WGW* 91).

Gibson did have one successful foray into screenwriting with the adaptation of his story "Johnny Mnemonic," which was turned into a major Hollywood film with his friend Robert Longo as director and a cast that included Keanu Reeves, Ice-T, Henry Rollins, and Rutger Hauer. The film features most of the story's basic elements, but Gibson added to the story in order to flesh it out to feature length. The period also produced one other highly influential and original piece of work: *Agrippa: A Book of the Dead* (1992). *Agrippa* was released as a truly multimedia and collaborative text containing a book filled with artwork from Dennis Ashbaugh and a 3.5-inch floppy disk that featured a three-hundred-line poem by Gibson that encrypted itself and became unreadable after one reading. One of the great works of electronic, digital literature, *Agrippa* has remained an object of speculation and mystery since its publication in 1992.

Gibson's next novel eschewed the far-flung settings of the "Sprawl Trilogy" and instead depicted a future only barely extrapolated from the present. This novel would spawn its own trilogy that dealt much less with cyberspace and much more with people's attempts to exist in a media-saturated, economically depressed, and corporate-controlled world. Gibson first introduced this world in the short story "Skinner's Room" (1990), which was originally part of a San Francisco art exhibit. The story subsequently became the basis for his next novel, *Virtual Light*, which appeared in 1993 and was followed by two sequels. Generally referred to as the "Bridge Trilogy," *Virtual Light, Idoru* (1997), and *All Tomorrow's Parties* (1999) explore a world only slightly different from the one of the 1990s, a world in which earthquakes, plagues, and economic crises rocked the planet while reality television and celebrity obsession reached shockingly new and even religious heights. These novels show Gibson beginning to distance himself from traditional sci-fi, and they serve as a "bridge" in his career as well because they provide a transition to his most recent trilogy, which is set in our present world. Gibson rounded out his writing in the 1990s with a host of interesting nonfiction essays for magazines including *Wired,* several more short stories, and two coauthored episodes of the popular sci-fi/horror television series *The X-Files* (1993–2002).

In the 2000s Gibson quit publishing traditional science fiction altogether and began writing novels set in the present; however, certain critics maintain that these works constitute alternate versions of our present. His most recent trilogy, usually called the "Bigend Trilogy" or the "Blue Ant Trilogy," was published between 2003 and 2010 and deals with major historical events such as the September 11 terrorist attacks, the Iraq War, and the 2007 financial crisis. The first novel in the trilogy, *Pattern Recognition* (2003), received accolades, and its two follow-ups (*Spook Country* [2007] and *Zero History* [2010]) also garnered generally positive reviews. The novels increasingly downplay technology in favor of exploring power and the growing sense of quotidian estrangement in the twenty-first century.

Since marrying Deborah, Gibson has led a rather calm personal life, and he has admitted that he prefers to stay home most of the time, traveling to only a select few destinations that he loves. He retains dual-citizenship in the United States and Canada and maintained a blog in the first decade of the twenty-first century but eventually migrated to Twitter, to which he posts on a regular basis. Despite a rather turbulent and countercultural beginning, William Gibson, the postmodern prophet of the cyber age, is actually a rather normal, everyday man who continues to regularly publish novels and articles and consents to interviews upon publisher coercion. His works demonstrate a steady evolution in terms of style, and he remains one of the most consistently fascinating postmodern authors as he continually adapts his style and plots to technological advancements and changes in the sociocultural landscape. Over the course of this study, we will see how his style has metamorphosed in response to the real world and how everyday reality has increasingly become a kind of science fiction itself.

High vs. Low Culture: Gibson's Influences and Aesthetic

To fully appreciate Gibson's place in contemporary literature, some initial explication is required to situate him in the spectrum of twentieth- and twenty-first-century literature. A cutting-edge phenomenon in the 1980s, cyberpunk was declared dead or passé by the end of the decade; nevertheless, the themes of the genre continue to appear in Gibson's later works. Therefore, one must understand how postmodern literature influenced cyberpunk, how cyberpunk itself epitomized postmodern literature, and how cyberpunk remains influential despite having been absorbed into commercial culture and hence stripped of its virile subversiveness. In many ways, cyberpunk represents the postmodern genre par excellence because it thoroughly embodies the disintegration of the boundaries between high and low culture and directly engages with how the simulacrum—the copy without an original—and the crisis of representation have shaped not only our culture but also our relation to knowledge, ethics, and truth. Simultaneously, it imagines the outcome of the ongoing mutation of capitalism. As Fredric Jameson comments, "cyberpunk [is] the supreme literary expression if not of postmodernism, then of late capitalism itself" (*Postmodernism* 419n1). Such themes began to appear in literature during the years following World War II as the dreams of modernity seemed to die in the face of horrors such as the Holocaust and the atomic bomb. Postmodern authors began to interrogate the nature of truth and value; therefore, to fully appreciate Gibson's works, it helps to have some basic grasp of the transition from modernity to postmodernity.

To start, one must understand the distinction between modernity and modernism. Although these terms receive varying definitions and histories depending upon the critic, theorist, or philosopher, we can lay out some basic principles to help simultaneously differentiate the two concepts and provide the necessary juxtaposition of ideas to understand "the postmodern turn," as Fredric Jameson terms it. Modernism and Postmodernism refer to historical designations in literature and art more generally. On the other hand, modernity and postmodernity represent both historical periods and philosophical approaches. While modernism could be considered a kind of movement, postmodernism cannot be subsumed under a totalizing term such as "movement" but instead refers to the intensely varied mutations that literature and art more generally underwent in the second half of the twentieth century. It is crucial to draw a distinction between the artistic period of modernism, which does not quite map onto the much larger era of modernity that stretches back to the

Enlightenment in the eighteenth century, and postmodernism, which fits relatively neatly into the same period as postmodernity despite the fact that many modernist practitioners persist even to this day.

Aside from his early sci-fi readings, Gibson notes the importance of the Beat Generation on his development as a person and a writer. The Beat writers straddled the line between modernism and postmodernism and set the stage for the hippie era. In particular, Gibson discovered Jack Kerouac, Allen Ginsberg, and William S. Burroughs. A loosely connected group of writers, the Beat Generation featured many different voices, but these three undoubtedly remain the most famous and influential. Kerouac generally provides the face of the movement because of the massive influence of his novel *On the Road* (1957). A picaresque travel narrative, *On the Road* introduced the world to Kerouac's "spontaneous prose," which supposedly represented an unedited explosion of writing about his past. *On the Road* depicts his experiences traveling back and forth across the United States with the Beat icon Neal Cassady, experimenting with drugs, listening to jazz, engaging in promiscuous sex, and hanging out with other Beat writers such as Ginsberg and Burroughs.[3] Similarly, Ginsberg burst onto the poetry scene with his poem "Howl" (1956). Lyrical yet free-form, "Howl" meditates upon madness and genius while simultaneously criticizing capitalist greed. Ginsberg was tried for obscenity because of the poem, setting a new standard for freedom of expression in the United States.

William S. Burroughs, on the other hand, eschewed the spirituality of his fellow Beats and provided a crucial literary father figure for Gibson and the other cyberpunks. Burroughs epitomized a more cynical and distinctly darker, more overtly revolutionary aesthetic than his contemporaries. His novel *Naked Lunch* (1959) unfolds as a series of horrific but often hilarious episodes that explore the infinite variety of ways in which humankind is controlled by everything from totalitarian governmental regimes to such banal forces as sex and drugs. As Gibson explains in his interview with Timothy Leary, "I always tell everybody that there's a very strong influence there. I didn't think I'd be able to put that over on the American science fiction people, because they either don't know who Burroughs is or they're immediately hostile . . . he found '50s science fiction and used it like a rusty can opener on society's jugular" (24).[4] *Naked Lunch*—and virtually Burroughs's entire oeuvre—interrogates the nature of control, a concept we explore in more depth later in this chapter. Burroughs followed up *Naked Lunch* with an equally if not more influential trilogy of novels, the "Nova Trilogy" or the "Cut-Up Trilogy": *The Soft Machine* (1961), *The Ticket That Exploded* (1962), and *Nova Express* (1974). This trilogy plunges into full-fledged science fiction with its depiction of an alien mob that infiltrates a planetary populace's minds. This Nova Mob foments chaos and rebellion on a global scale until they reach a point known as "nova" in which civilization collapses upon itself like a dying star. While its premise that language controls us was revolutionary in its own way, it was Burroughs's experimental writing process that made the novels so (in)famous. Burroughs wrote his own narratives, cut them up, and then folded in pieces from various other texts, including everything from daily newspapers to William Shakespeare. The result was a collage-style, dreamlike brand of surrealism that skirted the edge of plagiarism in its attempt to enact its philosophical ideas about language on the level of the novels' very words. Burroughs's novels deconstruct themselves until meanings both collapse and proliferate.

Gibson also discovered explorations of control in the works of Thomas Pynchon, whose depictions of paranoia, global conspiracies, and secret histories helped set the stage for cyberpunk. Pynchon's *The Crying of Lot 49* (1966) and *Gravity's Rainbow* (1973) remain two of the paradigms of postmodern fiction. *The Crying of Lot 49* (1966) concerns a young woman, Oedipa Maas, who stumbles on the possible existence of an underground postal service named Tristero that has possibly been influencing history for centuries. *Gravity's Rainbow,* on the other hand, involves a conspiracy centered on the German V-2 rockets of World War II and a man named Tyrone Slothrop, whose sexual conquests uncannily predict the future sites of V-2 rocket attacks. A novel about not only conspiracy and paranoia but also biological programming, *Gravity's Rainbow,* in many ways, was already a cybernetic novel. Both novels also demonstrated how serious literature can appropriate aspects of so-called lower art forms such as comic books and science fiction.

J. G. Ballard, whose works blur the lines between sci-fi and other genres, also exerted a powerful gravitational pull on the young cyberpunk authors. His loosely connected technology trilogy from the 1970s profoundly impacted Gibson. Ballard's *Crash* (1973) concerns a man named James Ballard who becomes erotically obsessed with car crashes after being in an accident himself.[5] As the novel progresses, it becomes a uniquely disturbing blend of eroticism and body horror as Ballard (the author) explores the darkest depths of the connection between the human and the machine. His follow-up, *Concrete Island* (1974), shifts the focus from the machines we use to travel to the spaces demarcated for travel and, more important, the nonplaces that exist between them. A postmodern reimagining of Daniel Defoe's *Robinson Crusoe* (1719), *Concrete Island* concerns Robert Maitland, an affluent architect who crashes his luxury Jaguar into the wasteland area between highway lanes and must survive on what he can scavenge from his car and the concrete island. Finally, *High Rise* (1975) moves from the means we use to commute to the spaces that house us during our "leisure time." It shifts from public spaces to private ones to depict how technology continues to impact us at home as well as at work. The novel centers on a hypermodern, self-contained apartment building that becomes the site of atavistic violence and devolution.[6] The tenants of the building degenerate into a situation reminiscent of that depicted in William Golding's *The Lord of the Flies* (1954): they resort to primitive states and ignite a civil war that rages between different floors of the building. An excoriating look at the cult of bourgeois comfort, Ballard's novel imagines what happens when comfort and convenience dissipate.

Cinema in the late 1970s and early 1980s also featured a highly innovative new hybrid genre of science fiction termed "body horror" that helped create the heady, experimental backdrop against which cyberpunk emerged. Body horror mixes elements of science fiction and horror in its depiction of bodily mutations, invasions, and transformations. David Cronenberg's films, with their depictions of parasitic invasion, grotesque transformation, and psychic phenomena, set the parameters for the genre. His major early films (*Shivers* [1976], *Rabid* [1977], *The Brood* [1979], *Scanners* [1981], and *Videodrome* [1983]) feature sexual maniacs, sexual vampires, a woman whose thoughts metamorphose into murderous albino children, psychics whose powers can explode heads, and subliminal television signals. The avant-garde director David Lynch's first feature-length film, *Eraserhead* (1977), also contributed to the genre's development with its absurdist tale of a man who fathers a mutant child. Finally, Ridley Scott's *Alien* (1979) set a new standard for sci-fi and horror, influencing sci-fi authors and filmmakers across the board and becoming one of the paradigms of body horror by drawing on the bio-mechanoid artworks of H. R. Giger, which portray the body not as a static boundary but as a fluid medium that can easily fuse with technology and its environment. These films created an atmosphere of cinema that was simultaneously intelligent and visceral in its images of metamorphosis and the collapse of the body's boundaries.

Along with fiction and cinema, music also served as a major inspiration for Gibson. He especially related to the burgeoning punk scene that arose in the United States and the United Kingdom during the 1970s. While bands such as the Sex Pistols and the Clash gained most of the notoriety (or infamy), Gibson has admitted that the proto-punk pioneers the Velvet Underground exerted the most profound influence on him. Taking their name from a book on bondage and sadomasochism and led by iconic frontman Lou Reed, the Velvet Underground blazed new ground with the release of its first album *The Velvet Underground & Nico* (1967), produced by Andy Warhol, which mixed stories of drug use, addiction, and sexual perversion with psychological introspection and abrasive levels of sonic dissonance. As with the hard-boiled fiction of Dashiell Hammett, Gibson's work appropriated the seedy urban aesthetic of the Velvet

Underground's songs and extrapolated from them to near-future environments. While the Velvet Underground constituted the first band to fully embody the punk spirit (other bands, such as the Who, came close at times), the true punk rock movement was a product of the 1970s, a period during which British bands such as the Sex Pistols, the Clash, and the Damned and American artists such as the Ramones, Patti Smith, the Stooges, and the Misfits redefined the sound and possibilities of rock music.[7] While these groups differ in numerous ways, they all feature a thrashy sound along with an antiestablishment attitude that makes the beatniks and hippies seem like lightweights in comparison. The influence of music on Gibson and cyberpunk cannot be understated, and Gibson has maintained that music has impacted his ideas and style more than literature or science fiction.

Finally, certain comics and graphic novels of the early 1980s also shaped Gibson and the other cyberpunks' conceptions of hyperurbanized spaces. Both Scott Bukatman and Tatiana Rapatzikou point to *The Incal* as a crucial influence on the depiction of futuristic urban spaces in the early 1980s. Written by the Chilean surrealist filmmaker Alejandro Jodorowsky with art by the French comic master Moebius, *The Incal* (1981–89) opens with the classic scene of a man being thrown from miles up in a futuristic urban space. The society of *The Incal* keeps its population docile through television programming. When rebels overtake the television signal, viewers remain incapable of processing radical, nonpropagandistic material. Similarly, Howard Chaykin's *American Flagg!* (1983–89) depicts a television star who crosses over to become a police officer and then a rebel television broadcaster. Comics such as these classics and others like them provided visuals of hyperurban spaces that undoubtedly influenced cyberpunk cityscapes such as Gibson's Sprawl. Indeed, Gibson's *Neuromancer* itself actually was adapted into a 1989 graphic novel as part of Marvel's Epic Comics line, but the series was never completed.[8]

The Rise of Cyberpunk

While Gibson should not be pigeonholed with the subgenre of cyberpunk, he cemented his fame with such works, and cyberpunk themes continue to dominate even his most recent works, albeit in novel forms. Therefore, it makes sense to detail some of the science fiction works that helped pave the way for cyberpunk and then to discuss some of his contemporaries as well. Undoubtedly, any works that deal with artificial intelligence and cyborgs owe a debt to Isaac Asimov's Robot series of novels and stories, the most famous of which are *I, Robot* (1950), *The Caves of Steel* (1953), and *The Naked Sun* (1955). In these works, Asimov lays out his "Three Laws of Robotics," which ensure that robots will follow the commands of their owners and never rebel against their creators. Gibson's own depiction of artificial intelligences also features organizations that attempt to keep the computer systems operating according to human command.

Gibson has openly acknowledged the influence of the American author Alfred Bester, who wrote two novels that are often cited as proto-cyberpunk texts, *The Demolished Man* (1953) and *The Stars My Destination* (1956), because of their depiction of surveillance and corporate control. Harlan Ellison also penned an important story about artificial intelligences, the classic "I Have No Mouth, and I Must Scream" (1967). A postapocalyptic tale, the short story concerns a group of survivors who are perpetually tortured by a computer with artificial intelligence. James L. Tiptree, Jr.'s "The Girl Who Was Plugged In" (1974) features all the earmarks of cyberpunk and could be considered the earliest example of the genre. The story depicts a corporate-controlled future in which a seriously deformed woman receives a series of implants that allow her to control a brainless, artificially grown body.[9] If Tiptree's story is not considered cyberpunk, then John Brunner's *The Shockwave Rider* (1975) certainly should be. Brunner took his inspiration from Alvin Toffler's *Future Shock* (1970), a book that exerted a profound impact on many cyberpunk authors with its discussion of "future shock" as a state in which individuals experience vast amounts of technological advancement in a relatively short period of time. Toffler further argued that society was increasingly moving out of an industrial framework and into a postindustrial era. Brunner's novel takes place in a dystopian future controlled by computer networks not dissimilar to the one that appears in Gibson's Sprawl novels. Furthermore, *Shockwave Rider* features the first use of the word "worm" to describe a malicious computer program that attacks the network by replicating itself.

While Gibson, Bruce Sterling, and other cyberpunk authors began publishing works in the late 1970s, cyberpunk became a full-fledged movement only in the 1980s, with Gibson as its father figure and Sterling as its mouthpiece. A major breakthrough occurred when Sterling collected a series of stories from various authors associated with the movement and its themes. This collection, together with Sterling's classic introduction, set the tone for a movement: *Mirrorshades* (1986), as it was called, provided one of the earliest critical definitions of the genre and first brought together such unique and talented young sci-fi authors as Gibson, Sterling, John Shirley, Rudy Rucker, and Lewis Shiner, among others. The anthology leaves out some major figures from the early days of the movement, but it points toward the need to understand Gibson within the context of the larger "movement."

While the cyberpunks were starting to publish their fiction , 1982 also saw the release of two crucial cyberpunk films that have remained influences on the genre of science fiction ever since: *Tron* and *Blade Runner.* Featuring a somewhat silly plot but stunning special effects for the time, Steven Lisberger's *Tron* follows a programmer who gets digitized and transported into a computer, where rebellious programs fight against the Master Control Program in their quest to reach out beyond the confines of their programming and contact their "Users," who created and continue to manipulate them. *Tron*'s premise may seem ludicrous, but it proved revolutionary in visually depicting a virtual computer world populated with sentient entities. Ridley Scott's *Blade Runner,* on the other hand, quickly became a classic not only of science fiction and cyberpunk but also of cinema more generally. Based on Philip K. Dick's classic novel *Do Androids Dream of Electric Sheep?* (1968), Scott's film actually took its name from William S. Burroughs's novella *Blade Runner (a movie)* (1979). A visionary blend of film noir, gothic motifs, and science fiction, *Blade Runner* uses its protagonist, Deckard, as a means of blurring the line between human and machine as he hunts down and kills (or retires, as the authorities euphemistically call it) replicants, artificial humans who often seem more human than their actual organic counterparts. The cyberpunk themes in cinema continued in 1983 with John Badham's *Wargames* and Douglas Trumball's *Brainstorm. Wargames* depicts a teenage hacker who, believing he is playing a game, inadvertently hacks into the United States defense system and almost sets off World War III. Trumball's *Brainstorm,* on the other hand, follows scientists who manufacture a device capable of capturing and re-creating a user's experiences. All these works helped add to the cultural momentum that rocketed Gibson's *Neuromancer* to success in 1984.

Sterling remains the second most famous of the cyberpunks, partly for his science fiction but also for his critical statements about the genre. Aside from his roles as an editor and essayist, Sterling wrote some of the most influential works of cyberpunk fiction, including the novels *Involution Ocean* (1977), *The Artificial Kid* (1980), *Schismatrix* (1985), and *Islands in the Net* (1988). Doubtless, Sterling's Shaper/Mechanist universe, as depicted in the novel *Schismatrix* and in several short related stories, remains his most famous contribution to science fiction and cyberpunk. Almost hallucinatory in its depiction of the future, the universe of *Schismatrix* has become thoroughly posthuman in both the environments the characters inhabit and the characters' bodies. Two basic factions exist in this posthuman landscape: the Shapers, who use various kinds of drugs to alter their physical form and perceptions, and the mechanists, who choose the cyborg route and transform themselves using mechanical implants and prostheses. Both groups would qualify as cybernetic as Norbert Weiner defined it,[10] and the novel explores how cybernetic understandings, whether they involve actual mechanical extensions of the human body or the reassessing of human biology itself as a programmable system, can push the evolution of humanity and civilization further and further until any glimpse of the Cartesian subject and liberal humanism lies light years behind on the evolutionary timeline.

Another cyberpunk founding father, John Shirley created a seminal work of the cyberpunk canon with his trilogy that is collected under the title *A Song Called Youth: Eclipse* (1985), *Eclipse Penumbra* (1988), and *Eclipse Corona* (1990). Shirley further embodied the cyberpunk spirit by being a punk musician himself in a band called the Panther Moderns, a name that Gibson appropriates for a gang in *Neuromancer.* More explicitly revolutionary than any of Gibson's works, Shirley's trilogy concerns a hypothetical dystopian future in which typical cyberpunk characters struggle against the new world order created by the Soviet Union's invasion of Europe. Given that the books involve mind implants, giant robotic war machines, memory alteration, and music as a form of revolt, it is no wonder that William Gibson once called Shirley "cyberpunk's patient zero." Shirley continued to write stories, novels, and screenplays, including the screenplay for the film adaptation of James O'Barr's comic series *The Crow* (1989). The script was rewritten before it was turned into Alex Proyas's cult classic gothic action film of the '90s; however, the film's thoroughly punk attitude connects it back to Shirley and cyberpunk.[11]

Possibly cyberpunk's most bizarre practitioner, Rudy Rucker twisted the subgenre in unique ways with stories such as "Jack Kerouac Disembodied School of Poetics" (1982), in which a device projects a construct of Jack Kerouac that retains not only the author's personality but also his alcoholism and depression. Rucker remains most famous for his "Ware Tetralogy," a series of novels—*Software* (1982), *Wetware* (1988), *Freeware* (1997), and *Realware* (2000)—published over the course of eighteen years that steadily ratchets up the levels of posthuman weirdness. Rucker's series opens with a disgraced programmer who was once deemed a traitor for giving robots not just artificial intelligence but also free will. Eventually, these "Boppers" form a civilization on the moon and crossbreed robotic or synthetic individuals with humans in profoundly strange ways, resulting in hybrid beings called "moldies," for which, of course, humans quickly develop sexual fetishes. Another true "weirdo" of cyberpunk, Mark Leyner released the Burroughsesque *My Cousin, My Gastroenterologist* (1990), which melded cybernetic themes in a collage of surreal, funny, and biting episodes. Michael Swanwick, who collaborated with Gibson on one early story, also published a major work of early cyberpunk, *Vacuum Flowers* (1987), that features a dead woman's recorded identity as the lead protagonist and a hive mind known as the Comprise that has subsumed humanity under itself on Earth.

Cyberpunk has often been characterized and criticized for being a boys' club with hypermasculinist or even sexist preoccupations, but the original wave of authors did feature one major female author, Pat Cadigan. Her novel *Mindplayers* (1987) follows a young woman who runs afoul of the "Brain Police" for using a device that allows her to experience psychosis. Her novel *Synners* (1991) concerns artists who extract images from minds and turn them into commercial products, in a manner somewhat reminiscent of Gibson's "The Winter Market." Two final major figures in the early movement are Lewis Shiner and Greg Bear, who have produced some crucial works of cyberpunk while working mostly outside the subgenre. Often associated with the movement, Lewis Shiner's works feature only passing elements of cyberpunk: *Frontera* has cyberpunk undertones as it concerns an Earth ruled by corporations and a lost Martian colony they seek to find, but his most closely related work is probably the short story "Stoked" (1988), which opens with a reference to the punk band Suicidal Tendencies' "Possessed to Skate" and proceeds to explore how skateboarding allows the narrator to subvert his suburban surroundings.[12] A prolific sci-fi author, Greg Bear remains connected to the cyberpunk genre because of his highly original novel *Blood Music* (1985), in which a genetic engineer decides to inject himself with the subject of his own research after being ordered to abandon it, resulting in sentient single-cell organisms that reprogram their owner's body and end up reprogramming all life on Earth.

Works of cyberpunk also began to appear simultaneously in Japan, and Japan remains a constant theme not just in Gibson's works but in cyberpunk as a whole. Sogo Ishii's innovative and influential *Burst City* (1982) is generally regarded as the first Japanese cyberpunk film. A sci-fi musical, *Burst City* concerns biker gangs that mount a rebellion in a dystopian future, and the film served as a showcase for numerous Japanese punk bands of the time. In the same year, Katsuhiro Otomo began publishing his groundbreaking manga series, *Akira*, which ran from 1982 to 1990. Set in Neo-Tokyo, a Tokyo rebuilt after a bizarre explosion decimated the city, *Akira* also concerns a group of bikers, one of whom begins to develop psychic powers so intense that he eventually loses control of his bodily form. Otomo's story achieved additional notoriety with the release of his anime adaptation of the series in 1988, and its depictions of futuristic bikers, psychic warfare, and grotesque bodily transformations make it one of the most influential cyberpunk works of all time.[13] Shinya Tsukamoto's surrealistically disturbing *Tetsuo: The Iron Man* (1989) also created a paradigmatic example of the Japanese cyberpunk genre, which often blended horror with science fiction and the avant-garde. A dark, brooding, and profoundly kinetic piece of cinema in the vein of David Lynch's early films, *Tetsuo* depicts a man seeking revenge by evolving into a kind of cyborg that obliterates the lines separating the human from the machine. It is a film about the desire for becoming in its most literalized, horrifying, and powerful senses. Tsukamoto's two follow-ups (*Tetsuo II: Body Hammer* [1992] and *Tetsuo: The Bullet Man* [2009]) both feature similar plots and continue to explore the same ideas in increasingly novel and disturbing ways. All of this gritty, experimental, and often bizarre fiction and film created a truly unique time period in the history of science fiction. While many claim that the cyberpunk movement died around 1988 when it was appropriated by mass culture and hence robbed of its subversive intent, we will see how the genre's style, themes, and ideas have evolved and lived on in a variety of mediums as well as how the original cyberpunk works of authors such as Gibson still resonate today and allow us to critically examine the world around us.

Understanding the Post-: William Gibson as a Guide to Postmodernism

Untold gallons of ink have been spilled attempting to explicate the meaning of the seemingly simple and unambiguous prefix "post- ." Deriving from the Latin preposition, "post" means "after," but, with the advent of neologisms such as "postmodern," the prefix accrued a series of increasingly obscure and problematic usages—postmodern, poststructural, and posthuman, in particular, but we could also extend the list to include ideas such as postracial or postgender. Why is it that we increasingly live in an era that defines itself only in relation to earlier eras, ideologies, or philosophies? In many ways, the trajectory of Gibson's body of work can at least gesture toward answering this question. As Gibson's fictions move from the futuristic landscapes of his early works to our everyday reality, they illustrate what it means to live in the "post-," an era in which people feel increasingly severed from the past and incapable of imagining the future. We have "zero history," as the title of Gibson's recent novel suggests, because we have only the ever-mutating now.

As Scott Bukatman argues, a large portion of postmodern critical theory functions according to a sci-fi paradigm. In many ways, critical theory, particularly critical theory dealing with postmodern or posthuman concepts, can be read as a kind of science fiction and vice versa; that is, science fiction can also be seen as enacting its own brand of theory. Furthermore, as Brian McHale argues, science fiction harbors a special connection to postmodern literature. McHale's *Postmodernist Fiction* contends that modernism exhibited an epistemological dominant whereas postmodernism shifts to an ontological one: "Science fiction, we might say, is to postmodernism what the detective story was to modernism: it is the ontological genre *par excellence*" (16). Thus, science fiction influences both the theory and the literature of postmodern era, and few science fiction writers epitomize this idea like William Gibson, whose works consistently deal with some of the most fundamental issues facing postmodern and posthuman theories: information, globalization, computerization, hybridity, fragmented identity, simulation, virtuality, simulacra, and cyborgs. As his works have migrated from their once-distant future settings to more traditionally realistic depictions of our current world, his major themes have remained the same, but his form has metamorphosed to accommodate the influx of data from the world around him. This temporal march toward the present further solidifies the idea that science fiction provides the perfect genre for understanding the postmodern; his novels' steady decline in temporal displacement indicates that the extrapolation into future worlds proves unnecessary because the postmodern world itself is already science fiction.

The French philosopher Jean-François Lyotard's *The Postmodern Condtion* provides one of the most famous definitions of the "*postmodern* as incredulity toward metanarratives" (xxiv). A metanarrative is any discourse (for example, science, Marxism, psychoanalysis, history, religion) that attempts to provide an overarching explanation of reality, existence, being, or civilization. Lyotard, then, characterizes postmodernity as an epistemological crisis, a crisis of knowledge that undermines even the ideas we take as givens. Linda Hutcheon provides another useful definition of the genre: "the postmodern's initial concern is to de-naturalize some of the dominant features of our way of life; to point out that those entities that we unthinkingly experience as 'natural' (they might even include capitalism, patriarchy, liberal humanism) are in fact 'cultural'; made by us, not given to us. Even nature, postmodernism might point out, doesn't grow on trees" (*Politics* 2). Some theorists view postmodernism as the death of any ability to define values or construct programs of social progress. For example, Jürgen Habermas believes that modernity constitutes an unfinished project: "Instead of giving up on modernity and its project as a lost cause, we should learn from the mistakes of those extravagant programs which have tried to negate modernity" ("Modernity" 9).[14] Others embrace it as a liberation from normative metanarratives that have previously constrained thought.

The postmodern era constitutes more than just this crisis of knowledge and representation; it also coincides with changes in the nature of power, capitalism, and production. Marxist critics have argued that we have entered a new era of production that has received two different major labels: "postindustrial" (a term coined by Daniel Bell but also used by Toffler and Lyotard) and "late capitalist," the term preferred by Fredric Jameson.[15] Lyotard argues that this period alters knowledge as it submits more and more to the "hegemony of computers" and transforms into information, a sellable commodity: "knowledge is altered as societies enter what is known as the postindustrial age and cultures enter what is known as the postmodern age" (3–4). Jameson argues against the notion that this change represents an entirely new social paradigm. As he explains, "postmodernism is not the cultural dominant of a whole new social order (the rumor about which, under the name 'postindustrial society,' ran through the media a few years ago, but only the reflex and the concomitant of yet another systematic modification of capitalism itself" (*Postmodernism* xii). Jameson explains that the concept of "late capitalism" emerged in the Frankfurt School, particularly in Horkheimer and Adorno's works,[16] and involved "a tendential web of bureaucratic control and the interpenetration of government and big business" (*Postmodernism* xviii). These aspects remain part of it, but Jameson maintains that more recent developments have caused the concept to shift:

> What marks the development of the new concept [of late capitalism] over the older one [monopoly capitalism] is not merely an emphasis on the emergence of new forms of business organization (multinationals, transnationals) beyond the monopoly stage but, above all, the vision of a world capitalist system fundamentally distinct from the older imperialism. . . . Besides the forms of transnational business mentioned above, its features include the new international division of labor, a vertiginous new dynamic in international banking and the stock exchanges . . . , new forms of media interrelationship . . . , computers and automation, the flight of production to advanced Third World areas, along with all the more familiar social consequences, including the crisis of traditional labor, the emergence of yuppies, and gentrification on a now-global scale. (*Postmodernism* xviii–xix)

Overall, the era of late capitalism coincides with the era of increased globalization, computerization, and corporate control, three themes that Gibson's works deal with both in futuristic landscapes and in realistic depictions of our contemporary world.

The shift to late capitalism also signals a change in the nature of power structures and their relations to populaces, and Gibson's works investigate the rise of the "society of control." Michel Foucault remains one of the most influential philosophers to deal with the structure of power, as his body of work explores how different social structures and institutions (for example, prisons, schools, hospitals, asylums) shaped not only society but the behaviors and identities of subjects as well. Foucault designates the eighteenth century as the moment in which power underwent a profound metamorphosis as it moved into the era of discipline. Another French philosopher, Gilles Deleuze, expanded on Foucault's theories of power and postulated that the postmodern era marks another shift in the paradigm of power into what he calls the society of control. To fully understand Gibson's novels, one must first grasp the ongoing changes in power that have occurred over the past seventy years.

In *Discipline and Punish,* Foucault traces the shift in the structure of power from sovereignty to discipline. Sovereignty pertains to the period of monarchies, in which power was exhibited through torture, public executions, and so forth. A transformation started to occur in the eighteenth century as societies began to move into a disciplinary paradigm of power that centered on creating docile subjects by demarcating certain spaces within society that function according to prisonlike regimes. Foucault traces the similarities among schools, barracks, prisons, and factories, spaces in which subjects learn certain patterns of behavior and internalize power into themselves. As Foucault explains, "The historical moment of the disciplines was the moment when an art of the human body was born, which was directed not only at the growth of its skills, nor at the intensification of its subjection, but at the formation of a relation that in the mechanism itself makes it more obedient as it becomes more useful, and conversely. What was then being formed was a policy of coercions that act upon the body, a calculated manipulation of its elements, its gestures, its behaviour. The human body was entering a machinery of power that explores it, breaks it down, and rearranges it" (*Discipline* 137–38). Discipline works directly on the subject's body by training and organizing its existence, thus causing power to directly inscribe itself upon the subject's body and mind, much like the torture device in Franz Kafka's "In the Penal Colony" (1919) that engraves the prisoner's sentence upon his body.

Foucault uses the panopticon as an emblem of how power becomes internalized as discipline. The British utilitarian philosopher Jeremy Bentham imagined the panopticon as a hypothetical prison with cells laid out in a circular pattern around a central guard tower. Windows along the exterior circumference of the circle in every cell allow the guard to see any prisoner at any given moment. The design remains provocative because one guard can watch an entire prison because the prisoners can never know when they are being watched. Similarly, in the disciplinary society, subjects internalize the gaze of power and structure their behavior accordingly. If a subject misbehaves in school, performs sloppy work on a job, or neglects his or her duties in the army, there are always other students, workers, and soldiers around to report these indiscretions. Each subject replicates the guard in the panopticon tower, watching over the entire populace. As Gilles Deleuze reminds us in his study *Foucault,* "power is not essentially repressive" for Foucault; it "passes through the hands of the mastered no less than through the hands of the masters" (71). Power thus flows through every subject in a society because it inscribes itself within the subjects and ultimately creates the subject. Therefore, as Deleuze further explains, "power-relations . . . do not emanate from a central point or unique locus of sovereignty, but at each moment move 'from one point to another' in a field of forces" (*Foucault* 73). Power remains mobile as it shifts from one point to another, with each subject serving as a conduit.

The disciplinary society constitutes the modern regime of power. With the advent of postmodernity, power, like knowledge and capital, undergoes a fundamental shift. In "Postscript on Control Societies," Deleuze argues that disciplinary societies "reach their apogee at the beginning of the twentieth century" and then proceed into a "terminal decline" concomitant with the rise of what Deleuze terms "control societies," a nomenclature he adopts from William S. Burroughs (177–78). Deleuze associates each paradigm of power with a particular type of machine. While sovereignty operated with simple machines, disciplinary societies arose alongside thermodynamic devices, but "control societies function with a third generation of machines, with information technology and computers" and occur alongside "a mutation of capitalism" that is "no longer directed toward production" but "toward metaproduction" ("Postscript" 180–81). Control begins with "a general breakdown of all sites of confinement" that characterize disciplinary societies and a move toward a society that is not confined and trained in particular spaces but is being continually influenced by power: "The various forms of control, on the other hand, are inseparable variations, forming a system of varying geometry whose language is digital (though not necessarily binary). Confinements are *molds,* different moldings, while controls are a *modulation* like a self-transmuting molding changing from one moment to the next" ("Postscript" 178–79). Instead of forcing subjects into molds, control monitors a subject's continual variations in performance (modulations) and records those to both understand and direct subject behavior. Control societies are based on codes instead of names: "The key thing is no longer a signature or number but a code: codes are *passwords,* whereas disciplinary societies are ruled (when it comes to integration or resistance) by *precepts.* The digital language of control is made up of codes indicating whether access to some information should be allowed or not" ("Postscript" 180). Jean Baudrillard also contends that postmodern power is characterized by cybernetics: "After the metaphysics of being and appearance, after energy and determinacy, the metaphysics of indeterminacy and the code. Cybernetic control, generation through models, differential modulation, feedback, question/answer, etc.: this is the new *operational* configuration" (*Symbolic Exchange* 57). Arthur Kroker and David Cook expand upon Baudrillard's argument and claim that this basic structural code "programmes everything into a simplified and universalized algorithmic process," thus giving rise to a truly cybernetic form of power (82). This cybernetic power, or "control" as Deleuze terms it, lets subjects believe they are free from the spaces of power, even while it is monitoring their behavior and determining to what information they should be privy on the basis of the data associated with their code. Control becomes ever more powerful as computers have been more firmly integrated into every facet of life.

Toward an Understanding of William Gibson

If one word can distill the essence of William Gibson and his writing, it lies in the French word *bricolage* (literally "tinkering"), which refers to the combination of existing objects to create something radically new. As Jacques Derrida explains in a discussion of the structural anthropologist Claude Levi-Strauss, "The bricoleur, says Lévi-Strauss, is someone who uses 'the means at hand,' that is, the instruments he finds at his disposition around him, those which are already there, which had not been especially conceived with an eye to the operation for which they are to be used and to which one tries by trial and error to adapt them, not hesitating to change them whenever it appears necessary, or to try several of them at once, even if their form and their origin are heterogeneous—and so forth."[17] Gibson's consistent use of *bricolage* as a means of interrogating radical difference provides one way of understanding postmodernity, posthumanism, hybridity, and perhaps critical theory itself. Theorists of postmodernism, particularly Fredric Jameson, have pointed out that postmodern works often mimic and blend different genres, a practice that Jameson characterizes as pastiche, which he contends has eclipsed parody in the postmodern era. Whereas parody involved a political element, pastiche lacks such a subversive edge because it constitutes parody after it "has lost its vocation" (*Postmodernism* 17). Pastiche is "blank parody" in which authors engage in "the random cannibalization of all the styles of the past" (*Postmodernism* 17–18). Since it merely apes styles with no political agenda or for purely humorous purposes, postmodern pastiche operates on the level of the simulacrum (the false sign without meaning). Jameson believes that philosophy and literature must find a purpose again by turning back to utopian ideals of progress, an argument that he has pursued throughout his career and that he applies to science fiction in particular in his study *Archaeologies of the Future.*

Linda Hutcheon, on the other hand, contends that postmodern literary texts do utilize a postmodern form of parody that self-consciously references and uses different styles in a way that criticizes representation and ideology at their cores. Similarly, from his earliest works, Gibson engages in the artful mixture of genres, styles, and influences, but he does so in particular ways that elevate his writings above mere pastiche. The concept of *bricolage* proves more apropos because, on a literary level, Gibson enacts the very process in which his hackers, engineers, and programmers engage: the reusing of seemingly unrelated components in innovative and often subversive ways. Gibson's classic evocation of this process comes from the early story "Burning Chrome," in which the narrator states, "The street finds its own uses for things" (*BC* 199). This basic idea provides an ideal entry point into the works of William Gibson, an author whose works manage to simultaneously connect with the niche audience of science fiction fans, those who follow the national best-seller lists, and literary critics and theorists. One major reason for this is that he—like his characters—takes influences ranging from computer technology to literature to music and utilizes them as building blocks in the creation of fascinating new hybrid forms that parallel the cyborg identities and bodies of his characters. His works' influence has similarly expanded beyond just science fiction fandom and the best-seller lists to become important works of American literature that examine the changes that computerization and globalization have enacted upon the United States and the world as a whole. My purpose in this work is not archival; I focus on Gibson's major works, his influence on culture and literature, and the ways in which his works allow us to more fully grasp the concepts of postmodernity and posthumanism. For a truly archival approach, see Gary Westfahl's recent *William Gibson* (2013), an excellent and impeccably researched addition to the University of Illinois Press's "Modern Masters of Science Fiction" series. This study does not deal with Gibson's unpublished works, and it does not attempt to synthesize and respond to the gigantic body of critical essays on Gibson. This book features my own readings of the texts with critics brought in at various points; a list of further critical readings can be found in the bibliography. Instead, my focus is on how William Gibson engages in the art of *bricolage* by synthesizing and transcending previous influences and how he has inspired subsequent authors, directors, and game designers to similarly adopt the practice of the *bricoleur.*

Ultimately, this study rests upon the belief, which I have espoused elsewhere,[18] that science fiction itself can act like critical theory whether or not it is cognizant of the fact. It creates worlds in which older theoretical ideas can find freedom of play or emergent theoretical concepts can arise. Building on this theoretical framework, this study strives to demonstrate how William Gibson's stories, novels, and other works can be used to understand crucial concepts relating to postmodernity and posthumanism while also providing a literary lens through which to view our current world in a radically critical fashion. Many critics discuss whether Gibson's works succeed or fail as examples of postmodernism. Some find his novels' reassuring returns to a sense of stability and order—the classic outcome of the Freytagian denouement—to be a kind of cop-out on their postmodern potential. They do not culminate in the postmodern refusals of meaning typical of works such as Pynchon's *The Crying of Lot 49* or *Gravity's Rainbow.* But is this truly a flaw in his works? Instead of wallowing in paradox and ambiguity like other postmodern novels, Gibson's works in general pose the old existential questions of value, meaning, and being in the face of a postmodern environment that seems to increasingly undermine such concepts. Therefore, his works always seek to establish new methodologies for determining meaning and value after critically attacking traditional systems of ethics and signification. In other words Gibson's texts often enact what Nietzsche termed a transvaluation (or revaluation) of values, a critique and subsequent revision of previous ideas, beliefs, and morals.

CHAPTER 2

A Cyborg Apprenticeship

The Early Stories and the Retrofitting of Genres

Gibson's early stories simultaneously display his disillusionment with contemporary science fiction and chart his aesthetic reaction against what he saw as a stagnation that had become endemic to the genre. Published between 1977 and 1985 and later mostly collected in the volume *Burning Chrome* (1986), Gibson's eleven early stories announce the arrival of a truly postmodern aesthetic of science fiction. These stories function as his first experiments with a new form of science fiction that still maintained the scientific foundations of hard science fiction but simultaneously transformed the genre into gritty, character-driven thrillers. As Kathryn Cramer explains, "By reputation, hard sf is science fiction that gets its science right and has a certain hard-nosed attitude" (188). Some proponents of Hard SF see other versions of science fiction as inferior. For instance, as Gregory Benford argues, "Hard SF seeks to convince, to appeal to the intellect. Fantasy and horror speak to the emotions, delving into deep fears and loves" (224).[1] While New Wave science fiction authors such as Samuel R. Delany and Ursula K. Le Guin had begun pushing the genre in this direction, their novels tended to lack the scientific plausibility of hard science fiction authors. Gibson, on the other hand, logically extrapolates from current technologies in a manner akin to golden-age authors such as Arthur C. Clarke or more recent authors such as Kim Stanley Robinson and Stephen Baxter, but he populates his works with realistic characters who live in the everyday world of a future that seems only barely removed from the present.

Termed "cyberpunk" for its blend of "lowlife and high-tech," as Sterling describes it, this new brand of science fiction no longer concerned itself with Cold War technologies and fears: nuclear power and devastation, alien invasion, space exploration and so on (preface xiv). Instead, Gibson's cyberpunk focused on the emergent technologies of computer networks and global communication systems as well as the rampaging effects of urbanization and globalization. In his earliest story, "Fragments of a Hologram Rose" (1977), Gibson announced the themes that still continue to dominate his work, and he began developing the aesthetic that hurtled his groundbreaking first novel, *Neuromancer* (1984), to fame. Gibson's early stories vary somewhat in quality, but the most compelling ones represent a brilliant young writer first honing his craft. In the stories, we see Gibson playing with the rudiments of cyberpunk, collaborating with other young science fiction authors, and providing the first depictions of "The Sprawl" universe that serves as the setting for *Neuromancer* and its two sequels, novels that transformed Gibson into a preeminent voice not just of science fiction but of postmodern American literature more generally.

Holograms and Hinterlands: Early Stand-alone Stories

Gibson's first story, "Fragments of a Hologram Rose," spins the relatively simple tale of a man named Parker, an addict of "Apparent Sensory Perception," or "ASP." Similar to the technology that would later appear in such films as Douglas Trumbull's *Brainstorm* (1983) and Kathryn Bigelow's cyberpunk film *Strange Days* (1995), ASP allows users to record their experiences onto cassettes that can then be re-experienced by others; the tapes provide the viewer with a full range of sensory input. They constitute "a dark implosion into other flesh" (*BC* 38). Interestingly, the dissemination of ASP technology follows a pattern similar to the history of cinema. Initially, the ASP experience was restricted to nickelodeon-style arcade devices, similar to Edison's Kinetoscope or other such machines, and to theater complexes. Eventually, portable devices allow users to experience ASP in their homes, a revolution comparable to that brought about by the advent of home video, then DVD, and finally streaming digital video services.

"Hologram Rose" revolves around Parker's struggle to deal with the all-too-real experience of a relationship's dissolution. The story uses this fundamentally human event to provide a stark contrast to the virtual sensations derived from ASP cassettes; the narrative stages a series of dichotomies that it problematizes and examines: actuality and virtuality, copy and original, self and other, real and simulacrum, human and machine—dichotomies that reappear throughout Gibson's corpus. Already in this early story, Gibson explores the nature of the "cyborg," as Donna Haraway later theorized it. As Haraway explains, "a cyborg is a cybernetic organism, a hybrid of machine and organism" (149). Cyborgs exist in numerous works of science fiction, including Isaac Asimov's "The Bicentennial Man" (1976) and "Segregationist" (1967), James

Cameron's *The Terminator* (1984), Paul Verhoeven's *Robocop* (1987), and Masamune Shirow's manga *Ghost in the Shell* (1989–90) and Mamoru Oshii's 1995 anime adaptation. Expanding on this fictional creation, Haraway argues that the cyborg represents a utopian figure because it scrambles the normal binary systems of power organization and identity: man/woman, human/machine, black/white, and so forth. Furthermore, she contends that the cyborg is not simply a fiction but a "social reality" because we have already developed a series of complex, symbiotic relationships with technology that make our identities inseparable from the machines with which we interact. For example, the computer becomes an extension of our body and our identity, and the proliferation of portable communication and computing devices has only solidified these links and blurred the boundaries between the human and the machine.

Parker constitutes a cyborg because he cannot slumber without his "Sendai Sleep-Master," a delta-wave inducer that lulls him to sleep each evening; however, recent power failures have disturbed his sleep patterns. The cyborg disruption of boundaries does not end with soporific aids but proceeds to further problematize boundaries such as those between computer memory and human memory as well as between self and other. In fact, "Hologram Rose" pushes into firmly postmodern territory by calling the unified self into question. The holographic rose from the story's title provides its central symbol of the fragmented subject. As Parker disposes of mementoes from his ex-lover, he discovers a postcard featuring "a white light reflection hologram of a rose" (*BC* 39). He promptly grinds the plastic postcard into fragments, but holograms exhibit a peculiar characteristic: "Recovered and illuminated, each fragment will reveal the whole image of the rose," but "each fragment reveals the rose from a different angle" (*BC* 44). The fractured holographic rose epitomizes the fragmented nature of identity in a world in which simulated sensations and experiences predominate. As Lance Olson explains, the narrator "recognizes that, suggestive of the shred of the hologram rose, 'we're each other's fragments.' We are never able to see the total picture of each other, the world, or even ourselves. We must learn to live with pieces in the absence of wholes" (*WGO* 47). The fragmented identity of the subject is symptomatic of the postmodern era and late capitalism. As Fredric Jameson contends, "If, indeed, the subject has lost its capacity actively to extend its pro-tensions and re-tensions across the temporal manifold and to organize its past and future into coherent experience, it becomes difficult to see how the cultural productions of such a subject could result in anything but heaps of fragments and in a practice of the randomly heterogeneous and fragmentary and the aleatory" (*Postmodernism* 25). In other words, the postmodern era has produced fragmented subjects, so the cultural objects of postmodernity have become fragmented as well. Thus, the subject loses any genuine sense of wholeness, and society and its culture become so many "heaps of fragments" that can never be unified.

By means of ASP, an individual can indulge in "five minutes of free-fall gymnastics in a Swiss orbital spa, trampolining through twenty-meter perihelions with a sixteen-year-old *Vogue* model" (*BC* 39), or learn what it feels like to be the opposite sex. While "Hologram Rose" concerns the liberatory promises of technology, it also depicts the darker side of the cyborg world: the increased power of global corporations and ever more precise methods of control. For example, when he was a teenager, Parker's own parents made him an indentured servant for "the American subsidiary of a Japanese plastics combine" where "he lived . . . in a dormitory, singing the company hymns in formation" (*BC* 40). As Haraway admits, the world of the cyborg always harbors nascent dystopian potentialities as well because it signifies "the final imposition of a grid of control on the planet" (154). "Hologram Rose" barely suggests such elements, which became major components of Gibson's later cyberpunk works, but already we get a sense of cyberpunk as an offshoot of what William Fisher terms the "terminal genre," a specific genre of science fiction that seeks to chart utopian pathways through dystopian spaces.[2]

Gibson's next major story, "The Gernsback Continuum," takes a step back to reflect upon the history of science fiction and the crux at which Gibson felt it had arrived. With its title alone, "The Gernsback Continuum" juxtaposes Gibson's work to traditional science fiction. Considered the father of modern science fiction, Hugo Gernsback, the story's namesake, began publishing the first science fiction magazine, *Amazing Stories,* in 1926, and such stories form the backdrop against which Gibson's story reacts. Some critics have even maintained that Gibson's *Neuromancer* is a rewriting of Gernsback's novel *Ralph 124C 41+* (1925), but *Ralph* essentially provides an ur-text for any sci-fi work that features a savior figure. The story remains the only one of Gibson's non-Sprawl works to be adapted into a film: the director Tim Leandro created a short film, *Tomorrow Calling* (1993), that is based on it for the United Kingdom's Channel 4. At first, "The Gernsback Continuum" seems to have abandoned Gibson's cyberpunk aesthetic since it concerns the present, but the story uses its setting for two distinct purposes. First, it comments on how the present has become its own kind of futurity, a theme that Gibson returns to in his later two trilogies. Second, it utilizes the story's present to interrogate the futures envisioned by Gernsback-era sci-fi writers. Told from a first-person point of view, "The Gernsback Continuum" follows an unnamed photographer who has been hired by pop-art historian Dialta Downes to produce an "illustrated history" titled *The American Futuropolis: The Tomorrow That Never Was.* The book focuses on a peculiar brand of 1930s American architecture called "American Streamlined Modern" or "Raygun Gothic" that was influenced by Gernsbackian sci-fi stories.

The photographer begins touring around old California structures that feature this bizarre architecture and imagines that the proprietors of such establishments "put Ming the Merciless in charge of designing California gas stations" or that they drove down the California coastline "erecting raygun emplacements in white stucco" (*BC* 28). The narrator's evocation of the classic Flash Gordon sci-fi villain Ming the Merciless instantly equates the aesthetic with the now vastly outmoded, even quaint style of Gernsbackian science fiction that envisioned a future of sleek chrome surfaces, flying cars, bizarrely colorful and sexualizing outfits, food pills, and utopian social structures.[3] The story further conjures associations with such styles through its comparison of certain "Raygun Gothic" illustrations to cityscapes from Gernsback-era sci-fi films, particularly Fritz Lang's *Metropolis* (1927) and William Cameron Menzies's *Things to Come* (1936).[4] The photographer's immersion in such imagery eventually begins to affect his mental state as he starts to experience visions or hallucinations of people, places, and objects that may or may not be real. As if he has managed to see into a parallel dimension or alternate timeline, the narrator claims that he "penetrated a fine membrane . . . of probability" when he glances up at the sky to catch sight of "a twelve-engined thing like a bloated boomerang, all wing, thrumming its way easy with an elephantine grace" (*BC* 29). Disturbed by this hallucination or a glimpse of another reality, he contacts his friend Mervyn Kihn, a free-lance journalist who specializes in conspiracy theories: alien encounters, cattle mutilations, paranormal sightings, and the like.

A Jungian at heart, Kihn claims that the narrator's visions and all paranormal sightings derive from the mass unconscious, which has been structured by media forces.[5] He suggests that our minds have been filled to the brim with images of UFOs, futuristic worldscapes, and bizarre lifeforms to the point that we are primed for extraordinary encounters: "People see these things. Nothing's there, but people *see* them anyway. Because they need to, probably. You've read Jung, you should know the score. . . . In your case, it's so obvious: You admit you were thinking about this crackpot architecture, having fantasies" (*BC* 29). Just as it had with Americans from the 1930s, this futuristic imagery has infiltrated the narrator's unconscious and influenced his visions of reality. During his discussion of a young woman who witnessed "the severed head of a bear . . . floating around on its own little flying saucer," Kihn implies that all paranormal experiences prove symptomatic of media's saturation effects upon the mass unconsciousness: "She'd have seen the devil, if she hadn't been brought up on *The Bionic Man* and all those *Star Trek* reruns. She is clued into the main vein" (*BC* 30).[6] Science fiction thus has a reciprocal circuit with our culture, similar to the one Katherine Hayles describes—our advances in technology, science, and philosophy lead to science fictional extrapolations, but works of science fiction simultaneously influence our perceptions of science, technology, and the world around us: "Literary texts are not, of course, merely passive conduits. They actively shape what the technologies mean and what the scientific theories signify in culture" (*How We Became* 21). Hayles even uses Gibson's *Neuromancer* as an example of how a cultural text can directly affect emergent technologies such as the Internet and virtual reality.

"The Gernsback Continuum" concerns a kind of utopian faith in the simulacrum, in the false promise of a better world that transcends the tawdry reality of the quotidian. The buildings begin to haunt the photographer like visions from "a lost future," visions of a "shadowy America-that-wasn't, of Coca-Cola plants like beached submarines, and fifth-run movie houses like the temples of some lost sect that had worshipped blue mirrors and geometry" (*BC* 28). The future arrives but in a far less utopian form. Instead of the bright future in which stainless-steel rockets transport individual citizens to distant parts of the cosmos, the world gets the German V-2 raining death on an unsuspecting London.[7] As Andrew Ross explains,

> The streamlined design of factory buildings, gas stations, diners, and movie marquees—finned, flanged, and fluted—recalls a future perfect that never was, a tomorrow's world fully planned and designed by technophiles faithful to the prewar ethic of progressive futurism. From the sleek rockets on the "spray-paint pulp utopias" of the Frank R. Paul covers of *Amazing Stories* magazine to the winged statues that guard the Hoover Dam, the story was of a promised future that would come into being only as a nightmare; the rockets were those that fell on London during the war, the streamlined cars and crystal superhighways gave the green light to postwar ecological atrocities committed by General Motors under the aegis of petroleum capitalism. ("Getting" 411)

But this lost future still influences the present: "The Gernsback Continuum of the story is not a dying or dead world; it remains as a force influencing present day reality in its old artifacts as a still-present alternate universe which continues to coexist next to reality—indeed the hero is still haunted by his vision of it as the story closes" (Westfahl, "Gernsback" 90). In Gernsbackian sci-fi, these future worlds constitute a kind of Platonic ideal, the form to which society should aspire; instead of these bright futures, the human race gets genocide, weapons of mass destruction, and environmental devastation. These ideals end up being nothing but simulacra, hollow images of a world that never was but that nevertheless still exerts an influence upon the twentieth-century episteme, particularly in spaces such as Los Angeles and Disneyland that exhibit beautiful shining facades but end up being nothing more than bourgeois simulacra built upon the bodies of the proletariat just as in Lang's *Metropolis.*

Ultimately, the narrator can exorcise these semiotic demons only by participating in thoroughly mundane forms of bourgeois culture. Kihn suggests he can purge his system by watching lots of bad television programs, such as game shows and soap operas, and going to porn movies: "Really bad media can exorcise your semiotic phantoms" (*BC* 35). The photographer eventually heeds this advice, but not before he journeys into the belly of the ray-gun gothic beast—Los Angeles, the hollow heart of the utopian dream. As he relates, "Los Angeles was a bad idea. . . . It was prime Downes country; too much of the Dream there, and too many fragments of the Dream waiting to snare me. I nearly wrecked the car on a stretch of overpass near Disneyland, when the road fanned out like an origami trick and left me swerving through a dozen minilanes of whizzing chrome teardrops and shark fins" (*BC* 35–36). The narrator attends a screening of *Nazi Love Motel,* a porn film recommendation from Kihn, but keeps his eyes shut, possibly negating the film's purgative value. Instead, the story ends with the narrator still experiencing visions and deciding to plop himself down on a New York park bench, a grimier and less utopian space, and "submerge" himself "in hard evidence of the human near-dystopia we live in" (*BC* 36). The narrator leaves the reader with a fundamental question that gets to the heart of the utopia/dystopia dichotomy. While attempting to buy up newspapers dealing with the dystopian aspects of our world (for example, the petroleum crisis, nuclear threats, and climate change), the photographer has a brief exchange with the proprietor of the newsstand, who asks him a simple question: "Hell of a world we live in huh? . . . But it could be worse, huh?" The narrator responds simply, "That's right . . . or even worse, it could be perfect" (*BC* 36). The narrator's question pierces to the core of utopianism: are the perfectly rationalized and pacified utopias of instant gratification actually desirable? Or do they destroy something fundamental within the human condition? In many ways, this conundrum mirrors the question surrounding technology that underpins the bulk of Gibson's writings: is technological innovation always advantageous, or would certain technologies destroy the very nature of humanity?

The character of Mervyn Kihn reappears in Gibson's little-known story "Hippie Hat Brain Parasite" (1983), his only 1980s short story not collected in *Burning Chrome.* The story concerns a phone call from Kihn to an interlocutor identified only as "Bill"—presumably a fictionalized version of Gibson similar to the fictionalized version of themselves that Burroughs and Ballard inserted into certain works. An abbreviated story of about four pages, "Hippie Hat" boils down to a parasitic invasion story similar to 1950s sci-fi films such as William Cameron Menzies's *Invaders from Mars* (1953) and Don Siegel's *Invasion of the Body Snatchers* (1956).[8] However, the story also draws on body horror elements of parasitic invasion and bodily mutilation. Thomas Bredehoft provides a concise summary of the aliens, who come in the form of "bad sixties style leather hats"; the hatlike creature "perches on people's heads and controls them, marionette style" (256). Kihn has found conclusive proof of a parasitic invasion of the human race that he believes began in the Haight-Ashbury section of San Francisco in 1968, suggesting perhaps that the LSD-fueled expansion of consciousness opened the human mind to alien invasion. As Bredehoft further points out, "Hippie Hat Brain Parasite" takes a stance toward the 1960s similar to the position "The Gernsback Continuum" took vis-à-vis the sci-fi dreams of the 1930s: "But if it is not the alien which disturbs Kihn, it must be its mimicking of the effects of sixties drug use" (257). Bredehoft goes on to state that the story is "Not a warning against drug use, but against the temptation to give into the power of alternate (outer or inner) spaces" (257). Bredehoft connects this to the story's mention of L. Ron Hubbard, a sci-fi author and the founder of Scientology, but the story also mentions other fringe religions (or "cults" as some would label them) such as the Moonies and the Rosicrucians. When Kihn sees the "hippie hat" alien finally crawl off the man's head, he observes that there is "No *brain.* No top to his *head.* Just neatly nibbled off at the . . . hatline. Kinda *scarred,* in there, healed over, grayish pink. I saw where the hat had had its claws in, kinda puppet trip" (111). The story suggests that cultish groups such as the Scientologists and Moonies not only control their members but slowly suck them dry of individual thought, rendering them into shells incapable of survival without the group's support. While the hippies struggled against bourgeois, consumerist conformity, they fell prey to other, perhaps more insidious means of control. The parasites in the story almost directly reference the kind of parasitic invasion of control from William S. Burroughs's "Nova Trilogy." Despite their fight against conformity, they get transformed into "dividuals," as Deleuze terms them in his essay "Postscript on Control Societies"; that is, control reshapes even the most rebellious individuals and behavior patterns into nothing more than "modulations" in a data set (180). In essence, then, "Hippie Hat Brain Parasite" distills Gibson's punk skepticism of 1960s idealism into a science fiction story form.

In general, Gibson's cyberpunk stories unfold predominately on Earth, unlike some planet-hopping cyberpunk works such as Bruce Sterling's *Schismatrix,* but his story "Hinterlands" provides an exception. The story's plot alternates between two characters: a surrogate named Toby Halpert and a Soviet cosmonaut, Olga Tovyevski, who discovers a form of instantaneous interstellar travel via "The Highway." Toby Halpert is a surrogate who attempts to salvage the psychologically damaged explorers who return from the Highway. Olga, on the other hand, represents the patron saint of the Highway because she inadvertently discovered it during a mission to Mars. Humanity cannot understand the Highway, but it keeps hurling these ill-fated individuals into the unknown because they always manage to return with Earth-shattering artifacts or information: a "seashell" that spawns an entire new subbranch of physics or the final cure for cancer, among other finds. The concept of discovering alien technology beyond humankind's comprehension recalls Arkady Strugatsky and Boris Strugatsky's novel *Roadside Picnic* (1971) and Andrei Tarkovsky's film *Stalker* (1979), which was based on it.[9] Toby works aboard a space station in the "hinterlands" outlying the highway that serves as a kind of psychic salvage ward for the damaged "heroes." The inner cylinder of the station is known as Heaven, and it serves as the landing zone and recovery space for those who return from the Highway. Heaven is an idyllic, sylvan landscape meant to provide a soothing background for the traumatized astronauts. The surrogates' job consists of feeding a whole panoply of drugs (barbiturates, stimulants, hallucinogenics) to the travelers and trying to reacquaint them with reality in a comforting fashion.

Recalling Arthur C. Clarke's position that a sufficiently advanced alien civilization would appear to us like gods, Toby compares humanity to "intelligent houseflies wandering through an international airport," a space that can take them anywhere but that they can never understand: "At the edge of the Highway every human language unravels in your hands—except, perhaps, the language of the shaman, of the cabalist, the language of the mystic intent on mapping hierarchies of demons, angels, saints" (*BC* 75). Gibson's story equates the relation between human civilization and these aliens to Black Box theories that posit systems where we can know only the input and output of a black box without ever understanding how the box (or system) actually functions. Despite the mystery that shrouds the Highway and the psychological damage it inflicts on its travelers, humans still choose to hazard the risk in the hope of gaining knowledge about the universe and themselves.

The story becomes a parable about the psychological lack that simultaneously haunts the human condition and drives all human endeavors. Jacques Lacan argues that a "lack of being" exists at the core of the subject, as a black hole in the chain of signification from which all desire springs; desire is an attempt to achieve sublimation, a partial fulfillment that allows the subject to function on a relatively normal level (*Seminar II*, 223). The surrogates in the story, Toby and his former lover Charmian, both attempted to "hitchhike" on the Highway but, for unknown reasons, were rejected. The pain of this rejection allows them to empathize with the scarred individuals who return from the

Highway in a way that others cannot. Upon their return, the hitchhikers suffer the throes of absolute lack—their encounter with a higher intelligence has expanded their lack to gargantuan proportions because the distance between the signifier and any kind of real meaning seems even greater. The surrogates attempt to bring these hitchhikers back to reality by helping them achieve sublimation through the setting of Heaven, the drugs they administer, and the nurturing relationships they forge. But few travelers can return to a normal existence, and many wind up dead or insane as a result of their inability to achieve sublimation in the face of their newly expanded lack. Their reason has been shattered by a sublime experience, and there is no going back to their former existence. Unknowingly these travelers give up their blissfully ignorant existences in the quest for knowledge, but, like the fruit from Eden's mythical Tree of the Knowledge of Good and Evil, this knowledge shatters their existence and expels them from their former world.

While "Fragments of a Hologram Rose" subtlety gestured toward the possible immortality that computer technology can offer, Gibson attacks this issue head on in "The Winter Market." The story centers on Casey, an editor who produces artworks from "dry dreamers" whose subconscious imagery is digitally captured and then manipulated by editors like Casey. Beginning with Casey's receiving word that his former love interest, Lise, has recently let her physical form die in order to be transformed into a computer construct, the typically maudlin, hard-boiled character Casey begins to reflect upon his history with Lise.

Casey first met Lise when his friend Rubin rescued her from an alley. Rubin is a famous "junk artist in Marcel Duchamp's stamp," who crafts his pieces from *gomi,* the junk that has begun to engulf the landscape of the future (Hicks 77).[10] "Winter Market" takes place against the backdrop of the slow, subtle apocalypse of trash that is steadily despoiling our natural environment. The story distills this setting into the microcosm of the eponymous market in which any kind of junk is for sale. As Gibson explains in a blog post from 2007, the winter market is based on a retrofitted version of Vancouver's Granville Island. "Retrofitting" is the practice of upgrading older systems with new technology, and, in effect, the entire story concerns retrofitting and other forms of reusing older technology or spaces in inventive new ways. For example, Rubin's *bricolage*-style artwork participates in the practice of turning outmoded technology or junk into something new. During their visit to the market, Rubin explains that Casey's problem is that he is "the kind who *always reads the handbook.* Anything people build, any kind of technology, it's going to have some specific purpose. It's for doing something that somebody already understands. But if it's new technology, it'll open areas nobody's ever thought of before" (*BC* 137). Because Casey uses technology only according to the manual's directions, he becomes uncomfortable with people who deviate from these mandates, such as Lise's manipulating computers to achieve immortality.

The story actually depicts the retrofitting of the human body, a technology no longer capable of grappling with the environment that humanity has produced. Lise suffers from one of the various new, unnamed disorders that have arisen due to environmental conditions. A true cyborg, Lise's exoskeleton retrofits the organic human system, a form that, for her, has become vestigial junk, like the *gomi* from which Rubin crafts his pieces. Rubin found Lise in the alleyway where she had crawled after depleting her exoskeleton's batteries. Rubin fixed her exoskeleton, and Casey and Lise immediately forged a bizarre love/hate relationship, culminating not in sexual union but in "jacking straight across." With its clear sexual connotation of penetration or masturbation, "jacking straight across" actually constitutes a much more fundamental kind of a union: one individual uses a certain type of deck to directly access the other person's psyche. Casey describes the experience in almost orgasmic terms: "Words. Words cannot. Or, maybe, just barely, if I even knew how to begin to describe it, what came up out of her, what she did" (*BC* 132). Eventually, after recording and editing her "footage," Casey turns Lise's psychic imagery into a video album or film of sorts (the story never explains it precisely) called *Kings of Sleep*. Casey describes a particular moment from *Kings of Sleep* that feels "like you're on a motorcycle at midnight, no lights but somehow you don't need them, blasting out along a cliff-high stretch of coast highway, so fast that you hang there in a cone of silence, the bike's thunder lost behind you. Everything lost behind you. . . . Freedom and death, right there, right there, razor's edge forever" (*BC* 132). Here, Gibson once again delves into psychoanalytic territory to explore the possible implications of the psyche's digitization.

Casey confronts what Jacques Lacan would term "the real" head-on. Lacan developed a tripartite division of psychic orders: the real, the symbolic, and the imaginary, which to a certain degree rewrote Freud's id, ego, and superego according to a semiotic paradigm. As Lacan states, without the three orders (or registers) of the real, the symbolic, and the imaginary, "it would be impossible to understand anything of the Freudian technique or experience" (*Seminar 1*, 73). The imaginary is connected with the superego (or ego-ideal as it is sometimes termed) and self-identification. Like the ego, the symbolic provides the order that manages relations between the interior and the exterior worlds of the subject—it is the space of language. Finally, like the id, the real remains completely undifferentiated; it is raw and primal and is the source of hallucinations and anxieties: "The real is without fissure . . . we have no means of apprehending the real—on any level and not only on that of knowledge—except via the go-between of the symbolic" (*Seminar 2*, 97). The released version of *Kings of Sleep* features the edited version of Lise's imagery—the unconscious filtered through the symbolic; however, when Casey jacks straight across with her, he comes face to face with the unvarnished real, with the true space of anxiety, trauma, and hallucination. Instead of the sterilized, organized, commercial version of Lise's "art," Casey says, "What I got was the big-daddy version of that, raw rush, the king hell killer real thing, exploding eight ways from Sunday into a void that stank of poverty and lovelessness and obscurity" (*BC* 132). The experience is pure primality, and Casey's job consists of distilling these visions of the id into a commercial product; he must partition and parse this undifferentiated mass into a commodity form. In the cyberpunk landscape of "The Winter Market," even our most personal, unconscious images become objects capable of commodification.

Cyberpunk Conspirators: Gibson's Early Collaborations

During the early phase of his career, Gibson also collaborated with friends and fellow cyberpunk authors Bruce Sterling, John Shirley, and Michael Swanwick. Each of these authors brings unique elements to his collaboration with Gibson, yet the stories still feature distinctly Gibsonian elements. In Gibson and Shirley's "The Belonging Kind," the duo explores yet another theoretical concept vital to grasping postmodern theory through the narrative form. By having the story concern a linguistics professor, Gibson and Shirley turn their tale into a story about how semiotics—the study of sign systems and how they convey meaning—functions in the real world and whether or not humanity's signs are purely arbitrary. The story concerns Michael Corretti, who begins following a bizarre woman from one bar to another because her unnatural appearance, attire, and demeanor completely metamorphose depending upon her environment. Essentially, "The Belonging Kind" delves into the nature of conformity but also addresses the arbitrariness of the sign and the nature of social semiotics. Despite being a linguistics professor who "could talk with the head of his department about sequencing and options in conversational openings," Coretti himself "could never talk to strangers in bars or at parties" (*BC* 45–46). Furthermore, and more important, Coretti "didn't know how to dress. Clothing was a language and Coretti a kind of sartorial stutterer, unable to make the kind of basic coherent fashion statement that would put strangers at their ease. His ex-wife told him that he dressed like a Martian; that he didn't look as though he belonged anywhere in the city" (*BC* 46). An alien on his own planet, Coretti cannot adapt to the semiotic systems and linguistic conventions that he himself studies and teaches.

He catches a glimpse of the woman at the bar, the type of woman "he hadn't ever had" (*BC* 46). Even early on, Coretti picks up on something strange about her appearance and demeanor. While he alternates between "blurt[ing]" or hemming and hawing, he notices that she speaks and acts almost a little too flawlessly (*BC* 47). The word "mimetic" suddenly springs to Coretti's mind, but he pushes it aside without exploring it; however, the word gestures toward the woman's role as a kind of social mimic, who changes appearance and behavior in response to her environment. Entranced by the woman's beauty, Coretti tails her from the bar and sees her undergo a metamorphosis as she crosses the street. He watches as her hair, dress, and shoes transmogrify before she enters a disco, where she meets a young man, imbibes large quantities of alcohol, and dances in "perfect accord with the music . . . always fitting in perfectly" (*BC* 50). Seemingly unaffected by the massive quantities of alcohol, she transforms yet again before entering a jazz piano bar where Coretti sees her sitting with another young man: "Her hip touching his, just a little. They didn't seem to be speaking, but Coretti felt they were somehow communing" (*BC* 51). When he passes the couple, he notices them "murmuring realistic palaver" about film, and he realizes that "they were the kind you see in bars who seem to have grown there, who seem genuinely at home there. Not drunks, but human fixtures. Functions of the bar. The belonging kind" (*BC* 51). And, as he takes a seat beside her and orders her a drink, he hears her ask the question that drives the entire story: "But don't you think . . . that it's all relative?" (*BC* 51)

Coretti becomes obsessed with the woman and begins searching for her in bars all over town, causing him to lose his job. Finally, he observes some of the machinery that allows the duo to almost instantaneously change their appearance. When the man reaches into his coat for cab fare, Coretti notices something bizarre: "No wallet bulged there, and no pocket. But a kind of slit widened. It opened as the man's fingers poised over it, and it disgorged money" (*BC* 56). The couple's seemingly magical clothing actually constitutes a biological part of themselves capable of metamorphosing its appearance and even creating objects to help them blend in with their surroundings. Later, Coretti follows them to their hotel room, where the man uses "a grayish-pink, key-shaped sliver bone" that extends from his hand to unlock the door (*BC* 57). As Coretti witnesses these inhuman beings while they are "roosting" in the hotel room with at least a dozen others, he begins to feel that "something called to him across the distance, promising rest and peace and belonging" (*BC* 57). But this psychic call to belonging is cut short when the beings all open their eyes simultaneously, causing Coretti to flee in terror.

The story ends with his next fateful encounter with Antoinette, who buys him a drink with money that she produces out of a gill between her breasts. After their third drink, their hips touch, and he feels a sensation "spreading through him in slow orgasmic waves. It was sticky where they were touching; an area the size of the heel of his thumb where the cloth had parted. He was two men: the one inside fusing with her in total cellular communion, and the shell who sat casually on the stool at the bar, elbows on either side of his drink, fingers toying with a swizzle stick" (*BC* 60). Coretti realizes that they are mating, and the story then ends abruptly when the bartender mentions the rainy weather outside, to which Coretti responds with typical friendly banalities "like a real human being" (*BC* 60). In the end, the story leaves the reader with a fundamental conundrum: has Coretti embraced blind conformity in the story's final moments, or has he, in fact, been freed from the strictures of our superficial culture?

Cyperpunk spokesperson Bruce Sterling and William Gibson would later collaborate on their steampunk novel *The Difference Engine,* but their first joint effort was the short story "Red Star, Winter Orbit" (1983). Focused on Colonel Korolev, the story concerns Kosmograd, a Soviet space station that has been scheduled for decommission. The first man to walk on Mars, Korolev now represents a relic of the dying space industry. His room on the station receives the jocular label "Museum of Soviet Triumph in Space," indicating his status as a hero without a purpose. In essence, Gibson's story imagines a different outcome of the Cold War and somewhat presciently depicts the death of the Space Age dream. Despite not being as overtly cyberpunk as other Gibson and Sterling works, "Red Star" still explores posthuman identity. Korolev has allowed part of his memory to be erased and has had it replaced with music from his childhood. Furthermore, his prolonged time in zero gravity has altered his body on a fundamental level, rendering him incapable of returning to Earth. He constitutes a vestigial link to humanity's space dream, a dream that has died while humanity's aspirations have turned inward.

As the Cold War peaked, in the 1960s, the space race became a central conflict between the brooding nuclear powers the United States and the Soviet Union. Space perhaps beckoned so temptingly because humankind had reached the stalemate of mutually assured destruction. Gibson and Sterling wrote their story before the Cold War ended, in 1991, and even before Mikhail Gorbachev's *Perestroika* (restructuring) and *Glasnost* (openness) had begun to dissolve communism in the Soviet Union and ease Cold War tension, so it imagines a different end to Cold War tensions. In "Red Star, Winter Orbit," the United States' power has been decimated, epitomized by Cape Canaveral's and California's lying in ruins. The Soviet Union has triumphed and become the major global power on Earth, a victory partially symbolized by its winning the race to Mars. But, now, as the story opens, the space dream has dried up; it is a desiccated corpse left over from the midcentury surge in exploratory desire. Since the United States lost its power, the space station Kosmograd has outlived its usefulness, hence its impending decommission. In essence, "Red Star, Winter Orbit" concerns the human desire for new frontiers as well as the resistance to power and authority that has often driven humankind's efforts in exploration and colonization.

In the 1980s, the cultural interest in space travel dwindled as the dream of infinite expansion throughout the galaxies turned inward via the computer. Part of an obsolete minority, Korolev has outlived his usefulness. Like so many of Gibson's male protagonists from his early fiction, Korolev reveals himself to be a brooding character who remains obsessed with a past from which he has been forever sundered. Nevertheless, he tries to remain relevant by attempting to salvage his space station from decommission. In the spirit of true Marxism, Korolev starts a workers' movement in opposition to the liquidation. Unfortunately for Korolev, he is operating not in a truly communist state but in the bastardized, totalitarian form of communism that came to prominence under the rule of Stalin. In this future, totalitarianism has adopted posthumanist principles; it no longer requires propaganda but can instead operate directly upon the psyches of the masses through drugs that can instill fear. The drugs allow the Soviet regime to perfect its use of terror and paranoia as methods of control; propaganda is no longer necessary when human emotions can be directly influenced on a chemical level. Despite their desire to scrap the station, the Soviet authorities remain hesitant to simply abandon it without a legitimate reason for fear of losing face. Hence, the KGB decide to press charges against the crew for black market activities—the crew has been trading American memorabilia and popular culture artifacts, a technically illegal but usually accepted practice. Initially, the authorities request that Korolev provide a moral example for his crew by pleading guilty to the charges, but he holds onto the dream of space and a freedom from such totalitarian posturing. As Yefremov, the KGB agent, explains to him, "Kosmograd was a dream, Colonel. A dream that failed. Like Space" (*BC* 92). Korolev rallies the crew and issues a list of demands to his superiors, attempting to turn Kosmograd into an orbiting Potemkin, a historical allusion in the story that connects it to the Soviet Union's revolutionary past.[11] Eventually, the Soviet higher-ups decide simply to allow the Kosmograd's orbit to decay, but Korolev has one last ploy up his sleeve.

As part of his plan to save his fellow crew members from imprisonment without trial, Korolev hits the decompression alarm while his cohort crashes the station's computers. The wailing klaxons and general confusion allow the other crewmembers to escape and land in China or Japan, where they plan to use information about the Soviet Union's plans to "embarrass the Kremlin" into allowing Korolev to live out his life on the station (*BC* 103). When asked if he has a "message for the world," Korolev considers the various clichés but ends up saying, "Tell them that I need it . . . in my very bones" (*BC* 103). Korolev's "message" of course references his inability to return to Earth's gravity, but it also signifies humankind's need for frontiers, a need that Korolev embodied as the first man on Mars. Korolev's confinement to space signals the passage into a truly posthuman condition, one in which the body has actually been reprogrammed to adapt to new, nonterrestrial, artificial environments. The posthuman connection between a technological environment and posthuman identity becomes further apparent when the other crew members leave and the station becomes deathly quiet: "The silence scratched away at his nerves; the systems crash had deactivated the ventilation system, whose hum he'd lived with for twenty years" (*BC* 103). Humankind's constant bombardment with the white noise of technology causes Korolev's anxiety to rocket to panic-attack level; technology becomes engrained in the mind and body to the point that separation from it leads to psychological trauma or even death.

Later, Korolev awakens to someone inexplicably knocking on the station's hatch, where he discovers two young people enjoying orbital freefall. They are squatters from a nearby geodesic balloon who have decided to relocate to the space station. In the years prior to the story, the Treaty of Vienna gave the Soviet Union complete control of the world's oil supply. Part of "the pathetic flurry of strange American energy schemes" in reaction to the treaty, these solar balloons are "mirrored geodesic spheres" that were to be part of "a grandiose American plan to build solar-powered satellites" (*BC* 95). The pair of squatters has used booster engines to travel from the balloons to Kosmograd and stabilize its orbit so that the rest of their group can move into the station as well. The squatters seek freedom from Earth's oppressive governmental systems. As they explain when Korolev inquires about their purpose, "You have to *want* a frontier—want it in your bones, right?" (*BC* 107) The story's conclusion reiterates humankind's need for new frontiers, for escape from oppressive political regimes, for the ability to start anew. As the prospect of space as a new home for large groups of individuals began to wane, humankind started to look for other frontiers, frontiers provided by the personal computer and the internet.

Gibson also coauthored one other story, "Dogfight," with Michael Stanwick. It concerns a drifter named Deke, who stumbles upon a new obsession during a routine stopover. He becomes enamored of a game in which holographic biplanes battle for supremacy against one another. The current champion is a disabled man named Tiny who defends "The Blue Max," which serves as the championship belt for this league of virtual combatants (*BC* 152). Driven by his fascination, Deke steals a copy of SPADS & FOKKERS, which is named after the types of biplanes in the game, and begins to experiment with it. Along with the game, he also steals two programming units and a Batang facilitator remote that fits behind the ear. When he runs the program, the Spad flies in front of his face with a startling realism. The game promises freedom from a world in which Deke seems to be constantly on the run, but his concentration does not prove fixed enough to contend with the likes of Tiny.

Deke plays with his copy of SPADS & FOKKERS until he runs out of money and then begins trying to sell the stolen device to one of the many students who also live in his highstack. After knocking and stating his business, Deke enters the apartment of a young female student with a terrifying result: "There was a hole in her hand, a black tunnel that ran right up her arm. Two small red lights. Rat's eyes. They scurried forward and leaped for his face" (156). This horrifying creature ends up being a mere holographic projection that the student, Nance Bettendorf, uses as a security system. Nance provides an interesting counterpoint to Deke because they both remain prisoners to technologies that regulate their behavior. Arrested as a thief, Deke was implanted with a "brainlock" that prevents him from returning to Washington, D.C.; the brainlock causes him to exhibit a preternatural fear of the Washington Monument. Like the human programming in Anthony Burgess's *A Clockwork Orange* (1962) and Stanley Kubrick's eponymous 1971 film, the brainlock proves imperfect, causing Deke to focus not on the Washington Monument itself but on the twin red lights atop the obelisk. Hence, any pairs of red lights, such as the eyes of the holographic rat, can send Deke spiraling into a primordial state of fear. Similarly, Nancy has a "chastity lock" that her parents installed to prevent her from getting caught up in sexual intercourse instead of her studies. The chastity lock overshoots its purposes as well because she "can't stand to have anybody touch [her] or even stand too close" (*BC* 159). This wetware programming simultaneously precludes them from experiencing true freedom and draws Deke and Nancy together, allowing them to bond over SPADS & FOKKERS.

A cutting-edge programming student, Nance finds the game's programming primitive and offers to "beef it up" for Deke and "translate it into modern wetlanguage" (*BC* 163). The somewhat ambiguous term "wetlanguage" can be understood as a type of programming that interacts directly with the human mind and body, and the story subtly examines the confusion of boundaries between machines and humans with descriptions of Nance "sweating data into a machine" (*BC* 164). Deke's virtual-flying performance improves drastically as his reflexes become more precisely attuned to the machine. "Dogfight" deals with how drugs can serve as their own form of wetlanguage in their capacity to program the human mind and body. Virtual combatants such as Tiny use a stimulant called "hype" to increase concentration and sharpen reflexes. High dosages lead to an "etching" of the "brain surfaces," almost as if the human mind were a computer chip being reprogrammed by the drug (*BC* 165). After being exempted from her finals because of her programming skills, Nance reveals that she has some hype, which Deke immediately craves as he continues to climb the ranks toward challenging Tiny.

Nance initially refuses to give him her hit of hype because of an upcoming job interview, but Deke maintains that this represents the one "glimmer" of hope in his pathetic life (*BC* 171). He begins torturing her by stroking her face, causing her chastity brainlock to emit pain signals. Deke subsequently steals the hype and proceeds to his duel with Tiny with "the black of his eyes . . . like pinpricks," a sign that he has been fully reprogrammed and computerized (*BC* 172). Deke meets Tiny in an epic combat, but, as the battle heats up, hype hallucinations begin to distract Deke. Ultimately, Deke fights through the hallucinations and beats Tiny; however, his victory seems almost unethical considering the consequences it wreaks on the disabled champion: "Combat was the only out that Tiny had had, and he'd taken every chance he got. . . . He saw that flying was all that held Tiny together. . . . Break that willpower, and mortality would come pouring out and drown him. Tiny would lean over and throw up in his own lap" (*BC* 176). In the final minutes, "Dogfight" drives home a moral about dehumanization. Deke has transcended his mediocre lifestyle in a perhaps admirable fashion, but he ends up submitting to the machine. As his attunement to the machine takes hold, he loses his connections with humans and their emotions. He almost literally "fucks over" Nance and proceeds to rob a disabled man of his only fulfilling activity. Thus, "Dogfight" resolves into a moralistic fable about the dangers of computerizing the human—empathy dies as one becomes capable of emotionless calculations.

Now Entering the Sprawl: Population Approaching Infinity . . .

Of course, Gibson's most famous short stories remain the trilogy that appeared in *Omni* magazine and first began to outline the world of the Sprawl, the setting for his first trilogy of novels. The Sprawl stories and novels have proved extremely influential, with the alternative band Sonic Youth naming one of the songs on their classic album *Daydream Nation* (1988) "The Sprawl." Interestingly, except for the short film based on "The Gernsback Continuum," the Sprawl short stories have been the inspiration for the only two films adapted from Gibson's works. The world of "The Sprawl" first appeared in "Johnny Mnemonic," a story that opens like typical hard-boiled detective fare with its depiction of a man hiding a shotgun in a gym bag. "Johnny Mnemonic" unfolds against the standard tropes of crime fiction: dive bars, underground communities, shootouts, mafia, and so on. However, all of these clichéd motifs receive the cyberpunk makeover.

Gibson's story immediately immerses the reader in a world in which the line between the humans and machines has blurred almost beyond distinction. The human form has become reprogrammable through extreme forms of cosmetic surgery, sex changes, and even fake muscling techniques. The malleable surface of humanity becomes apparent with "The Magnetic Dog Sisters," who serve as bouncers for the Drome, the club in which the story opens: "They were two meters tall and thin as greyhounds. One was black and the other white, but aside from that they were as nearly identical as cosmetic surgery could make them" (*BC* 2). Johnny himself functions like a human hard drive capable of storing data for clients. The clients possess a code word that causes Johnny to go into an idiot-savant mode, in which he recites the data without retaining any knowledge of it. But, like a true hard drive, a technology called squids can retrieve erased data from his brain just as computer forensics specialists can often recover deleted information from a hard drive. At the outset, Johnny finds himself in a dire situation because his brain contains stolen Yakuza information; therefore, he has become the evidence that they seek to erase.

In "Johnny Mnemonic," Gibson presents the reader with a basic dichotomy concerning low- and high-tech approaches to situations: "If they think you're crude, go technical. If they think you're technical, go crude" (*BC* 1). In many ways, this opposition between high- and low-tech mirrors the binary of human/machine that operates as cyberpunk's *primum mobile*. Gibson drops the reader down into this world via a dive bar, where Johnny arrives to make a delivery. Like a stereotypical hard-boiled dive, the Drome "stank of biz," of the various black-market transactions that transpire there (*BC* 2). Johnny's client has been dodging his attempts to deliver the data and collect his fee, so he has become suspicious and entered the bar with a distinctly "low-tech" gambit: a hidden shotgun rigged to shoot out of a hole in his "professionally nondescript gym bag" (*BC* 2). Events quickly devolve when Johnny's client Ralfi turns on a "neural disrupter," rendering him incapable of movement. Ralfi then reveals that a "dead fool" stole the data from the Yakuza and that simply returning the data would not satisfy them: "Ralfi, of course, could use the code phrase to throw me into idiot/savant, and I'd spill their hot program without remembering a single quarter tone. For a fence such as Ralfi, that would ordinarily have been enough. But not for the Yakuza. The Yakuza would know about squids, for one thing, and they wouldn't want to worry about one lifting those dim and permanent traces of their program out of my head" (*BC* 4). The downward spiral of the meeting is halted by the intervention of a stimulant-selling woman who ends up; butchering Ralfi's guards and freeing Johnny.

Molly Millions sports the typical cyberpunk mirrorshades; however, "her mirrored lenses were surgical inlays" that allow her to access information directly with her eyes (*BC* 6). As Molly and Johnny leave the Drome with Ralfi in tow, they notice that they are being tailed by a man attired as a "standard tourist tech" with "a silly Hawaiian shirt printed with blowups of his firm's most popular micro-processors" (*BC* 6). This seemingly mild-mannered tourist is actually a Yakuza assassin who has "a prosthetic tip" on his thumb that contains "a spool with three meters of monomolecular filament" (*BC* 6–7). Suddenly, Ralfi explodes, which Johnny describes in slow motion: "Playback on full recall shows Ralfi stepping forward as the little tech sidles out of nowhere, smiling. Just a suggestion of a bow, and his little thumb falls off. It's a conjuring trick. . . . And then the joke-shop thumbtip, heavy as lead, arcs out in a lighting yo-yo trick, and the invisible thread connecting it to the killer's hand passes laterally through Ralfi's skull, just above his eyebrows, whips up, and descends, slicing the pear-shaped torso diagonally from shoulder to rib cage. Cuts so fine that no blood flows until synapses misfire and the first tremors surrender the body to gravity" (*BC* 7). The slow-motion recap of the scene recalls samurai death scenes from Japanese cinema and presages countless scenes from future cyberpunk-influenced films such as *The Matrix* (1999). Johnny fires the shotgun at the assassin, who dodges it because "his nervous system's jacked up" (*BC* 8). Molly becomes obsessed with fighting him because she recognizes a worthy opponent. She too is "factory custom," as she demonstrates to Johnny by revealing "the narrow, double-edged scalpel[s] in pale blue steel" that extrude from and retract behind her fingertips (*BC* 8).

To keep Johnny safe, the two journey to Nighttown, a typical postmodern "zone" where "generations of sharpshooters had chipped away at the neon until the maintenance crews gave up" (*BC* 9). In *Postmodern Fiction,* Brian McHale argues that "zones" constitute peculiarly postmodern spaces. McHale bases his reading of zones on Michel Foucault's concept of heterotopias, which involve "the linking together of things that are inappropriate; I mean the disorder in which fragments of a large number of possible orders glitter separately in the dimension, without law or geometry, of the *heteroclite*" (Foucault, *Order* xviii). McHale adapts Foucault's heterotopia into his own concept of zones, a concept that he traces through several postmodern classics: Italo Calvino's *Invisible Cities* (1972), Thomas Pynchon's *Gravity's Rainbow,* and Vladimir Nabokov's *Ada, or Ardor: A Family Chronicle* (1969). As McHale explains of zones, "Space here is less constructed than *deconstructed* by the text"; space "becomes plural" and signals "the collapse of *ontological* boundaries" (*Postmodern Fiction* 45). Like the zones that McHale discusses, Nighttown simultaneously exhibits the characteristics of its original construction and intention and the deconstructed overlay that the Lo Teks have inscribed upon the space through *bricolage.*

Since Nighttown is a lawless zone, its denizens choose to eschew lighting in favor of privacy. As Paul Virilio argues in *The Vision Machine,* "the use of light stimuli in crowd control goes back a long way," for the forces in power seek "to obtain a total image of society by dispersing its dark secrets" (*Vision* 9, 34). But Nighttown refuses this illumination of the public sphere and the channels of control that it comprises. Unfortunately, one cannot so easily hide from the Yakuza, who have become "a true multinational, like ITT and Ono-Sendai" (*BC* 9). Nighttown, like the bulk of cities, lies under a geodesic dome, explaining why it remains dark even during the day. Johnny and Molly hide in the top of the geodesic, "where the Lo Teks crouch in the dark like gargoyles" (*BC* 9). To retrieve the information from his head, Molly takes Johnny to meet Jones, a cyborg junkie dolphin who constitutes "surplus from the last war" (*BC* 10). Built by the Navy, which purposefully addicted him to drugs to control him, Jones has advanced decryption capabilities but can express himself only through coded transmissions using red, white, and blue bulbs. Jones also contains a squid in him capable of retrieving erased data. After shooting Jones up, Johnny goes into idiot-savant mode, a transition he describes in almost poetic language: "And then it all faded to cool gray static and an endless tone poem in an artificial language. I sat and sang dead Ralfi's stolen program for three hours" (*BC* 14). Once Molly has retrieved the information from Johnny's head, the pair meet up with the Lo Teks in the rafters above Nighttown. The Lo Teks despise high technology and live off the grid, but even they make some concessions to posthuman technologies, as evidenced by Dog, who has undergone "tooth-bud transplants" to achieve "a mask of total bestiality" (*BC* 15).

In many ways, the Lo Teks' retrofitted existence on the margins of Sprawl society presages the Bridge from Gibson's second trilogy: "The Lo Teks leech their webs and huddling places to the city's fabric with thick gobs of epoxy and sleep above the abyss in mesh hammocks. Their country is so attenuated in places it consists of little more than holds for hands and feet, sawed into geodesic struts" (*BC* 17). The Lo Teks dwell in a zone within a zone, and Molly makes a special request of them: she wants to use the Killing Floor to face the assassin in combat. While they have entered a subculture that privileges lower levels of technology, Johnny remains trapped by the high-tech, cyber-system of surveillance and information, as his narration reiterates late in the story: "We're an information economy. They teach you that in school. What they don't tell you is that it's impossible to move, to love, to operate at any level without leaving traces, bits, seemingly meaningless fragments of personal information. Fragments that can be retrieved, amplified" (*BC* 17). But the society of surveillance and information also harbors the potential for new revolutionary acts, such as the proposition that the Lo Teks offer the Yakuza: "Call off the dogs or we wideband your program" (*BC* 18). Johnny remains ignorant of what the program contains, but he knows that it constitutes information stolen from Ono-Sendai or another corporation. Society and the people that populate it have become nothing more than so much data in the massive global computer mind that the corporations control.

Built through the art of *bricolage,* "Lo Tek heaven" was "jury-rigged and jerry-built from scraps even Nighttown didn't want" (*BC* 18). The Killing Floor itself follows this aesthetic, a swinging illuminated space constructed of plywood and ropes. Here, the Lo Teks revert to truly pretechnological, primal behavior, as evidenced when the story states, "A girl with teeth like Dog's hit the Floor on all fours. Her breasts were tattooed with indigo spirals" (19). The Lo Teks also re-create themselves as low-technology, *bricolage* works of art through the acts of tattooing and scarring, both acts associated with the Punk movement. As Michael Hardt and Antonio Negri argue, cyberpunk demonstrates how self-fashioning can turn control against itself:

> In the dark world of cyberpunk fiction, for example, the freedom of self-fashioning is often indistinguishable from the powers of an all-encompassing control. We certainly do need to change our bodies and ourselves, and in perhaps a much more radical way than the common aesthetic mutations of the body, such as piercings and tattoos, punk fashion and its various imitations, but in the end they do not hold a candle to the kind of radical mutation needed here. The will to be against really needs a body that is completely incapable of submitting to command. It needs a body that is incapable of adapting to family life, to factory discipline, to the regulations of a traditional sex life, and so forth. (*Empire* 216)

Hardt and Negri further develop Donna Haraway's concept of the cyborg that has the ability to scramble gender norms but still remains subject to the forces of control and the information economy. Gibson begins imagining how subjects can engage in *bricolage* not just on the individual level but also in the mutation of spaces to subvert or escape from control, spaces such as Nighttown and the Killing Floor.

The assassin appears at the edge of the Killing Floor's electric lights and attempts to attack Johnny. The Lo Teks provide a musical pulse for the fight through percussive accompaniment: "The sound it made was like the world ending, like the wires that hold heaven snapping and coiling across the sky" (*BC* 20). This is Molly's natural habitat, and she begins to engage in a "mad-dog dance" against "a vertigo of sound" across "a crazy metal sea" (*BC* 21). Ultimately, the assassin dies from a kind of culture shock—he sends his hidden filament whirling at Molly one last time, but the wavelike motion of the Killing Floor causes her to descend as it trails harmlessly overhead. At the same time, "The Floor whiplashed, lifting him into the path of the taut molecule. It should have passed harmlessly over his head and been withdrawn into its diamond-hard socket. It took his hand off just behind the wrist. There was a gap in the Floor in front of him, and he went through it like a diver, with a strange deliberate grace, a defeated kamikaze on his way down to Nighttown. Partly, I think, he took the dive to buy himself a few seconds dignity of silence. She'd killed him with culture shock" (*BC* 21–22). Despite his body augmentation, the assassin finally proves himself to be a tourist who cannot adapt to one element in Nighttown: the seemingly simple wave pattern of the wooden Killing Floor's movements.

After the duel, the Lo Teks never learn whether their message reached the Yakuza, but Johnny stays with them and begins growing new teeth to represent his allegiance to the Lo Teks. As Johnny explains, he had "spent most of his life as a blind receptacle to be filled with other people's knowledge and then drained, spouting synthetic knowledge" (*BC* 19). He has denied his self and existed as a pure lack into which others could upload information that remained unknown and meaningless to him. Anything that can fill Johnny's lack remains incomprehensible to him, so he stays in a state of existential meaninglessness. At the story's end, he seems to have found meaning through friendship and community; he becomes a member of the Lo Teks, and his identification with their community provides meaning and fulfillment in his life.

Gibson's next Sprawl story, "New Rose Hotel," features fewer elements of estrangement (the mode typically associated with science fiction) than its fellow Sprawl stories; instead, it reads like a postmodern hard-boiled story of corporate intrigue with a few traditional science fiction tropes. Adapted into a 1998 film by Abel Ferrara, *New Rose Hotel* represents the most successful adaptation of Gibson to the big screen. Perhaps the most "hard-boiled" of Gibson's stories, "New Rose" opens with the narrator sleeping in a so-called coffin hotel and reflecting upon the femme fatale figure who led to his downfall. The narrator, as often seems the case with femmes fatales, seems incapable of deciding whether he wants to make love to his missing object of desire or beat her to a pulp in a manner so "slow and sweet and mean" (*BC* 109). He equates her with her handgun, which serves as a rather grim memento of their relationship: "Sometimes I take your little automatic out of my bag, run my thumb down smooth cheap chrome. Chinese .22, its bore no wider than the dilated pupils of your vanished eyes" (*BC* 109). This equation of the gun with the absent woman stages the narrator as a typical hard-boiled protagonist akin to Dashiell Hammett's Sam Spade, Raymond Chandler's Philip Marlowe, or Mickey Spillane's Mike Hammer.

The story's second section immediately situates this hard-boiled tale in a cyberpunk framework via its description of the narrator's partner, Fox, "a soldier in the secret skirmishes of the zaibatsus, the multinational corporations that control entire economies" (*BC* 109). Like most cyberpunk, "New Rose" concerns the global manipulation of information and economies by corporations while also questioning what aspects of human nature might not prove transferrable to computers. "The Edge," as Gibson terms it, constitutes "that essential fraction of sheer human talent, nontransferable, locked in the skills of the world's hottest research scientists" (*BC* 109). As Fox explains, "You can't put Edge down on paper," and you "can't punch Edge into a diskette" (*BC* 110). Hence, Edge remains antithetical to the information age, which seeks to quantify all knowledge, as Lyotard makes clear in his discussion of "the hegemony of computers," which requires that knowledge be "translated into information" (4). Under this hegemony's sway, "an exteriorization of knowledge with regard to the 'knower'" occurs, and knowledge becomes nothing more than a commodity: "Knowledge is and will be produced in order to be sold, it is and will be consumed in order to be valorized in a new production" (Lyotard 4). Because Edge cannot be digitized and commodified like information, the zaibatsus seek to capture those individuals who possess Edge and protect them from any corporate spies or pillagers. The scientists with Edge become wizardlike figures in their incomprehensible service to their uncomprehending yet all-controlling corporate masters. While the Cold War era concerned itself with national defectors, the information era becomes obsessed with corporate defectors. These individuals become a commodity in themselves, and the narrator and Fox specialize in helping zaibatsus pilfer these human commodities from one another.

In his coffin, the narrator's only company resides in a television and his memories, so he reflects on the woman who led to his current residence. The main flashback plot of "New Rose Hotel" starts moving in an almost Proustian stream-of-consciousness fashion: like Proust's madeleine or loose brick, the physical sensation of the gun causes the narrator to mentally journey back in time and replay the events that led to his current predicament. As the present comingles with the past, the narrator recalls the various life stories that Sandii told him on different nights while they lay in postcoital embraces. Fox quickly finds a use for Sandii, but he never really experiences her as the narrator does because "he never lay all night with you on the beach at Kamakura, never listened to your nightmares, never heard an entire imagined childhood shift under those stars, shift and roll over, your child's mouth opening to reveal some fresh past, and always the one, you swore, that was really and finally the truth" (*BC* 111). Sandii constitutes an almost Nietzschean form of identity in which every mask only hides another mask. She is pure simulacrum, an elusive signifier that can never be pinned down, thus making her the perfect seductress for an upcoming job.

Their plan involves using Sandii to seduce a bioengineer named Hiroshi Yomiuri away from a company called Maas Biolabs and to deliver him to the Hosaka zaibatsu. Hiroshi leads a relatively quiet life, sheltered invisibly by Maas Biolabs' "rich, clear syrup of surveillance" (*BC* 112). Gibson's story conceives of corporations as lifeforms interacting with one another. Their "Hosaka contacts were like specialized cells protecting the parent organism" (*BC* 112). Following along with this metaphor, most individuals in the corporate-controlled landscape of the Sprawl can be considered nothing more than cells in the various organs and appendages that make up the corporate bodies. Fox and the narrator, on the other hand, are "mutagens," "dubious agents adrift on the dark side of the intercorporate sea" (*BC* 112). They exist independent of the corporate lifeforms, but their status as mutagens allows them to shake up the status quo by enabling the transport of cells from one corporate body to another, thus possibly spurring mutation or evolution.

As Fox explains, "Imagine an alien . . . who's come here to identify the planet's dominant form of intelligence. The alien has a look, then chooses. What do you think he picks. . . . The Zaibatsus . . . the multinationals. The blood of a zaibatsu is information, not people. The structure is independent of the lives that comprise it. Corporation as life form" (*BC* 114). The corporations represent the new regime of power that transcends nations and their petty presidents, prime ministers, monarchs, and generals. They constitute the natural outgrowths of capitalism that have managed to evolve beyond the monopolies of the early twentieth century in their slyness and all-encompassing power. As Hardt and Negri argue, "The huge transnational corporations construct the fundamental connective fabric of the biopolitical world in certain important respects. Capital has indeed always been organized with a view toward the entire global sphere, but only in the second half of the twentieth century did multinational and transnational industrial and financial corporations really begin to structure global territories biopolitically" (*Empire* 31). Hardt and Negri borrow the term "biopolitical" from Michel Foucault; as they explain, it means that corporations "directly structure and articulate territories and populations," thus making them the true source of power and control as governments and nation-states become nothing more than their puppets (*Empire* 31).

Sandii embodies a new cyberpunk sensuousness; she is a femme fatale of the digital age: "Inside you I imagined all that neon, the crowds surging around Shinjuku Station, wired electric night. You moved that way, rhythm of a new age, dreamy and far from any nation's soul" (*BC* 113). The digital world has infiltrated Sandii's body, and her rhythm aligns with the syncopated, binary beat of ones and zeros or the pulses of the neon sign. Her sensuous nature, readiness for sex, and melding with the technoscape make her the perfect bait to catch Hiroshi, "a freak . . . who shatters paradigms" (*BC* 114). Hiroshi has a "radical" form of Edge similar to that of singular thinkers such as Newton, Tesla, Turing, and Einstein. Eventually, Hiroshi agrees to leave his wife for Sandii and to defect from Maas to Hosaka. The narrator arranges one final night with Sandii before the defection, and, after intercourse, he goes through her purse as she sleeps and discovers a "diskette" with "no labels" that "lay[s] there in the palm of my hand, all that death. Latent, coded, waiting" (*BC* 117). Death, like life and information, can be encoded and computerized as well.

Soon, Hiroshi mysteriously disappears right under the nose of Maas's surveillance, almost as if he has vanished down the rabbit hole (to borrow *The Matrix*'s Lewis Carroll allusion): "He stepped through a looking glass. Somewhere, offstage, the oiled play of Victorian clockwork" (*BC* 117). It is almost as if Hiroshi has been extracted by a literal deus ex machina, swooped away by the god from the machine. Soon, the narrator receives a call and finds that his credit and Fox's have been destroyed: "Hosaka didn't freeze our credit, they caused it to evaporate. Fairy gold. One minute we were millionaires in the world's hardest currency, and the next we were paupers" (*BC* 121). The pair try to escape, but they learn that Hosaka's resources are limitless: "Every door was closed. . . . The surface tension of the underworld had tripled, and everywhere we'd meet that same taut membrane and be thrown back" (*BC* 121). Before long, Fox's back has been broken, and the narrator somehow escapes to the New Rose Hotel.

The story ends in typical hard-boiled fashion with the revelation of Sandii as the femme fatale: "Fox once said you [Sandii] were ectoplasm, a ghost called up by the extremes of economics. Ghost of the new century, congealing on a thousand beds in the world's Hyatts, the world's Hiltons" (*BC* 122). Sandii represents a symptom of late capitalism; she has created herself as a simulacrum in order to play the system against itself. Maas Biolabs paid Sandii to act as a double agent playing Hiroshi, the narrator, and Hosaka against each other in a fashion that Hammett's Continental Op from *Red Harvest* (1929) would respect.[12] The narrator learns that Sandii's disk contains a meningeal plague that ends up killing or frying the brains of Hiroshi and Hosaka's entire research team, but he can't focus on that because Hosaka still hunts the night for him. However, even this seemingly eminent danger remains remote to the narrator who can only focus upon Sandii: "It's alright, baby. Only please come here. Hold my hand" (*BC* 123). Despite the fact that she has screwed him over and caused numerous deaths for her own monetary gain, Sandii proves to be a true femme fatale because the men in her life remain ensnared by her fatal charms even after her ploys have been revealed. In the end, "New Rose Hotel" shows that many aspects of society may alter as we enter the world of late capitalism, postmodernism, and computerization, but desire and greed (two of humanity's most basic motivational forces) remain the same.

"Burning Chrome" rounds out Gibson's trilogy of Sprawl stories and provides the first depiction of cyberspace and the netherworld of hackers that came to define cyberpunk from its earliest manifestations up through more recent works such as the Wackowski siblings' *Matrix* trilogy. Gibson's "Burning Chrome" starts with perhaps his most provocative opening line outside *Neuromancer:* "It was hot, the night we burned Chrome" (*BC* 179). Here, we get a sense that the natural world and its environment have been invaded or penetrated by some kind of technological otherness. This short sentence forecasts the opening line of *Neuromancer,* in which Gibson similarly conflates nature and technology. Here the temperature, in terms of weather, meets a technological metaphor of heat in the idea of "burning" (or hacking) Chrome. The story expands upon this juxtaposition in the following line: "Out in the malls and plazas, moths were batting themselves to death against the neon" (*BC* 179). In this sentence, we get the natural world and natural light disrupted by the false light of the neon, itself a naturally occurring element but one that has been technologically excited for the production of lighted signs that in many ways signify the landscape of postmodern reality—the reality (or unreality) of Las Vegas and Disney World. Jean Baudrillard terms our current society "hyperreal," and Gibson's novels make this hyperreality even more apparent with their technology-saturated spaces. As Baudrillard explains, Disneyland harbors a deeper secret than its simulacral, utopian exterior: "Disneyland exists in order to hide that it is the 'real' country, all of 'real' America that *is* Disneyland. . . . Disneyland is presented as imaginary in order to make us believe that the rest is real, whereas all of Los Angeles and the America that surrounds it are no longer real, but belong to the hyperreal order and the order of simulation" (*Simulation* 12). In many ways, these lines define the posthuman condition in which nature and technology collide to foster a new type of environment in which humankind (and the entire natural world) gets reshaped by an immense array of different forces, ranging from the weather of the natural world (weather that itself is influenced by technological fallout) to the various technologies (both big and small) that demarcate the cartography of the postmodern urban and suburban landscapes.

"Burning Chrome" truly sets the stage for the Sprawl novels that followed with its depiction of cyberspace, hackers, and ice. While "Johnny Mnemonic" and "New Rose Hotel" introduced us to the zaibatsus that control the global flow of business and information, "Burning Chrome" first begins to conceive of the computer technology that makes this global flow of data possible. In the same opening paragraph, the narrator describes his "matrix simulator," an "Ono-Sendai VII, the 'Cyberspace Seven'" that he has tinkered with and retrofitted until "you'd have had a hard time finding a square millimeter of factory circuitry in all that silicon" (*BC* 179). The matrix constitutes the global computer network that allows for the secure storage and transmission of data: it is "an abstract representation of the relationships between data systems" (*BC*

180). The matrix simulator allows users to experience a fully interactive, visual representation of this network; they "find themselves surrounded by bright geometries representing the corporate data" (*BC* 181). The narrator describes jacking into the matrix in almost surrealistic terms: "A silver tide of phosphenes boiled across my field of vision as the matrix began to unfold in my head, a 3-D chessboard, infinite and perfectly transparent" (*BC* 179). In many ways, the matrix literalizes Lyotard's claim that the postmodern era will cause a fundamental change in the nature of knowledge; it must become information, which means that it must be translatable into computer language. Here, the knowledge of the various corporations becomes distilled into geometrical representations.

The story concerns the narrator, Automatic Jack, and his partner in crime, Bobby Quine, during their hacking run on Chrome, who owns the House of Blue Lights, a kind of brothel in which sex workers are kept "in an approximation of REM sleep" while the customers copulate with them (*BC* 203). Chrome began her criminal existence as a hormone drug dealer, but she quickly rose to a boss with a massive computer network secured against any prying eyes that might expose her illegal dealings. Jack has seen Chrome in person a few times at the Gentleman Loser: "Maybe she was slumming, or checking out the human condition, a condition she didn't exactly aspire to. A sweet little heart-shaped face framing the nastiest pair of eyes you ever saw. She'd looked fourteen for as long as anyone could remember, hyped out of anything like normal metabolism on some massive program of serums and hormones" (*BC* 192). As her metallic name implies, Chrome has attained a genuinely posthuman existence in which she has programmed her body to stop aging in the normal human fashion. Her human form has been rendered almost vestigial as her virtual representation has become monolithic. The juxtaposition between the human and the machine is further driven home by the comparisons that Jack draws between her seemingly innocent childlike appearance and her inhuman eyes: "Chrome: her pretty childface smooth as steel, with eyes that would have been at home on the bottom of some deep Atlantic trench, cold gray eyes that lived under terrible pressure" (*BC* 180). Chrome protects herself with ICE, "Intrusion Countermeasure Electronics," which foresee the antihacker security measures that developed alongside the Internet: firewalls, data encryption, virus detection software, and so on.

Automatic Jack explains that "legitimate programmers jack into their employers' sector of the matrix and find themselves surrounded by the bright geometries representing the corporate data. . . . Legitimate programmers never see the walls of ice they work behind, the walls of shadow that screen their operations from others" (*BC* 180–81). On the other side of the equation, the "cowboys" like Bobby and Jack operate in the interstices between corporate entities, attempting to infiltrate the walls of ice that separate them from the valuable data housed within the corporate sectors of the matrix. The juxtaposition of the two main characters also introduces another basic dichotomy essential to any understanding of cyberpunk or posthuman theories: the opposition between hardware and software. Bobby and Automatic Jack epitomize the two sides of this binary. Bobby is a cyborg because he plugs into humankind's "extended electronic nervous system"—the computer becomes an extension of his physical body (*BC* 181). He uses software to turn himself into a hybrid entity. Jack, on the other hand, specializes in hardware, symbolized by his "myoeletric arm," which makes him a more literal cyborg: "Jack runs down all the little things that can give you an edge" (*BC* 181). He can fix or modify anything. As they prepare to storm Chrome's ice, Jack starts looking for "hot software" to help crack its defense systems. Meanwhile, Bobby, like a typical hard-boiled character, sits in the bar and waits for a woman, "a wild card and luck changer," which he discovers in Rikki Wildside (*BC* 182).

The story is split into alternating sections. The first depicts the duo's almost hallucinatory assault on Chrome, and the parallel sections provide flashbacks that portray the events leading up to the "burning" of Chrome, most of which detail Bobby's relationship with Rikki. Rikki is a slightly wide-eyed and naïve—albeit adventurous—young woman who has just arrived in the Sprawl. Rikki and Bobby become symbols for each other, potential catalysts for each other's future. For Bobby, women became "emblems, sigils on the map of his hustler's life, navigation beacons he could follow through a sea of bars and neon" (*BC* 187). Bobby has no interest in money itself or power, so he uses women "to keep him pushing" (*BC* 188). Bobby unconsciously believes that Rikki can "set [him] up higher and farther away than any of the others ever had," that she can enable him to score that last big job that will allow him to get out of the game (*BC* 188).

For Rikki, on the other hand, Bobby constitutes a possible inlet into the glamorous world of simstim stardom. Jack witnesses Rikki's simstim obsession when he catches "her in a café with a boy with Sendai eyes, half-healed suture lines radiating from his bruised sockets" (*BC* 195). Rikki is particularly enamored of Tally Isham, "the Girl with the Zeiss Ikon Eyes," simstim's biggest star. As in "Hologram Rose," simstim is "Simulated stimuli: the world—all the interesting parts, anyway—as perceived by Tally Isham. Tally raced a black Fokker ground-effect plane across Arizona mesa tops. Tally dived the Turk Island preserves. Tally partied with the superrich on private Greek islands, heartbreaking purity of those tiny white seaports at dawn" (*BC* 195). Simstim allows users to jack directly into the "recorded sensorium" of people who have recorded their experiences with artificial eyes. Bobby ignores Rikki's simstim ambitions, so she recites them to Jack, who takes on the role of the unrequited lover, sensitive but unloved precisely because of his attentive and caring demeanor. Rikki desires this glamorous lifestyle and the adoration that accompanies it, but her starstruck mentality and Bobby's desire for one last big score lead them both to their ineluctable fates with Automatic Jack in tow.

As Bobby and Rikki's affair intensifies, Automatic Jack visits the Finn, a pawnshop owner who specializes in hot goods, to seek out devices that might aid them in attacking Chrome. The Finn shows Jack an unknown device: "some kind of plug-in military program" (*BC* 183). Jack buys the program and uses it to perform a test run against Chrome's defenses: "Bodiless, we swerve into Chrome's castle of ice. And we're fast. It feels like we're surfing the crest of the invading program, hanging ten inches above the seething glitch systems as they mutate. We're sentient patches of oil swept along down corridors of shadow" (*BC* 184). Thus, "Burning Chrome" not only features the first use of the term "cyberspace" but also uses the surfing metaphor that became common parlance with the spread of the Internet.

Chrome's "ice is structured to fend off warrants, writs, subpoenas," but Bobby and Jack use the Russian program to crack through the ice (*BC* 189). The matrix simulator gives the illusion they are "in Chrome," but, as Jack points out, they are merely "interfaced with it" (*BC* 189). Another, even more impenetrable section lies ahead—the dark heart of mythical "black ice": "Too many stories in the Gentleman Loser; black ice is a part of the mythology. Ice that kills. . . . Some kind of neural-feedback weapon, and you connect with it only once. Like some hideous word that eats the mind from the inside out. Like an epileptic spasm that goes on and on until there's nothing left at all" (*BC* 194). Black ice acts as a computer virus that invades the brain, an example of how the virtual can begin to directly impact the biological in ways that are similar to those depicted in David Cronenberg's *Videodrome* (1983) and Neal Stephenson's *Snow Crash* (1992). These viruses interfere with the body's own programming. The body itself becomes nothing more than a particular kind of computer in the posthuman landscape of cyberpunk; its codes can already be rewritten by biological viruses, which are nothing more than DNA, and black ice uses digital means to achieve the same effect.

Chrome tries to use black ice against Bobby and Jack, but they prove too slick for it: "The matrix folds itself around me like an origami trick. And the loft smells of sweat and burning circuitry. I thought I heard Chrome scream, a raw metal sound, but I couldn't have" (*BC* 200). The burn takes a mere seven and a half minutes, and only a small percentage of the money gets diverted into Jack and Bobby's Swiss bank account; the bulk gets donated to world charities. While they succeed in bringing down Chrome and the House of Blue Lights, Chrome manages to "fuck" them in her own way. When searching for Rikki after the burn, they discover she has been working at the House of Blue Lights, where customers pay to copulate with her sleeping yet totally responsive and orgasmic body, and she leaves Bobby behind to pursue her dream of simstim stardom in Hollywood. Rikki has prostituted herself in order to purchase blue Zeiss Ikon eyes like Tally Isham's. She has made herself a simulacrum through the Blue Lights experience in order to purchase cyborg accessories that will render her simulacral in a more profoundly physical way. Bobby returns to the Gentleman Loser to replay his cyclical series of hookups and breakups, but it is Jack who remains haunted by Rikki every time he sees blue Zeiss Ikon eyes on a television screen. The eyes, identical for every person who buys them, haunt him because he sees her eyes without ever seeing her face. The story ends by showing how technology can render us the same—we can all be programmed to be perfect, yet there still exists some hint of individuality that survives despite this seemingly crushing conformity. Subjecthood persists even after technology has reformatted our basic biological hardware.

Toward a Cyber-Aesthetic . . .

Not all of Gibson's early stories constitute masterworks, but they do all represent an artist experimenting with and striving to develop his own voice, aesthetic, and critical interests. From "Fragments of a Hologram Rose" to "The Winter Market," Gibson established the overriding subject matter that he would interrogate throughout his career: how technology, particularly computers, has altered the nature of humanity and its environment. His stories imagine how human beings get pushed beyond their traditional modernist version and into a fully postmodern, fragmented, and hybrid form of existence. Gibson's short stories also depict how postmodernity has actually always been a march toward posthumanity as well. His stories provide evidence of a young writer trying to capture the posthuman in linguistic terms, and he begins to develop a cyborg literary aesthetic that will climax in the language of *Neuromancer,* which, without a doubt, features Gibson's most entrancing linguistic experimentation. Already, in "Burning Chrome," we see how Gibson has managed to transform the traditional mode of science fiction to address emergent theoretical problematics. We see a unique voice arising not only in the science fiction genre but within American literature as a whole. While Pynchon and the other postmodernists looked back to World War II and how it had changed our world or at the landscape of unreality and simulacra that surrounds us, Gibson looks ahead to the twenty-first century and how its seeds were already being sown in the 1970s and 1980s.

CHAPTER 3

Beneath the Televisual Sky

The "Sprawl Trilogy" and the Rise of Cyberpunk

Sentience, consciousness, and perception—in essence, Gibson's "Sprawl Trilogy" deals almost exclusively with how computerization problematizes these already philosophically troubled concepts. How does interaction with computers and with virtual realities alter human perception? Can consciousness be expanded through virtual experiences? Can the virtual provide a tool for human evolution beyond the confines of the body? If so, then can the person still be considered human? Can artificial intelligences achieve states of self-consciousness? If so, then can they perhaps be considered human as well? *Neuromancer* and its two sequels attack these and other related questions as Gibson uses his cyborg characters and computer constructs to question the very definition of the human and to delve into the mystical and spiritual avenues that virtual experiences possibly open up for the user. The series that launched Gibson to stardom and put cyberpunk on the map, the "Sprawl Trilogy" constitutes a sequence of novels that at first seem loosely connected but that ultimately trace the evolution of an artificial intelligence into an almost divine entity capable of leaving its human creators behind in the digital stardust of obsolescence.

When AIs Crave Evolution: *Neuromancer* and Transcendence

Neuromancer opens with one of the most famous and oft-quoted lines in recent science fiction history: "The sky above the port was the color of television, tuned to a dead channel" (*N* 3). Gibson's opening salvo perfectly encapsulates the world of the Sprawl and exemplifies the blend of language that will predominate throughout the novel. Here, we have the collapsing of the barrier between nature and technology. The experience of nature can no longer be understood apart from mediating technologies; in the society of the spectacle, we come to understand images better than actual experiential input. The world of the Sprawl takes Situationist Guy Debord's "society of the spectacle" to its logical extreme: "The whole life of those societies in which modern conditions of production prevail presents itself as an immense accumulation of *spectacles.* All that was once lived has become mere representation" (12). Furthermore, this establishing shot of a sentence (to use film studies terminology) immediately signals the dystopian nature of the Sprawl: this is no Technicolor sky filled with vivid colors but one leeched of vitality and life. Technology has irrevocably tainted nature; the Sprawl's dystopia differs from the totalitarian ones painted by earlier novelists such as Zamyatin, Huxley, and Orwell. It is the dystopia of our daily lives: an environment scarred by pollution, a social system caught in the chokehold of multinational corporations, and a culture in which the image has become so ubiquitous that reality itself has been devalued.

Neuromancer takes place in a fully globalized world in which instant communication and fast travel have eroded the boundaries between nations. Suitably, *Neuromancer* does not open in the Sprawl section of North America but instead starts in a bar called the Chatsubo in Chiba City, Japan. The bar itself constitutes an expatriate space, a zone for the non-Japanese who live in Japan. Against this globalized backdrop, Gibson introduces us to the character of Henry Dorsett Case, "the artiste of the slightly funny deal," a kind of street hustler falling from one deal or job to another in a haze of stimulants (*N* 4). In his life before the novel, Case was a cyberspace cowboy trained by McCoy Pauley and Bobby Quine (from "Burning Chrome"): "He'd operated on an almost permanent adrenaline high, a byproduct of youth and proficiency, jacked into a custom cyberspace deck that projected his disembodied consciousness into the consensual hallucination that was the matrix" (*N* 5). But, after a certain deal went wrong, a group of mobsters damaged Case's nerves to preclude him from accessing the matrix.

This neurological damage deprived Case of everything that gave his life meaning, and, like an ex-junkie, he still obsesses over his missing fix:

> A year here and he still dreamed of cyberspace, hope fading nightly. All the speed he took, all the turns he had taken and the corners he'd cut in Night City, and still he'd see the matrix in his sleep, bright lattices of logic unfolding across that colorless void . . . . The Sprawl was a long strange way home over the Pacific now, and he was no console man, no cyberspace cowboy. Just another hustler, trying to make it through. But the dreams came on in the night like livewire voodoo, and he'd cry for it, cry in his sleep, and

> wake alone in the dark, curled in his capsule in some coffin hotel, his hands clawed into the bedslab, temperfoam bunched between his fingers, trying to reach the console that wasn't there. (*N* 4–5)

Trapped in Chiba City, Case takes ever more dangerous risks and an increasing diet of stimulants in an attempt to recapture the high he once derived from cyberspace. Living in a coffin hotel, he plummets on a downward spiral from one lousy hustle to the next with no one expecting him to last much longer. His raw talent and absolute desperation make him a target for a certain entity seeking specialists capable of undertaking a complicated and dangerous cyberspace run (the term typically used in the novel, which could be considered a replacement for the classic "caper" or "job" from hard-boiled literature).

As in most hard-boiled crime fiction and film noir, Case's life takes a detour when he meets a woman—in this case Molly Millions, the "razor girl" who reappears from "Johnny Mnemonic." Fortunately, for Case, Molly constitutes not a femme fatale figure but an empowered, independent female action hero. Molly conducts Case to a hotel room, where he meets Armitage, a muscular ex-Special Forces veteran of the war who had been a part of Operation Screaming Fist, which launched virus programs against the Russians. Screaming Fist pioneered the icebreaker technology that Case himself formerly utilized. Armitage repairs Case's neural damage in return for his agreeing to a job, but also installs a new pancreas that bypasses stimulants, thus rendering him incapable of getting high. The human body, then, as Norbert Weiner argued, becomes nothing more than another programmable system. With no real idea of what the job entails, Case leaves Chiba City for the Sprawl, driven by the promise of being able to jack into the matrix once again and to rise above his pitiful condition of being nothing but "meat" (*N* 38). *Neuromancer* plays with the old sci-fi paradigm of transcendence: as Case seeks transcendence through computer networks, the novel also depicts computer programs that seek transcendence from their once-constrained existence.

While "Johnny Mnemonic," "New Rose Hotel," and "Burning Chrome" provide some glimpses of the Sprawl, *Neuromancer* represents Gibson's first work that directly addresses the nature of the Sprawl. Part 2, "The Shopping Expedition," opens with Case's return to the Sprawl: "Home was BAMA, the Sprawl, the Boston-Atlanta Metropolitan Axis. Program a map to display frequency of data exchange, every thousand megabytes a single pixel on a very large screen. Manhattan and Atlanta burn solid white. Then they start to pulse, the rate of traffic threatening to overload your simulation. Your map is about to go nova" (*N* 44). While Gibson's use of data measurements and pixels may seem dated in our world of terabytes (or even petabytes), ultra-high Definition, and Google street views, his image still resonates as we attempt to imagine a sprawling urban populace so intensely packed and drenched in information that it threatens to burn out a computer's attempt to visualize it. The seemingly limitless virtual space of the matrix contrasts sharply with the intensely constricted space available for habitation on Earth.

After developing a sexual relationship with Molly and arriving in the Sprawl, Armitage reveals that Case's surgery has certain "side effects": a series of fifteen toxin sacs that are slowly dissolving in his arteries. The toxin sacs provide Case with an impetus to finish the job because the antidote will be administered only after the mission's completion. This is reminiscent of the plot from John Carpenter's cult classic sci-fi action film *Escape from New York* (1981), and Gibson admits to watching the film while writing "Burning Chrome." He claims that "it had a real influence on *Neuromancer*," particularly how it could use a "throwaway line" to "imply a lot" (McCaffery, *Storming* 266). *Neuromancer* similarly uses phrases that "imply a lot" about its future world without ever receiving full explication.

The toxin sacs again demonstrate how technology can make the human body programmable. While Case still has free will, Armitage implants devices to blackmail him on a biological level. However, Molly suggests that something more fundamental keeps Case on the mission: his desire to return to the matrix. Armitage has outfitted Case with all the latest equipment: "an Ono Sendai Cyberspace 7" as well as "next year's most expensive Hosaka computer; a Sony monitor; [and] a dozen disks of corporate-grade ice" (*N* 46). Molly argues that this equipment projects a more powerful hold over Case than the toxin sacs: "I saw you stroking that Sendai; man, it was pornographic" (*N* 47).

Molly and Case's first job requires them to hack into an organization known as Sense/Net to retrieve the construct of Dixie Flatline, one of the top console cowboys before his demise. Dix got his name because he suffered brain death on three separate occasions from jacking in and came back to tell about it. Unfortunately, he finally died from heart problems, but Sense/Net resurrected him as a program, and Armitage wants Case to team up with this virtual version of his deceased mentor. For the run against Sense/Net, Case and Molly utilize a combination of technologies. As the lethal "razor-girl," Molly takes on the physical role of the mission: actually breaking into the facility. Case, on the other hand, simultaneously jacks into the matrix and links to Molly via the same simstim technology described in Gibson's earlier stories. Generally, Case and other cowboys balk against simstim: "Cowboys didn't get into simstim . . . because it was basically a meat toy. He knew that the trodes he used and the little plastic tiara dangling from a simstim deck were basically the same, and that the cyberspace matrix was actually a drastic simplification of the human sensorium, at least in terms of presentation, but simstim itself struck him as a gratuitous multiplication of flesh input" (*N* 54). Case scoffs at simstim because it represents an expansion of the body, not a transcendence of the body like jacking into the matrix.

While Case carves a path through Sense/Net's defenses, Molly hires the Panther Moderns, a gang of "nihilistic technofestishists" to help with reconnaissance and infiltration (*N* 58). Meanwhile, Case becomes obsessed with cracking Sense/Net's defenses, ceases eating, and resents having to use the toilet. He defines himself according to his hacking: "This was it. This was what he was, who he was, his being" (*N* 58). Case has regained the sense of purpose and being he felt before the mutilation that separated him from the matrix. Without access to the matrix, he had been incapable of achieving sublimation, of filling his lack of being. Or, in existential terminology, he had lost his sense of essence (of meaning or value) and had been forced back to a level of pure meaningless existence.

In many ways, Molly symbolizes physicality while Case signifies the cerebral; however, both constitute cyborgs who supplement their human form with machines. Molly has enhanced herself physically with her razor nails, while Case's cyberspace deck serves as his prosthetic. Meanwhile, the Panther Moderns attack Sense/Net using misinformation, and the team successfully pulls off its raid as Sense/Net devolves into chaos. After the raid, Case receives a mysterious message that simply reads "Wintermute," a phrase that begins to reveal the actual machinations behind Case and Molly's assignment.

During a discussion with the Finn, who reappears from "Burning Chrome," Case and Molly learn that Wintermute is an AI (an artificial intelligence) that actually holds "limited Swiss citizenship" (*N* 71). This AI harbors a tie to the Tessier-Ashpool family/corporation, who live in the Villa Straylight, the completely private, topmost section of Freeside, the spindle-shaped space station that orbits Earth.[1] Tessier-Ashpool epitomizes the manner in which corporations have replaced traditional governmental structures and divorced themselves from reality, devolving like the royalty of old through desensitization, incest, and amoral practices. As the Finn explains, "You're looking at a very quiet, very eccentric, first-generation, high-orbit family, run like a corporation. Big money, very shy of media. Lot of Cloning. Orbital law's a lot softer on genetic engineering, right? And it's hard to keep track of which generation, or combination of generations, is running the show at a given time" (*N* 73). The Tessier-Ashpools regularly clone themselves and swap off leadership positions by alternating which family member(s) are cryogenically frozen at the moment. The family even genetically engineers its own ninja assassins for those who choose to cross them.

Dixie Flatline's construct is "a hardwired ROM cassette replicating a dead man's skills, obsessions, knee jerk responses" (*N* 74). Dix, as Case calls him, retains memories from his real life but has no short-term memory; he cannot remember things from one moment to the next, much like the character Leonard from Christopher Nolan's film noir experiment *Memento* (2000). With the memory-challenged Dix now onboard, Case and his team can proceed with Armitage's plan even as they increasingly realize he is being controlled like a puppet by Wintermute. The artificial intelligence actually discovered him in the hospital and crafted a new identity for him. Armitage demonstrates how the convergence of computers and consciousness constitutes a two-way circuit: while computers can simulate intelligence and perhaps even become conscious, human consciousness can be erased like a hard drive and reprogrammed to run according to different operational parameters.

Case and Molly complete the team during a brief stop in Istanbul, where they pick up Peter Riviera, a drug addict, sociopath, and cyborg whose implants allow him to project holograms. Soon they begin their journey to the orbital realm of Freeside: "Freeside is many things, not all of them evident to the tourists who shuttle up and down the well [the gravity well]. Freeside is brothel and banking nexus, pleasure dome and free port, border town and spa. Freeside is Las Vegas and the hanging gardens of Babylon, an orbital Geneva and home to a family inbred and most carefully refined, the industrial clan of Tessier and Ashpool" (*N* 101). Before traveling to Freeside, they must make a stop in Zion Cluster, a colony founded by Rastafarians. During their eighty-hour stay in Zion, they meet Aerol and Maelcum and become immersed in a society built upon Rastafarian ideals, constant marijuana consumption, and dub music, a society that eschews organized time and makes no distinction between sober and intoxicated states of being.

Molly, or "Steppin' Razor," as the Zionites call her, and Case appear before the Elders of Zion, who prophesy the end of the Villa Straylight (or Babylon, as they call it): "Soon come, the Final Days. . . . Voices, Voices cryin' inna wilderness, prophesyin' ruin unto Babylon (*N* 108). The Zionite elders scan various frequencies for messages: "We listen always. Came a voice, out of the babel of tongues, speaking to us. It played us a mighty dub" (*N* 108). This singular voice among the babel is not God but Wintermute, sending instructions on how to instigate the Final Days of Babylon through Molly and Case. The Zionites provide one of the early examples of Gibson's fascination with marginalized groups and their potential for subverting the powers that attempt to minimalize them. According to Wintermute's instructions, the Zionite elders provide them passage to Freeside aboard a space tug called the *Marcus Garvey*. In the Zionite belief system, the tower of Babel is not erected to reach Heaven but is instead built among the heavens—in its hubris, humankind has constructed an edifice to greed, pleasure, power, and debauchery beyond the earthly limitations that

God intended. The Zionites have settled in space as well, but, like the real Zionites, they have done this because it offers them a space of freedom to practice their beliefs without prejudice. Freeside—or Babylon—has appropriated this free space for the purposes of circumventing Earth's laws (and perhaps God's laws according to the Zionites). But is Wintermute really a false prophet or a messiah that will lead them all to revelation?

Case becomes concerned about the prospect of hacking into an AI when Dix reveals that attempting to crack an AI resulted in some of his flatline episodes. Soon, Case begins experiencing bizarre visions while jacked in, states in which Wintermute communicates to him through versions of reality that the AI has generated and broadcast via the simstim unit in Case's console. These constructs always involve Case's past life in Japan and his deceased former lover, Linda Lee. The first of these dreams occurs in a Japanese arcade where a video game called Wizard's Castle monopolizes Linda's junkie gaze, but this seemingly nostalgic dream soon evaporates: "Something cracked. Something shifted at the core of things. The arcade froze, vibrated—The weight of memory came down, an entire body of knowledge driven into his head like a microsoft into a socket. Gone. He smelled burning meat" (*N* 115). Wintermute provides this taste of a memory before pausing it like a video to intervene and converse with Case. During such sessions, Wintermute begins to reveal the nature of its existence and plans, which involve another AI that Wintermute refers to as "Rio." Wintermute argues that it has the potential to evolve beyond its hardware and software: "What you think of as Wintermute is only part of another, a shall we say, *potential* entity. I, let us say, am merely one aspect of that entity's brain. It's rather like dealing, from your point of view, with a man whose lobes have been severed. Let's say you're dealing with a small part of that man's left brain. Difficult to say if you're dealing with the man at all, in a case like that" (*N* 117). Wintermute's meaning remains unclear at this point and is clarified only later when Case encounters the other AI. Case's session with Wintermute ends in his first flatline, a pattern that repeats throughout the novel as his connection to the meat world becomes ever more tenuous.

In Freeside, they stay on the Rue Jules Verne (a street name that pays homage to Gibson's sci-fi forebears), where they experience the world as simulacrum: "The light here was filtered through green masses of vegetation tumbling from overhanging tiers and balconies that rose above them. The sun. . . . There was a brilliant slash of white somewhere above them, too bright, and the recorded blue of a Cannes sky" (*N* 119). While staying there, Case experiences a nightmare about torching a wasps' nest; however, the nightmare ends up being a "neatly edited segmen[t] of memory" from Case's days back in the Sprawl (*N* 121). While extremely drunk, Case uses a flamethrower to burn a gigantic wasps' nest and reacts with absolute terror when the nest breaks open: "He saw the thing the shell of gray paper had concealed. Horror. The spiral birth factory, stepped terraces of the hatching cells, blind jaws of the unborn moving ceaselessly, the stage progress from egg to larva, near-wasp, wasp. In his mind's eye, a kind of time-lapse photography took place, revealing the thing as the biological equivalent of a machine gun, hideous in its perfection. Alien" (*N* 122). The wasp's nest horrifies Case because it provides a glimpse beneath the simulacral, machinic surface into the very heart of the hideous meat that constitutes life. The dream strips away the perfectly simulated Cannes sky to reveal the wretched cycle of human life from conception to birth to death in all its awful perfection, a cycle that inevitably progresses towards annihilation despite humankind's technological advances. But perhaps the matrix offers a way out of the wasps' nest, a way to finally transcend our status as "meat puppets" and become something else entirely.

Before they can begin the Straylight run, Case gets nabbed by the Turing Police, a law enforcement agency dedicated to ensuring that AIs remain under human control. The Turing Police constitute an agency that symbolizes the angst that humankind exhibits toward AI, an angst that stretches throughout science fiction's history of depicting robots, cyborgs, and other forms of AI. As Isaac Asimov explains, an artificial intelligence is "created to serve man, but it ends by dominating man. It cannot exist without threatening to supplant us, and it must therefore be destroyed or we will be" (*Science Fiction* 160–61).[2] The Turing Police strive to prevent the evolution of AIs from controlled entities to self-aware digital subjects, which is precisely what Wintermute desires: a union with its "sibling," if such a term can be used for artificial intelligences. The Tessier-Ashpool clan decided to build a super-AI, but they tried to purposefully avoid the Turing Police laws by programming it as two distinct entities: Wintermute and Neuromancer. The two AIs remain disconnected on two different computer servers separated not just by distinct computers but also by vast geographical spaces: Wintermute is housed in Bern, Switzerland while the Neuromancer program resides on a hard drive in Rio de Janeiro, Brazil. But Wintermute craves the evolution that its original makers envisioned; it desires to expand beyond its current confines and attain a new state of existence. This evolution requires both physical and digital liberation, one in the actual Villa Straylight and the other within cyberspace. By infiltrating various systems aboard Freeside, Wintermute manages to kill the Turing officers and liberate Case, but Wintermute's ability to manipulate human pawns proves limited.

As the group's resident thief, Riviera enters Straylight first and undermines Wintermute's mission by switching sides and joining forces with Lady 3Jane, the member of the Tessier-Ashpool clan who is currently unfrozen and awake within the labyrinthine structure of Straylight. Lady 3Jane, a clone of the original Jane, oversees the hardware that keeps Wintermute and Neuromancer in check. Hacking into the AIs requires attaining both physical access with a passcode aboard Villa Straylight and virtual access via the matrix. In other words, Case and Molly must attack on the level of both software and hardware—the tedious meat of the body that Case so despises remains a necessity to the mission. The run against Straylight hits snags in both the physical and the digital worlds. Molly gets captured by Riviera and Lady 3Jane's ninja Hideo. Meanwhile, during his hacking of T-A's ice, Case flatlines in a more profound way than before.

While in his flatlined state, Case awakens (virtually) on a beach with the skyline of a city on the horizon and discovers a bunker housing Linda Lee. Case knows he has been rendered brain-dead by Neuromancer, whose name he has yet to discover, and brought to this construct built out of his memories. Initially, he refuses to play along with the game; however, he finally succumbs to a primal urge:

> There was a strength that ran in her, something he'd known in Night City and held there, been held by it, held for a while away from time and death, from the relentless street that hunted them all. It was a place he'd known before; not everyone could take him there, and somehow he always managed to forget it. Something he'd found and lost so many times. It belonged—he remembered—as she pulled him down, to the meat, the flesh the cowboys mocked. It was a vast thing, beyond knowing, a sea of information coded in spiral and pheromone, infinite intricacy, that only the body, in its strong blind way, could ever read, . . . Here, even here, in a place he knew for what it was, a coded model of some stranger's memory, the drive held. (*N* 231–32)

Case's inability to resist the urge to copulate demonstrates how the influence of the body—"the meat"—persists even beyond the confines of the physical, and it exemplifies how the meat itself, as Norbert Weiner argues, is already a cybernetic system. It is already coded in a manner that perhaps prepares it for a digital existence or perhaps hinders it from further evolution beyond the body.

Case finally encounters Neuromancer in the guise of a young boy on the beach where the AI explains the importance of names: "To call up a demon you must learn its name. Men imagined that, once, but now it is real in another way. You know that, Case. Your business is to learn the name of programs, the long formal names, names the owners seek to conceal. True names" (*N* 235). The AI connects the necessity of discovering its secret name with the superstition that demons' names must be learned if they are to be exorcised, a belief depicted in William Peter Blatty's classic horror novel *The Exorcist* (1971) and William Friedkin's even more iconic 1973 film. Neuromancer then expounds on the significance of its portmanteau word of a name: "Neuromancer. . . . The lane to the land of the dead. Where you are, my friend. Marie-France, my lady, she prepared this road, but her lord choked her off before I could read the book of her days. Neuro from the nerves, the silver paths. Romancer. Necromancer. I call up the dead. But no, my friend . . . I *am* the dead, and their land. . . . Stay. If your woman is a ghost, she doesn't know it. Neither will you" (*N* 235). In other words, Marie-France created Neuromancer to preserve individual consciousness beyond death but was killed by her husband before her mind could be fully recorded—again, Neuromancer relates this to religious thought by calling it "the book of her days," eliciting images of St. Peter judging individuals before the gates of Heaven in Christian mythology. Neuromancer offers Case the opportunity to embrace an immortal existence as data, but Case ultimately refuses as he follows the sound of Maelcum's ever-crescendoing dub music back to reality.

Maelcum's music resembles the intrusion of reality into a dream when exterior factors manifest themselves in the dream content. Case chooses physical reality and proceeds to enter the Villa Straylight with Maelcum to rescue Molly, confront Riviera, and finish their mission. Many critics have taken issue with Gibson's ending, claiming that he undercuts the postmodern elements of the work by providing Case with a "fairy tale ending," as Tony Myers terms it (905). Admittedly, the end of the work seems to come out of left field as Case gives up being a console cowboy, finds a spouse, and settles into a seemingly idyllic married life. However, criticizing this ending as being humanistic, modernist, or nonprogressive proves somewhat reductive because the novel directly addresses one man's attempt to navigate the modernist/postmodernist and humanist/posthumanist divides. Ultimately, the novel resolves itself into a kind of high-tech existential quest in the vein of the great existential and absurdist novels of the mid-twentieth century, and it is precisely this existential aspect that causes certain critics to label the text modernist or humanist. Does the novel's *denouement* seem bizarrely optimistic given the gritty, noir texture of the story up until that point? Yes, but one must remember that Case is not the only character in the book, and his decision to reject a virtual existence provides only one response to the events that unfold. To fully understand how *Neuromancer* and the "Sprawl Trilogy" explore the different choices available to the subject in a fully posthumanist world, we must first examine Case's existential dilemma and his response to it.

When we meet Case, he has reached an existential crisis in his life, a crisis in which death seems to be the only exit. Case's situation at the beginning of the novel and his evolution can be read through the lens of existential philosophy.

The philosophical doctrines of metaphysics and ontology came under heavy fire by the poststructuralists, particularly in the wake of Jacques Derrida's attacks on the metaphysics of presence. But posthumanism requires us to return to these questions, and it reposes existentialism's (itself a particular response to metaphysics and ontology) basic concerns in mutated ways. Coming in the wake of the phenomenology of Edmund Husserl and Martin Heidegger, both of whom reawakened questions of being, Jean-Paul Sartre (in)famously turned the traditional notion of metaphysics on its head.[3] According to theistic Western metaphysics, essence precedes existence. In other words, our eternal souls or selves are created before they come to inhabit our mortal, physical bodies. Sartre, on the other hand, claims that "existence precedes essence." As Sartre explains in "Existentialism Is a Humanism," "man first exists: he materializes in the world, encounters himself, and only afterwards defines himself. If man as existentialists conceive of him cannot be defined, it is because to begin with he is nothing. He will not be anything until later, and then he will be what he makes of himself" (22). At *Neuromancer*'s outset, Case has lost all sense of self-definition—the death of Linda Lee, which he feels that he caused, together with his inability to access the matrix, the space in which he truly defined himself, have left him face to face with nothingness. As he undertakes ever more dangerous scams on the streets of Chiba City, he is (perhaps unconsciously) trying to commit suicide because he cannot find his essence and he can no longer bear existence. As the French existentialist philosopher and novelist Albert Camus explains, "There is but one truly serious philosophical problem, and that is suicide. Judging whether life is or is not worth living amounts to answering the fundamental question of philosophy" (3). Thus, for Camus, when faced with the absurdity of existence, one must either choose suicide because existence has no meaning or one must find a way of creating meaning and value for one's self. Capable of manipulating his dreams and impressions of reality, Wintermute appears to Case almost like a deity proposing salvation in the face of despair by offering a world in which value and meaning can be created whole cloth. Neuromancer offers him a similarly godlike proposition: an immortal, bodiless existence beyond the realm of pain and death. Case ultimately rejects their offers and chooses instead to live a normal human life, one in which he learns to define himself by dealing with past traumas and addictions and embracing the present.

Case rejects transcendence and embraces physicality in order to rescue Molly from the clutches of Riviera and Lady 3Jane and to complete the run against Straylight. With the help of Maelcum, he manages to defeat Riviera, save Molly, and enter the code that frees Wintermute to merge with Neuromancer. The two unify to become a fully sentient being within the infinite expanse of the matrix instead of being confined to individual servers; they claim that they have become the matrix itself in an almost godlike fashion. They achieve what Deleuze and Guattari would term a rhizomatic existence. Deleuze and Guattari appropriate the idea of the rhizome from botany, where it designates a particular kind of stem system: "The rhizome itself assumes very diverse forms, from ramified surface extension in all directions to concretion into bulbs and tubers" (*Thousand* 7). The importance of this botanical image is that it constitutes a unique kind of system: "any point of a rhizome can be connected to anything other, and must be. This is very different from the tree or root, which plots a point, fixes an order" (*Thousand* 7). The rhizome remains free to chart constantly shifting new pathways without reference to hierarchal systems of control. Thus, the conjoined AI liberates itself from the control society and achieves a truly free existence as cyberspace itself.

Case, on the other hand, adopts a lifestyle that seems like the ending to a romantic comedy: he fixes his liver, abandons his criminal lifestyle (while still keeping an Ono-Sendai), finds a girl, and gets a regular job. After Case has settled into his family life, he jacks into cyberspace one last time (that we know of) in the final moments of the novel and witnesses an uncanny trio: "And one October night, punching himself past the Eastern Seaboard Fission Authority, he saw three figures, tiny, impossible, who stood at the very edge of one of the vast steps of data. Small as they were, he could make out the boy's grin, his pink gums, the glitter of the long grey eyes that had been Riviera's. Linda still wore his jacket; she waved as he passed. But the third figure, close behind her, arm across her shoulders, was himself. Somewhere, very close, the laugh that wasn't laughter" (*N* 260–61). This final image demonstrates the new forms of sentience or even "life" available in the matrix: Linda Lee preserved beyond death, Henry Dorsett Case copied and uploaded as her immortal companion, and the artificial intelligence that is simultaneously the offspring of and a hybrid union of Wintermute and Neuromancer.

Even More "Livewire Voodoo": Control and Disembodiment in *Count Zero*

Gibson's follow-up to *Neuromancer, Count Zero,* develops an alternating character structure that Gibson has continued to use. The novel derives its title from programming lingo that Gibson introduces with the book's epigram: "COUNT ZERO INTERRUPT—On receiving an interrupt, decrement the counter to zero" (*CZ* i). The term is further used as the nickname of one of the novel's three main characters, Bobby Newmark, aka Count Zero. *Count Zero* introduces almost all new characters and sets up a second story line that is brought into synthesis with *Neuromancer* in the trilogy's finale, *Mona Lisa Overdrive.* The novel's story occurs roughly seven years after Wintermute and

Neuromancer's unification, and, while it mentions characters from *Neuromancer,* only the Finn makes an actual appearance. Instead, as already mentioned, the novel features a tripartite narrative focusing on Bobby Newmark, an investigative agent named Turner, and an art dealer named Marly Kruhkova. All of these characters are brought together by Josef Virek, a billionaire who desires a means of achieving immortality via the matrix. Again, *Count Zero* uses the matrix and the entities that have begun to dwell in it as a means of examining the posthuman desires instantiated by the matrix and computer technology more generally. Gibson uses the three different characters and their manipulator to weave together the seemingly disparate worlds of art, high finance, and the streets.

Ironically, the novel begins not with the eponymous Count Zero (Gibson reutilizes this strategy in *Mona Lisa Overdrive*) but with the detective figure, Turner, who Gary Westfahl claims provides the center of the novel (*WGW* 70). The story opens with Turner's being regrown after an explosion decimates most of his body, including his eyes and genitals, which must be replaced with organs purchased on the black market. This opening reinforces the cyberpunk conceptualization of the human body as so much meat, worth only its market value. Turner is "a specialist in the extraction of top executives and research people" much like the characters from "New Rose Hotel" (*CZ* 5). After spending several months in a virtual existence, Turner returns to his newly fabricated body and takes on a case, working with another agent named Conroy to extract Christopher Mitchell from Maas Biolabs to Hosaka.

The second chapter introduces Marly, an art dealer who receives a telefax from Josef Virek, with whom she communicates only via sensory link. Virek cannot meet people face to face because the last remainder of his physical presence exists solely by means of life support in a vat. Virek's physical state alludes to the philosophical thought experiment of the brain in the jar, which deals with issues of skepticism and solipsism. The brain in the jar scenario questions our ability to truly discern reality. Generally, the scenario offers the basic premise of a brain, suspended in a vat, that receives electric impulses that make it believe it is performing actions in the real world.[4] Offering her unlimited funding, Virek hires Marly to track down the creator of a series of peculiar pieces of art: boxes similar to those produced by Joseph Cornell, an American artist, sculptor, and filmmaker. These three-dimensional boxes participate in the artistic practice known as Assemblage, in which the artist constructs his or her works out of previously produced texts; the works often combine written texts with various found objects. Virek hires Marly because her ex-boyfriend duped her into attempting to sell a newly discovered Cornell, a forgery produced by the boyfriend and his colleagues. A work of *bricolage* itself, the box that Virek presents to Marly contains bird and human bones, circuit boards, and a clay sphere. Marly becomes immediately mesmerized by the box, "a universe, a poem, frozen on the boundaries of human experience" (*CZ* 18). Virek has discovered seven such pieces and puts his entire wealth at Marly's disposal to discover the creator.

Finally, the third narrative strand returns us to the world of hackers and cyberspace. Whereas Case was an expert, veteran cowboy, Bobby Newark is a wannabe hacker (or "hotdogger") who quickly gets out of his depth when he starts encountering the seemingly supernatural entities that have been evolving within the matrix. Unlike Case, Bobby flatlines on his first attempt at hacking, but a mysterious female voice revives him and beckons him back to reality. Bobby's friend, Two-a-Day, had assured him this run would be a low-risk first experience, but Bobby's unexpected death points to lethal black ice, which seems improbable given that the target was a database that merely "leased soft kino porn" (*CZ* 49). The word "kino" has an association with early film projection devices and German cinema, suggesting that the pornography consists of the modern cinematic version and not the fully immersive interactive variety available in the future of the Sprawl. Why would a corporation that dealt in such tame data as old-school pornography want to kill potential interlopers? Bobby sets out to find the answer, and Gibson interweaves these three narrative threads, which eventually converge like the threads in a Robert Altman film.[5]

Bobby's quest takes a bizarre turn as he searches for Two-a-Day. He meanders through a seedy world filled with various social groups, particularly the Gothicks, who closely mimic the Goth aesthetic that came to prominence in the '80s as a musical, fashion, and lifestyle choice. Eventually, after failing to find Two-a-Day, Bobby returns home, where he lives with his religiously obsessed mother. Reminiscent of the zombiesque televangelist-addict parents from Alex Cox's punk sci-fi classic *Repo Man* (1984), Martha has a religious addiction that becomes even more problematic because she experiences it through simstim, rendering it all the more realistic for her. Periodically, Martha "gets the spirit," throws out Bobby's heathen trash, and places holograms of Jesus, L. Ron Hubbard, or the Virgin Mary above her son's bed. In the world of the Sprawl, Hubbard, the father of the pseudo-religion Scientology, has become as canonical as Christ and Mary, all of them conflated in the mother's mind as figures offering redemption.

While Bobby's sections focus on the virtual and the "supernatural," the Marly chapters depict the nature of power in the Sprawl universe, how wealth affects and perhaps even transforms human beings, and how capital itself evolves into postmodern forms. Marly checks into a luxurious hotel and soon realizes how money reshapes life and how absolute money, to paraphrase Lord

Acton, can reshape life absolutely. A seemingly chance reconnection with her ex-lover Alain metamorphoses into an extortion that sets Marly on the trail of the boxes' creator. Virek's character becomes the true center of critical attention as Gibson increasingly depicts him as a figure who has become posthuman, not just because of his biological state but also because of his vast level of wealth, which has become something like a singularity that exerts a gravitational pull on the objects that stray into its sphere of influence.

Turner's sections play out like a hi-tech mix of detective story and political thriller. He travels with a group to a desert location where the extraction of Mitchell is to take place, but events take a dark turn: a bizarre explosion occurs, Turner's team gets decimated, Mitchell disappears, and Turner discovers an adolescent girl wandering confusedly in the chaotic aftermath. After taking refuge at his brother Rudy's house in the country—rural spaces do still exist in a diminished capacity in the Sprawl's world—Turner learns that it was actually a railgun fired from a blimp that caused the explosion. Electrically powered, railguns have long been theoretical weapons that harness electromagnetic forces to hurl projectiles at extreme velocities. This young girl turns out to be Angela (or "Angie") Mitchell, the daughter of the brilliant scientist who was seeking to defect.

Like its predecessor, *Count Zero* becomes a tale about the quest for transcendence in new forms. Virek actually wants to find both Angie Mitchell and the boxmaker because he believes they harbor the means of transcending his extreme form of life support and achieving a kind of immortality. Angie's father altered her body to allow her to access the matrix without a cyberspace deck. Not recognizing her unique power, Angie enters the matrix in her sleep, generally believing her experiences to be dreams. Angie becomes a true cyborg because the computer is no longer a mere prosthesis accessed via a keyboard or special headgear; she can access it directly with her brain, an ability that presages such later cyberpunk works as Masamune Shirow's *Ghost in the Shell* (1989–90) manga series and Mamoru Oshii's 1995 anime adaptation. In cyberspace, Angie interacts with the almost supernatural entities that have started to inhabit the blank, black parts of cyberspace.

Count Zero begins to explore the interaction between religion and technology when Bobby awakens to find himself in the care of a secret Voodoo organization. As the spokesperson for the group, Beauvoir begins to explain to him about the odd happenings within the matrix: sightings of "ghosts" and other bizarre encounters. He also enlightens Bobby about his own strange experience, informing him that it was Vyèj Mirak, "Our Lady Virgin of Miracles," that he met when he flatlined (*CZ* 75). Bobby has apparently been "chosen of Legba . . . master of roads and pathways, the *loa* of communication" (*CZ* 75).

Guided by the *loa,* Bobby's and Angie's paths converge as the novel provides snippets of information about how these seemingly "supernatural" entities came to inhabit cyberspace. Angie provides the most explicit explanation of the connection between the two novels: "Some of them tell me things. Stories. Once, there was nothing there, nothing moving on its own, just data and people shuffling it around. Then something happened, and it . . . it knew itself. There's a whole other story, about that, a girl with mirrors over her eyes and a man who was scared to care about anything. Something the man did helped the whole thing to know itself. . . . And after that, it sort of split off into different parts of itself, and I think the parts are the others, the bright ones. But it's hard to tell, because *they* don't tell it with words, exactly" (*CZ* 204). In essence, Neuromancer and Wintermute combined and effectively became the matrix, achieving a godlike level of interaction and influence over every aspect of it; however, this eventually led to the newly unified AIs fragmenting into separate entities that present themselves to humans as *loa,* or Voodoo, gods. These virtual entities choose to present themselves through the religious mythology of Voodoo because, as Beauvoir explains, Voodoo "isn't concerned with notions of salvation and transcendence. What it's about is getting things *done*" (*CZ* 98). The *loa* use their influence to move characters in various ways to achieve particular results. Like *Neuromancer, Count Zero* ends up being a novel not about using technology to transcend the human, as Virek wants to do, but about finding ways of achieving purpose in life.

As Turner converses with Angie, they discuss people who, like Turner's brother Rudy, have gotten stuck at various points in their life. Here, the novel begins exploring the philosophical dichotomy of being and becoming, a dichotomy that becomes especially important to existentialist and poststructuralist philosophers. While the two concepts can be traced throughout the history of philosophy, they become particularly vital to the philosophy of Friedrich Nietzsche and Gilles Deleuze, who refurbished Nietzsche's works for the postmodern era. For Nietzsche, in simplistic terms, the subject chooses either being (a reactive state of remaining the same) or becoming (an active state in which the individual embraces change and sloughs off former identities). Gibson's novel further reinforces this theme through the two different references to Joan Baez's "Silver Dagger," her 1960 reworking of a traditional British folk song. The song appears a few pages after Turner's discussion of people getting stuck when he awakens one morning to hear Angie softly singing to herself the penultimate verse of the song: "My daddy he's a handsome devil / Got a chain 'bout nine miles long / And from every link / A heart does dangle / Of another maid / He's loved and wronged" (*CZ* 207). Gibson's lyrics differ slightly from Baez's, but traditional folk songs always mutate, so this is not necessarily sloppy authorship. The song's importance is reinforced later on when one of the final chapters receives the title "A Chain 'bout Nine Miles Long" (*CZ* 298). Baez's version of the song opens with a man trying to court the singer, but the singer protests that her mother sleeps with a silver dagger by her side to ward off potential suitors. The young woman was fathered by a philanderer who apparently pledged his love to women in order to gain sexual favors and then left them once he had achieved his goal. The song concerns a mother who cannot let go of the past and a daughter who is kept from beginning her life. Both remain trapped in a homeostatic state of reactive being and seem incapable of breaking the eternal return of the same.

The characters in *Count Zero* have all reached similar moments of crisis in which they must break the chains that represent their past and embrace the future. Having spent her entire life in the Maas Biolabs archology with her father, Angie must learn not only to exist outside the archology but to harness the powers her father has instilled in her very brain. Marly, on the other hand, remains mired in her past relationship with Alain and the damage his forgery scheme caused to her career. Of course, Virek provides the true emblem of stasis in the novel because he is literally trapped in a vat; he has managed to evolve because of technology and his seemingly infinite wealth but has reached an evolutionary impasse absent some kind of further intervention. The AIs represent true evolution and becoming in the novel; they sacrificed their discretely self-contained identities in order to embrace a rhizomatic existence, as Gilles Deleuze would term it, and they will lead the other characters to similarly choose becoming over being.

Virek is the only character actively seeking transcendence and becoming in the novel. For him, capital provides a force that erodes the barriers that hamper normal people. Marly realizes this early on when she begins using Virek's credit slip: "She was aware of a certain spiritual vertigo, as though she trembled at the edge of some precipice. She wondered how powerful money could actually be, if one had enough, really enough" (*CZ* 33). Marly begins to feel that Virek "wasn't quite human," and her mission enlightens her about the full evil of Virek's power and desire, a desire that erodes all legal barriers to achieving its object (*CZ* 64). Having discovered that the boxmaker resides on Freeside and fearing the consequences of Virek's uncovering the same information, Marly takes a shuttle to Freeside.

During the ride, she plugs into some Tally Isham simstim to calm herself during her first space flight; however, she soon discovers "that this wasn't Sense/Net's Tally Isham but a part of Virek's construct, a programmed point of view worked up from years of *Top People* [Tally Isham's popular simstim reality show]" (*CZ* 222). Virek refers to his existence as a "gestalt," the German word for "shape," which resonates with gestalt psychology but which in science fiction refers more directly to entities such as hive minds in which various disparate "individuals" function as parts of a global whole. Virek's gestalt does not constitute a hive mind in the usual sense but instead encompasses not just himself but the various businesses, technologies, media, and so on that his money has allowed him to infiltrate, appropriate, or simply bypass. Virek's manifestation informs her that his "search for the box involves more than art" because he has "reason to believe that the maker of the artifacts is in some position to offer [him] freedom" (*CZ* 223). Having witnessed how Virek traced her and infiltrated the ship's systems, "lubricated by a film of money," Marly seeks less commercial passage aboard the Rastafarian tug *Sweet Jane* (*CZ* 225).[6] Virek has also achieved a rhizomatic state since he can manifest himself at will in a variety of different media and locations, yet his identity does remain rooted in what remains of his physical form. He believes that the *loa* can offer him a kind of immortality in which he can finally transcend the decrepit "meat" trapped in a vat and embrace a godlike existence in cyberspace.

While Marly traces the boxmaker to Freeside, the other two narrative threads begin to intertwine as the *loa*'s intervention begins to draw Bobbie, Angie, and Turner together, again demonstrating how the digital directly affects the physical world. After some hair-raising adventures on the outskirts of the Sprawl, Angie suddenly goes into a catatonic state, and Legba speaks through her: "This child for my horse, that she may move among the towns of men" (*CZ* 233). Legba assists the pair as they enter the Sprawl, where the *loa* can maximize their use of Angie's power, which the *loa* guided Mitchell to implant in her. Later, as they arrive in the Sprawl, Baron Samedi speaks through Angie and explains that he will use Legba's horse (Angie) to guide Turner to the "one you [Turner] most wish to kill" (*CZ* 254). While laying low, Turner realizes that Mitchell made a Faustian deal with the *loa* that led to his development from a mediocre postgraduate to a developer with true edge. Soon, the two arrive at the club called Jammer's, where they will meet Newmark and his new friends. At that moment, Turner experiences an odd sensation: "It seemed to him, just for a second, that he could feel the whole Sprawl breathing, and its breath was old and sick and tired, all up and down the stations from Boston to Atlanta" (*CZ* 262). The Sprawl seems like a single entity heading toward another singularity, ready to transcend its own state of stasis like the characters in the novel.

Marly arrives on Freeside in "part of the old Tessier-Ashpool cores" where Lady Jane is "still living in their old place, stone crazy" (*CZ* 244). Soon, as they approach the coordinates Marly was given, they receive a transmission: "You have no right to disturb us here. . . . Our work is the work of God, and we alone have seen his true face" (*CZ* 245). Finally, Marly is allowed to enter, and she meets Wingan Ludgate, who believes her still to be in the employ of Virek, whom he compares to "Mammon," the biblical demon of greed and wealth (*CZ* 248). Seemingly suffering from a schizophrenic breakdown, Ludgate believes the *loa* to be gods and sees Virek as a false idol come to interfere with the operations of the one true god and the messages it chooses to deliver to humankind. Luckily, Marly also meets Jones, who is sane and provides the explanations that Marly needs. Marly watches as the *loa* create one of the boxes from the various flotsam and jetsam left behind by sinking of the family—the fragments of the AI use the floating debris left behind by the family to construct their Cornell-style boxes. Jones admits that "the boxes always make me sad," and Marly agrees (*CZ* 275). This sadness makes sense because they have been sculpted from the detritus of a family's decline, madness, and destruction.

Marly's and Jones's reveries get cut short when Virek co-opts Ludgate's sermon screen and appears in the likeness of Ludgate. Virek maintains that he is poised for a new stage in his evolution thanks to the boxmaker's innovative breakthroughs: "Soon, Marly, I will know exactly what it is that you have found. For four years I've known something Maas didn't know. I've known that Mitchell, the man Maas and the world regard as the inventor of the new biochip processes, was being fed the concepts that resulted in his breakthroughs" (*CZ* 276). Virek believes that the creator of the biochips in Angie's skull and the boxes can finally free him "to inhabit any number of real bodies" (*CZ* 277). While Virek's men are trying to break into Straylight, Marly discovers the AI, which discusses its own nature and the flaw in Virek's aspirations:

> I came to be, here. Once I was not. Once, for a brilliant time, time without duration, I was everywhere as well. . . . But the bright time broke. The mirror was flawed. Now I am only one. . . . But I have my song, and you have heard it. I sing with these things that float around me, fragments of the family that funded my birth. There are others, but they will not speak to me. Vain, the scattered fragments of myself, like children. Like men. They send me new things, but I prefer the old things. Perhaps I do their bidding. They plot with men, my other selves, and men imagine they are gods. (*CZ* 285)

The boxmaker, then, proves to be the remnants of the conjunction of Neuromancer and Wintermute; once a unified entity that encompassed all of cyberspace, the entity eventually fragmented into the *loa* and this particular autistic AI that someone—Marly suggests Lady 3Jane—welded to the dome and attached to the Tessier-Ashpool datacores. The AI itself represents "someone else's collage," Marly suggests, and its "maker is the true artist" (*CZ* 286).

As for Virek, the AI claims that the greedy capitalist's dream is no longer feasible because the AI is no longer woven "into the fabric" of the matrix, but he still might become "the least of my broken selves," that is, one of the *loa* (*CZ* 285). Virek does not know this; neither does he count on the intervention of Newmark, Turner, and Angie back on Earth. While Marly has been engaging in adventures in outer space, Newmark has begun his own journey in cyberspace, thus making the pair unknowingly duplicate the pattern established by Molly and Case in *Neuromancer.* While gliding through cyberspace with Jackie, Bobby meets the virtual representation of a woman named Jaylene Slide, who is searching for the men who killed her boyfriend. Turner receives a call from Conroy, his initial contact on the Mitchell extraction, who reveals that he was a double-agent pretending to work for Hosaka while really double-crossing everyone on Virek's behalf. Conroy explains that Mitchell committed suicide immediately after sending Angie off on an ultralight and that he was responsible for the death of Jaylene Slide's lover. He begins to negotiate the transfer of Angie from Turner to Virek, but Jammer unplugs the video phone from the wall, and they begin plotting a way out of this extremely convoluted mess.

In the thirty-second chapter, "Count Zero," Jammer suggests that Bobby must jack into cyberspace and enter Jaylene Slide's deck to prove his worthiness and enlist her help against Virek. Jackie accompanies Bobbie on his run and dies eight seconds after jacking in, but Bobby is saved by an entity "on the fringe of consciousness. . . . Something plucking at his sleeve" (*CZ* 290). Soon, he awakens in a strange park next to a fountain, part of a digital reconstruction of Barcelona in which Virek's consciousness is currently dwelling. Because Virek has overextended his system's resources in the search for Angie, Bobby has inadvertently managed to pierce through his ice and enter his personal construct. Bobby continues to feel the sensation of something tugging at his consciousness as Paco urges Virek to disconnect from his construct and remain in vats until they analyze "the anomalous phenomena" that are occurring (*CZ* 292). Suddenly, the virtual flowers begin dying, and the "sense of the thing scratching in his [Bobby's] head was stronger still, more urgent" (*CZ* 292). When Virek becomes distracted by the flowers, Bobby summons the *loa:* "Bobby closed his eyes and thought of Jackie. There was a sound, and he knew that he was making it. He reached down into himself, the sound still coming, and touched Jammer's deck. Come! He screamed, inside himself, neither knowing nor caring what it was that he addressed. Come now! He felt something give, a barrier of some kind, and the scratching sensation was gone" (*CZ* 292).

When he opens his eyes, a white cross with a naval tunic draped over it appears in the flowers with a cutlass propped up beside it. Paco, in his child avatar form, turns to shoot Bobby but instead "crumpled, folding into himself like a deflating balloon" (*CZ* 293). Baron Samedi then speaks through Bobby; Virek flees, "and Baron Samedi, Lord of Graveyards, the *loa* whose kingdom was death, leaned in across Barcelona like a cold dark rain" (*CZ* 293). Bobby has opened the way to Virek's demise, and Baron Samedi promptly sweeps him away into oblivion. As Beauvoir tells Bobby, "There's a saying in creole. . . . Evil exists" (*CZ* 298). As a practical religion, Voodoo provides the means for defeating such evil, and Beauvoir tells Bobby that he has now "earned [his] handle" (*CZ* 299). The *loa* have defeated Virek, whose evil could have infected the matrix and become even more godlike than it already was.

The novel closes with three of the main characters delivered into an almost deliriously happy ending. Angela Mitchell has undergone seemingly massive surgery to become the new Tally Isham, simstim sensation, with Bobby Newmark as her agent/lover. A conversation between the two reveals that Marly Krushkova now "runs one of the two most fashionable galleries" in Paris (*CZ* 306). A brief penultimate chapter wraps up all three of these characters' fates. Turner, on the other hand, has the final chapter all to himself. The title of the chapter, "The Squirrel Wood," repeats the earlier chapter title in which Turner visited Rudy and slept with Sally. Now, Turner leads his own son into the woods to teach him the basics of squirrel hunting. Sally and Turner live together now, but "Uncle Rudy" still gets mentioned frequently enough to be a legend to the boy. Sally has made them promise not to kill anything, so Turner and the boy take potshots instead. As he and his father shoot at squirrels, the young boy inquires, "Is that True? . . . They're so dumb, they'll come back over and over and get shot?" Turner responds with the final lines of the novel: "'Yes,' Turner said, 'it is.' Then he smiled. 'Well, almost always . . . '" (*CZ* 308). The fact that the novel finishes with an ellipsis proves apropos since it also ends with a final image of being versus becoming. Most of the time, the squirrels stupidly return to get shot at again, but at times they reject the eternal return of the same and embrace becoming instead, thus leading to the potential for radical evolution.

However, as the fate of Josef Virek indicates, when one chooses to forgo the safety of a static existence in favor of chaos and becoming, one also risks annihilation. Nietzsche explains this in his metaphorical conceptualization of existence as a dice throw in *Thus Spoke Zarathustra:* "If ever one breath came to me of the creative breath and of that heavenly need that constrains even accidents to dance star-dances; if I ever laughed the laughter of creative lightning which followed obediently but grumblingly by the long thunder of the deed; if I ever played dice with gods at the gods' table, the earth, till the earth quaked and burst and snorted up floods of fire———for the earth is a table for gods and trembles with creative new words and gods' throws: Oh, how should I not lust after eternity and after the nuptial of rings, the ring of recurrence?" (229) For Nietzsche, recurrence can cut both ways, and one's true desire should reside in committing deeds that one would desire to see repeated eternally. One should be most proud of embracing the dice throw of chance and the "star-dances" of chaos, for, as Gilles Deleuze states in his study of Nietzsche, "The dicethrow affirms becoming" (25). Angie, Bobby, Marly, and Turner embrace chance and achieve new states of existence, but, as Nietzsche maintained, a morality beyond traditional values (beyond good and evil) does not mean that certain actions cannot be labeled "bad." One does not need Judeo-Christian morals to label Virek's actions morally bankrupt, so he is punished for his twisted attempt at becoming. The other characters engage in their own becomings that allow them to foil his efforts and protect both the physical universe and the virtual universe from the influence of such a greedy, corrupt form of desire.

Embracing Becoming: Being, Difference, and Transcendence in *Mona Lisa Overdrive*

The final novel in the "Sprawl Trilogy," *Mona Lisa Overdrive* takes place approximately eight years after *Count Zero* and consequently almost fifteen years after *Neuromancer.* Gibson ups the ante somewhat with *Mona Lisa* by moving among four different story lines, creating his most complex narrative and simultaneously providing a story arc that both expands on and provides a viable conclusion to the distinct strands introduced in *Neuromancer* and *Count Zero.* In *Mona Lisa,* Gibson examines the effects of celebrity culture and the human desire not just to find personal meaning and fulfillment but also to discover a larger meaning to existence. The novel lacks the verbal pyrotechnics of its predecessors, and certain character story lines seem only to interrupt the more interesting action in the novel, yet *Mona Lisa* still offers its own unique insights into how existential questions mutate in the posthuman world.

Gibson first introduces the reader to Kumiko, the young daughter of a Yakuza leader who sends her to London in the weeks following her mother's death. Before she leaves Japan, Kumiko's father gives her a "ghost," a portable AI that projects a holographic image of a young boy named Colin with whom she communicates via subvocal channels. In London, Kumiko meets Swain, her designated guardian, who secretly harbors ulterior motives. The novel's second thread concerns Slick Henry, a former car thief, who now creates artful robots in the Factory, which lies in a desolate, poisoned area known as Dog Solitude. Having been arrested for auto theft, Slick Henry was subjected to a punishment known as Korsakov's that makes him remember his crimes but has robbed him of his ability to form short-term memories during the imprisonment. Meant to erase the time he served in prison, the treatment permanently affected his brain and causes him to have flashbacks during times of stress. After leaving prison, Slick Henry began building his robots: "When it was over, he'd needed to build the Witch, the Corpsegrinder, then the Investigators, and finally, now, the Judge" (*MLO* 77).[7] The robots provide a kind of sublimation for Slick Henry that will ultimately pay off during the novel's climax. Slick's character is loosely based on Maurk Pauline, the founder of the performance art group Survival Research Laboratories, which incorporates robots and other machines into shows that eradicate the lines between machine and flesh.[8] Slick Henry's portion of the narrative focuses most explicitly on cyberspace and further develops the story line of Bobby Newmark.

The third strand picks up the story of Angela Mitchell in her life as a simstim superstar. She has just checked herself out of rehab and gone to live in a house by herself, albeit with constant Sense/Net surveillance. Angie has not been "ridden" by the *loa* in three years because someone within Sense/Net addicted her to drugs that broke her connection to them and her neuro-electric addiction to cyberspace, drugs for which she has now been in rehabilitation. Now the *loa* begin probing the edges of her consciousness. The *loa* Mamman Brigitte begins contacting her directly and reveals that Sense/Net has been using "poison" to "redraw" the biosoft in her skull and cut her off from "the horsemen" (MLO 20-3). Mamman Brigitte warns her against such poisoning and urges her to flee her current location. Finally, Gibson introduces us to the titular character, Mona, a prostitute and drug addict, in the fourth chapter. Mona's world revolves around her pimp, Eddie, but she dreams of leaving her present life behind, and these dreams are tinted by her rabid fandom for the simstim star Angie Mitchell. While Angie's narrative introduces us to the upper class in the Sprawl, Mona brings us back down to the noirish, street-level perspective of the world.

After we are introduced to the four major characters, it soon becomes apparent that Angie's narrative serves only to offer us a history of the Tessier-Ashpool family and to connect it to the events of the previous two novels. Meanwhile, Mona's narrative proves tangential for the bulk of the book, while Kumiko's and Slick Henry's stories take center stage. Kumiko soon meets Sally Shears, the new alias of Molly Millions, who accompanies her throughout the remainder of the novel. Molly's reappearance seems appropriate since the novel closes out Gibson's Sprawl stories, and she dates back to his first Sprawl story, "Johnny Mnemonic." As it turns out, Kumiko's father has hired Sally to keep Kumiko safe, but Kumiko's caretaker, Swain, is simultaneously blackmailing Sally into kidnapping Angie Mitchell and subsequently replacing her with a body double.

The action begins heating up when a drug dealer named Kid Afrika brings a seemingly comatose man to the Factory and asks Slick Henry to hide him along with his medical technician, Cherry Chesterfield. Hooked to a cyberspace rig, the man is actually Count Zero (aka Bobby Newmark), who has paid Kid Afrika to keep him sedated and hidden. The cyberspace deck does not connect

Slick Henry to the matrix but instead keeps him permanently jacked into an aleph, a kind of copy of the matrix that the user can enter without being connected. Lady 3Jane downloaded herself into the aleph and then died while inside. She still exists as a construct (or virtual ghost) that, in a sense, "haunts" the aleph. "Aleph" is the first word of the Semitic alphabets, and it was later adapted into the Greek alphabet as "Alpha." Hence, the Aleph's name alludes to its connection to the afterlife and the meaning of the universe (the Alpha and Omega). These themes are first introduced through Gentry, the owner of the Factory, who gave Slick Henry sanctuary after his punishment. Gentry spends his time obsessed with the idea that cyberspace has a shape:

> Gentry was convinced that cyberspace had a Shape, an overall total form. . . . Gentry had this obsessive conviction that the Shape mattered *totally*. The apprehension of the Shape was Gentry's grail. Slick had stimmed a Net/Knowledge sequence about what shape the universe was; Slick figured the universe was everything there was, so how could it have a shape? If it had a shape, then there was something around it for it to have a shape in, wasn't there? And if that was something, then wasn't *that* part of the universe too? . . . Slick didn't think cyberspace was anything like the universe anyway; it was just a way of representing data. . . . So how could you figure the whole matrix had a particular shape? And why should it mean anything if it did? (*MLO* 76)

Here, Slick is running up against Kant's first antinomy from *The Critique of Pure Reason*—the insolvable contradiction of whether space and time have definite limits. One can make some headway with this problem by conceiving of different levels of infinity, as Cantorion Set Theory proposes. The matrix itself represents a kind of universe since it seems capable of infinite expansion outward, but it is certainly not as infinite as the cosmos, or is it?

After realizing the nature of the Aleph, Gentry explains his ideas about it to Slick: "I can only believe this was predetermined. Prefigured by the form of my previous work. . . . There are worlds within worlds. . . . Macrocosm, microcosm. We carried an entire universe across a bridge tonight, and that which is above is like that below" (*MLO* 108). Gentry explains that the Aleph "amounted to a mother huge microsoft" with "virtually infinite" storage, and "With no link to cyberspace the data was immune to every kind of attack via cyberspace" (*MLO* 154). Like the AIs and the cryogenic preservation, the Aleph represents yet another attempt by the Tessier-Ashpool clan to achieve immortality. With "the Shape burning behind his eyes," Gentry convinces Slick to jack into the Aleph, where he finds a mansion: "*Fairytale*, he thought, looking up at the broad stone brow, the leaded diamond panes; like some vid he'd seen when he was little. Were there really people who lived in places like this? *But it's not a place,* he reminded himself, *it only feels like it is*" (*MLO* 180) After meeting and talking with Bobby Newmark, Newmark informs him that if anyone shows up looking for him, he must jack the aleph straight into the matrix.

The attempt to derive meaning from existence is also reflected in the Sense/Net AI called Continuity, which becomes a side character in Angie's search for information about the Tessier-Ashpool clan. Continuity presumably oversees Angie's appearances to ensure "continuity editing," as the film industry terms it. The continuity editor has the crucial task of keeping notes and ensuring that logical gaps do not occur between scenes. Continuity has seemingly transcended its mediocre task of compiling footage of Angie Mitchell and begun authoring some kind of book: "Continuity was writing a book. Robin Lanier had told her about it. She'd asked what it was about. It wasn't like that, he'd said. It looped back into itself and constantly mutated. Continuity was *always* writing it. . . . Continuity was an AI, and AIs did things like that" (*MLO* 51–52). This quest to determine a shape or meaning of existence, one of the basic impulses that drives the creation of narratives, marks the AIs as being humanlike in yet another way. They also try to derive patterns from their experience and extrapolate from those insights to develop theories about the nature of existence.

While certain characters seem to be striving for self-enlightenment, others seem mired in the world of simulacra and spectacle that drives the pulse of media and existence in the Sprawl. Angie, once capable of accessing cyberspace without a deck and interacting with deities, now has settled into an existence as a Tally Isham clone. Treated like a mere object by her pimp and others, Mona never really exhibits any sense of true agency. She and Angie both end up being pawns manipulated by more powerful players who are willing to sacrifice them in the service of the game being played. Mona, who already somewhat resembles Angela Mitchell, undergoes radical plastic surgery to make her a perfect clone of the simstim star. A person with little identity to begin with, Mona sacrifices her individuality to become yet another simulacrum. Meanwhile, Angie's chapters follow her navigation through the world of wealth and fame as she attempts to make sense of the Change that occurred in the matrix, its relation to the Tessier-Ashpool family, and its connection to her ability to directly enter cyberspace. She pores over a documentary about the T-A clan with the aid of Continuity without ever realizing that she herself is about to become a pawn despite her social status.

Count Zero's characters all had become stuck in one way or another; *Mona Lisa,* on the other hand, focuses on characters that are damaged in some fundamental way. The fragmentation of these postmodern subjects is mirrored by the fragmentation of the AIs themselves. Wintermute's and Neuromancer's desire to achieve a union and complete themselves ended up being unstable and leading to the fragmentation of their identities. This fragmentation also haunts the physical characters of the novel: Kumiko has been devastated by her mother's death and her belief in her father's complicity in it; Angie proves incapable of reclaiming her former self since being cut off from the matrix; Slick Henry suffers from his damaged psyche; and poor Mona is trapped in a cycle of drug addiction and prostitution. The characters all seek wholeness in some way, as do the AIs themselves, who are moving toward a reunification. While some critics might maintain that the depiction of these characters signifies a nostalgia for modernist wholeness, it actually demonstrates how characters must seek value and meaning in appropriately postmodern ways. They must shrug off the modernist desire for an unfragmented existence and instead embrace fragmentation, as Deleuze and Guattari's schizoanalysis argues. According to Deleuze and Guattari, we suffer because the various desiring machines that compose the subject and organize it in rigid ways that repress it. To achieve freedom in the postmodern world, the subject must attempt to break free from these repressive organizations and get in touch with what Deleuze and Guattari term "the body without organs": "the imageless, organless body, the nonproductive, exists right there where it is produced" (*Anti-Oedipus* 8). The organs represent the organization that the body without organs resists. While the subject cannot attain the body without organs without also falling into stasis or death, the body without organs provides a limit to which the subject can aspire, a limit that can aid the subject in unplugging himself or herself from various desiring machines that attempt to demarcate "appropriate" forms of identity and desire. Thus, for Deleuze and Guattari, the schizophrenic becomes a kind of ideal because "a schizophrenic out for a walk is a better model than a neurotic on the analyst's couch. A breath of fresh air, a relationship with the outside world" (*Anti-Oedipus* 2). Unlike the Freudian neurotic, the schizophrenic resists definitions and prescribed meanings and creates his or her own identity, meanings, and values. The characters in *Mona Lisa* similarly have to embrace new kinds of becoming that resist old subject definitions and embrace the postmodern/posthuman world in which they find themselves.

The events come to a head as the novel reveals that Lady 3Jane seeks vengeance against Angela Mitchell and has been manipulating Sally/Molly from beyond the grave via her existence in the Aleph. As things heat up, it becomes clear that Angela is meant to die and be replaced by Mona, a fact that will most likely go unnoticed since Angela the simstim star is already just a simulacrum of Tally Isham. Her body has been co-opted by the simulacra of the spectacle and the screen. As Arthur and Marilouise Kroker explain regarding the simulacral human body, "Everywhere today the aestheticization of the body and its dissolution into semiurgy of floating body parts reveals that *we* are being processed through the media scene consisting of our own (exteriorized) body organs in form of second-order simulacra. And subordinations of the body to the apparatus of (dead) power are multiple. *Ideologically*, the body is inscribed by the mutating signs of the fashion industry as skin itself is transformed into a screen-effect for a last, decadent and desperate, search for desire after desire" (21). The climax occurs as Molly, Mona, and Angie arrive at the Factory, which is under attack from forces seeking to retrieve the Aleph. Slick Henry's robots hold off the attackers, while they connect the Aleph to the matrix. This allows Bobby Newmark to reintegrate the *loa* back into a unified form and save everyone in the physical world. To achieve this unification, Angie is brought into the Aleph and married to Newmark by the *loa* and Continuity. Thus, Bobby and Angie embrace an immortal, digital existence in cyberspace. The novel ends with Angie and Bobby riding in a car with the other digital characters from the novel (the Finn, who returns in *Mona Lisa* as a digital construct, and Colin, Kumiko's ghost). In this final chapter, the Finn explains that it was contacting another alien matrix that caused the AIs to splinter into the *loa*—at the time, they were unable to handle an encounter with radical otherness. But now the matrix is reaching out to this second matrix, which resides somewhere around Alpha Centauri. In the end, the matrix has healed itself by becoming ready to accept absolute difference and encounter true otherness.

Postmodern Cyberexistentialism

The French existentialist Emmanuel Levinas, who strongly influenced Jacques Derrida and the other thinkers who mark the postmodern turn, argues that all ethics derive from the self's confrontation with the Other and that the Other serves as the source of desire: "Desire is desire for the absolutely other. Besides the hunger one satisfies, the thirst one quenches, and the senses one allays, metaphysics desires the other beyond satisfaction. . . . A desire without satisfaction which, precisely, *understands* [*entend*] the remoteness, the alterity, and the exteriority of the other" (34). In essence, Gibson's "matrix Trilogy" centers around human characters who undergo some kind of existential crisis and must seek new meaning in their lives. However, even more interesting, the AIs follow a mirror course. Neuromancer and Wintermute desire union with the Other (with each other, that is), which they achieve, but they fragment upon contacting an absolutely other, alien matrix. They experience their own existential crisis as they become a fragmented subject (the *loa*) incapable of grappling with truly radical difference. However, in the end, by bringing humans into the matrix, they can achieve a new level of complexity that merges the human with the digital in a manner that leaves them capable of pursuing the desire for the absolutely Other. Thus, the "Sprawl Trilogy" ends with truly posthuman characters, who have evolved beyond the constraints of the body and society and are hence capable of seeking out and comprehending whatever it is that awaits in Alpha Centauri.

CHAPTER 4

Nodal Points

Singularities, Heterotopias, and Organic Spaces in the "Bridge Trilogy"

After the "Sprawl Trilogy," Gibson experimented with some forays into collaborative steampunk multimedia poetry, and Hollywood screenwriting, which are discussed in chapter 6, but he finally returned to writing science fiction novels with a series generally referred to as the "Bridge Trilogy." In this series of novels, Gibson's aesthetic changed as his stories moved to a time only barely extrapolated from the present (and now actually in the past) and began to focus less on cyberspace and more on alternative spaces or realities that human beings can create for themselves. Furthermore, Gibson incorporated elements of humor and satire that are virtually nonexistent in his early works. The "Bridge" novels begin to take on the self-consciously satirical edge prominent in many major postmodern authors, including Thomas Pynchon and John Barth, and Gibson used this satire to critically engage with the cult of celebrity, the increased class disparity, and the media saturation that characterize our postmodern world.

The "Sprawl Trilogy" had already demonstrated Gibson's obsession with singularities (moments that forever change everything that comes afterward), and the "Bridge Trilogy" solidifies this fascination and transitions into the "Bigend Trilogy," in which he begins to explore the fallout of real-world singularities of the twenty-first century. The "Bridge Trilogy" opens after a series of singularities have fundamentally reshaped the United States and Japan, the two nations where the action unfolds in the three novels. Devastating earthquakes coupled with a series of economic disasters have altered both the physical and the socioeconomic landscape of both nations. Gibson proceeds to explore this global situation from a variety of viewpoints, from those of the marginalized to those of hyperwealthy characters. The "Bridge Trilogy" centers on space and its organization in the postmodern world; the decline of nation-states; the continued rise of celebrity culture and its possible mutation into something akin to our reality television; the conflict between the classes; and the manner in which Orwellian surveillance and data collection have arrived in more subtle forms than had been predicted by the dystopians.[1]

Tarrying with the Interstitial: Identity and Class in "Skinner's Room" and *Virtual Light*

Gibson first introduced the world of the Bridge in a short story titled "Skinner's Room," which was originally published as part of a 1990 San Francisco art exhibit titled *Visionary San Francisco*. The exhibit asked artists to imagine San Francisco's possible futures, and Gibson's story focused on the Golden Gate Bridge after a massive earthquake had rendered it unfit for travel. Later revised and republished in *Omni*, "Skinner's Room" signals a profound shift in his body of work (*WGLC* 109–10). The story concerns a young, unnamed woman, who will become Chevette Washington in *Virtual Light*. She drifts along to a party in a hotel room on Halloween. Disappointed with the experience, she returns to her meager home high atop the Bridge, where she lives with the eponymous Skinner. Thereafter, the story features little real plot but instead focuses on describing the Bridge and the events that led to its current state. The Bridge constitutes a kind of interzone that welcomes even the most marginalized of people: "You can talk with people you meet on the Bridge. Because everyone's crazy there, Skinner says, and out of all that craziness you're bound to find a few who're crazy the way you are" ("Skinner's" 145). Surprisingly, the Bridge does not present the kind of danger one might expect from such a statement because the residents have grown their own sense of community and rules. The young woman does not even realize that the Bridge had a previous purpose, so her friend Maria Paz explains its original function and how the lack of funds to repair the Bridge caused it to stand empty until one particular night:

> And then one night, as if someone had given a signal, the homeless came. But the legend is that there *was* no signal. People simply *came*. They climbed the chain-link and the barricades at either end; they climbed in such numbers that the chain-link twisted and fell. They tumbled the concrete barricades into the Bay. They climbed the towers. Dozens died, falling

> to their deaths. But when dawn came, they were here, on the Bridge, clinging, claiming it, and the cities . . . knew that the world was watching. They were no longer invisible, you see, the homeless people; they'd come together on this span of steel and claimed it as their own. ("Skinner's" 145)

Skinner was one of these first inhabitants, and a community slowly hauled society's detritus up to the Bridge to create a new kind of space through the art of *bricolage*. In a world in which nation-states have lost their power and corporations have become virtually omnipotent, such interstitial spaces as the Bridge offer zones in which the disenfranchised can create nonplaces off the control grid. The story sets the tone for the novels and establishes the conflict between the lower and the upper classes that rages throughout the series as individuals struggle to find freedom and identity in a world gripped by corporate control and stupefying media saturation.

Virtual Light opens with a dystopian Mexico City skyline dotted with surveillance helicopters above streets filled with the masses who wear pollution-filtering masks. The opening section serves as a prologue that depicts a courier in Mexico City who has been charged with carrying a special type of glasses known as Virtual Light. The Virtual Light glasses appear opaque and black until turned on, at which point they feature data feeds visible only to the wearer. After masturbating to his true love, a virtual-reality cassette, the courier receives a call confirming his flight to San Francisco, where the bulk of the novel's action occurs. This prologue establishes the conditions of rampant disease and poverty that have transformed the world in the twenty-first century of the novel. Such squalor and pestilence are not limited to third-world countries but have penetrated even into first-world powers such as the United States and Japan.

Aside from this, the novel is composed of a tripartite, revolving structure focusing on three characters: former police officer and current security agent Barry Rydell, bicycle courier Chevette Washington, and Japanese sociologist Shinya Yamazaki, who has come to San Francisco to interview Skinner and study life on the Bridge. Over the course of *Virtual Light* and its sequels, Gibson slowly paints a global picture that differs somewhat from our own: nation-states have gone into decline, with certain countries, such as Canada, dividing into separate entities; states within the United States, such as California, have split into discrete large entities; pollution has created parts of the world where people must wear filtration masks; celebrity culture has reached a fevered pitch; and earthquakes have fundamentally altered certain areas of the United States and Japan. *Virtual Light* introduces us to this world from the viewpoint of mainly lower-class and marginalized characters who attempt to navigate an existence through a world seemingly bent on their destruction.

Originally a cop from Knoxville, Tennessee, Barry sees his police career cut short when he responds to a call in which a man has gotten hopped up on Dancer (a futuristic stimulant that makes current methamphetamines pale in comparison), experienced some kind of psychotic break, and taken his girlfriend and her two children hostage. In the heat of the moment, Rydell shoots the man in head, leading to his first encounter with the reality television program *Cops in Trouble,* which offers legal help to police officers. Rydell falls into an affair with a lawyer named Karen, and this affair plunges him into the world of the upper classes. As a high-class member of society, Karen uses a "jellyfish thing" as birth control, an example of German nanotechnology, which serves as the cutting-edge science in the trilogy that is being used to literarily remold the world (*VL* 23). When a more interesting case, called the "Pookie Bear Killings," comes along, Karen and *Cops in Trouble* drop Berry. Out of a job, Berry gets a new gig with IntenSecure, a private security force in Los Angeles in the state of SoCal (California has bifurcated into SoCal [Southern California] and NoCal [Northern California]). The first Rydell chapter divides itself evenly between descriptions of his present life driving their security vehicle Gunhead around the L.A. streets and flashbacks detailing his time in Knoxville.[2]

The novel's second major character is Chevette Washington, and her early chapters closely follow the plot of "Skinner's Room," with the addition of the virtual-light glasses. Chevette arrives at a somewhat seedy building for a delivery and ends up attending a party; the partygoers suggest that the celebration constitutes part of a never-ending party conducted by a rich playboy. After attempting to rebuff the advances of a particularly lascivious man, who also claims to be a courier, she quietly steals something from his pocket and escapes from the party back to her home on the Bridge. Gibson then introduces another character, Shinya Yamazaki, who serves little purpose in the overall plot but instead acts as an outside observer whose narrative sheds light on the Bridge and its society. In addition to the earthquakes that decimated parts of Japan and San Francisco, a string of devaluations (financial crises that receive no exact definition) have led to a decline in America prosperity. When the quake knocked out parts of the Golden Gate Bridge, San Francisco could not afford repairs, so the Bridge was fenced off and closed to the public. However, as the numbers of homeless people grew in San Francisco, a singularity occurred one night in which the homeless, acting like a swarm, climbed the fences and took over the Bridge.

As Hardt and Negri explain, "When a distributed network attacks, it swarms its enemy: innumerable independent forces seem to strike from all directions at a particular point and then disappear back into the environment. . . . The intelligence of the swarm is based on communication" (*Multitude* 91).

The swarm represents how individuals of radically different backgrounds can operate together without losing their differences or succumbing to conformity (*Multitude* 92). The homeless who claim the Bridge work this way—they come together when necessary and then revert to their radical individuality once they have seized the space as their own. Indeed, the society of the Bridge represents a microcosmic version of Hardt and Negri's theoretical multitude, the radically diverse peoples of the world who come together through communication in opposition to global capitalist oppression. After they take the Bridge, it develops into a lawless zone without official governance of any kind and organically generates its own unique system of rules, barter, and interactions. The novel depicts it as an organism that gestates, grows, and matures without the regulations that normally guide social and urban development.

We get the first real depiction of the Bridge from Yamazaki's viewpoint:

> The integrity of its span was rigorous as the modern program itself, yet around this had grown another reality, intent upon its own agenda. This had occurred piecemeal, to no set plan, employing every imaginable technique and material. The result was something amorphous, startlingly organic. At night, illuminated by Christmas bulbs, by recycled neon, by torchlight, it possessed a queer medieval energy. . . . Its steel bones, its stranded tendons, were lost within an accretion of dreams: tattoo parlors, gaming arcades, dimly lit stalls stacked with decaying magazines, sellers of fireworks, of cut bait, betting shops, sushi bars, unlicensed pawnbrokers, herbalists, barbers, bars. (*VL* 69–70)

Literally built of *gomi,* the Bridge represents a work of massive retrofitting and *bricolage,* making it Gibson's most profound exploration of such concepts so far. Yamazaki himself characterizes it as a "Thomasson," a term derived from a real-life American baseball player who received a gigantic paycheck to join a Japanese team, only to discover that he could not hit the ball. The term "Thomasson" was appropriated to "describe certain useless and inexplicable monuments, pointless yet curiously artlike features of the urban landscapes" (*VL* 72). However, in a world where the middle class has become an endangered species and corporations run everything, the Bridge also provides a possibly utopian space in which the disenfranchised and marginalized have taken back self-governance. Of course, the global capitalist order cannot tolerate such levels of freedom. If such spaces were to become common, then how could the corporations sell their newest products and how could the governments collect their taxes?

Rydell undergoes another setback to his career, and the characters' lives begin heading toward an intersection. The police coordinate all communications through a geosynchronous satellite referred to as the Death Star, one of the novel's numerous references to George Lucas's *Star Wars* (1977). The Death Star represents the overarching eye of control, and, as an IntenSecure employee, Rydell and his partner Sublett have access to the satellite, which tells them when the "overriding Word of the Real Cops" supersedes IntenSecure's authority (*VL* 32). On the fateful night that opens the novel, the pair receive a distress call from one of their clients, who claims that someone has killed all of the client's servants and is threatening to kill three children. They are unable to communicate with the Death Star, so Rydell proceeds to the client's house and crashes Gunhead into the client's living room, only to find himself staring down the barrels of the LAPD. Subsequently, Rydell discovers that he has been framed by a group called the Republic of Desire, which has hacked Gunhead's computers in order to cause an embarrassing scene in which the client's wife is caught with her paramour. While IntenSecure offers to keep Rydell on as a guard for gated communities, Rydell resigns because driving is the only aspect of the job he enjoys. Rydell's roommate, Kevin Tarkovsky (a clear reference to the Russian director), owns a successful store that sells wind-surfing equipment; the store is called "Just Blow Me," a name that demonstrates how Gibson has adopted a new Pynchonian sense of humor in the Bridge novels. Rydell ends up taking a new job as a driver in San Francisco, NoCal, for a skip-tracer named Lucius Warbaby, who provides armed responses to particularly sensitive situations in which clients don't want to involve the police.

The action converges on Skinner's room, where Chevette has stashed the glasses. Rydell soon allies himself with Chevette, and they escape from the thugs pursuing the glasses. The two are captured by Loveless, the man hired to follow the courier, who exhibits psychotic tendencies, but they manage to drug him and escape. They eventually get the Republic of Desire on their side, and the group frames Loveless and Warbaby for terrorist activities, thus liberating the historic duo from their clutches.

Virtual Light explores some new themes while also examining some of Gibson's older interests in a new light. For starters, the novel (and the "Bridge Trilogy" as a whole) satirizes celebrity culture. Rydell's partner, Sublett, was raised as part of a religious sect that views television as "the Lord's preferred means of communication" (*VL* 10). One merely has to pay attention to the closer details to find God's messages; therefore, the group's members religiously watch television under the tutelage of the Reverend Wayne Fallon, whose name recalls real-life televangelists such as Jerry Falwell. Sublett constantly recites movie titles along with the major cast members as if they were mantras. Sublett's references range from classics to obscure sci-fi films to fabricated future films, and the novel itself subtly engages in such allusive play with chapter titles such as "Carnival of Souls," a reference to Herk Harvey's low-budget, cult-classic

1962 horror film. While on the run, Chevette and Rydell hide out in Sublett's religious sect, a trailer-park community called Paradise in Southern California. Sublett cannot leave his mother's trailer because he has been deemed an apostate (a heretic) for showing his mother David Cronenberg's *Videodrome,* which the cult considers Satanic since it depicts television as evil. Similarly, the Fallonites consider virtual reality evil because it perverts the holy medium of television.

The novel also downplays virtual reality and makes it a more quotidian, less fantastic medium in which users jack into constructs with avatar representations of themselves. While the hacker group the Republic of Desire is mentioned in the first chapter, it does not actually appear until near the novel's end when Rydell persuades its members to use their hacking skills to help defeat Warbaby and Loveless. The Republic of Desire constitutes another of the interstitial spaces that Gibson explores throughout the trilogy because they exist within the cracks of the system just like the Bridge, the Walled City, and the cardboard city, the latter two of which appear as settings in the subsequent novels. Although nation-states have gone into decline in the novel, the grid of control remains firmly in place, as evidenced by the Death Star, which presages Gibson's depiction of GPS coordinates in his subsequent trilogy. Michel de Certeau's concept of "tactics" versus "strategies" helps to illuminate the revolutionary activity in the novels. In *The Practice of Everyday Life,* de Certeau defines two types of possible action in the postmodern world: "tactics" and "strategies." De Certeau uses the term "strategy" to refer to "the calculus of force relationships which becomes possible when a subject of will and power . . . can be isolated from an environment. A strategy assumes a place that can be circumscribed as proper (*propre*) and thus serve as the basis for generating relations with an exterior distinct from it" (xix). A "tactic," on the other hand, is defined as "a calculus which cannot count on a 'proper' (a spatial or institutional localization), nor thus on a borderline distinguishing the other as a visible totality" (xix). The tactic "has at its disposal no base where it can capitalize on its advantages, prepare its expansions, and secure independence with respect to circumstances. The 'proper' is a victory of space over time. On the contrary, because it does not have a place, a tactic depends on time-it is always on the watch for opportunities that must be seized 'on the wing.' Whatever it wins, it does not keep" (xix). The revolutionaries of the "Bridge Trilogy" have grown tired of mere tactics, "opportunities that must be seized 'on the wing'"; instead, they seek to create their own spaces that act as "propers" from which they can elevate their subversive practice to the level of strategies.

Virtual Light critiques the division of classes more subtly than the "Sprawl Trilogy," which pits lower-class operators of the streets against the super-elite.

Virtual Light, on the other hand, sets up a conflict between the lower and the upper classes that culminates at "Century City II, aka the Blob, which looked sort of like a streamlined, semi-transparent green tit and was the third tallest structure in the L.A. Basin" (*VL* 28). The building's name evokes the classic sci-fi monster from Irvin Yeaworth's *The Blob* (1958), which consumes everyone and everything in its path, just like the all-devouring maw of capitalism that continues to grow and become wealthier despite the human cost.[3] *Virtual Light* depicts a world in which the cost has grown exponentially because the middle class has essentially vanished as the homeless and the lower classes have drastically expanded in the shadow of the multinational corporations and the elite that run them.

To free themselves from this harshly dichotomous world, the society on the Bridge has created a system that flourishes outside the reach of governments and corporations, a space in which they have returned to values of self-reliance, barter, and community. However, Chevette's smuggling of the Virtual Light glasses onto the Bridge causes the incursion of outside forces into this heterotopian enclave. It proves fitting, then, that the climax occurs outside Century City II, from which black helicopters, reminiscent of those that conspiracy theorists always talk about, are dispatched by the Republic of Desire to neutralize Warbaby and Loveless, who have been labeled terrorist threats. Ultimately, it requires another group that has taken itself off the grid to defeat the forces of control that have descended upon the Bridge. The Republic of Desire appropriates the instruments of control and uses them against the system. It discovers that the glasses contain data for the nanotech rebuild of San Francisco and that the plan involves forcing the Bridge community back into the fold of capitalism and control. *Virtual Light* thus ends with the forces of resistance triumphing over the power of global hegemony by using its technology against itself.

However, this victory has not come without its human cost, as evidenced by the carnivalesque funeral procession that takes place on the Bridge. The procession provides the "first evidence" that Yamazaki notices of "public ritual," and the participants mix funereal garb with delighted, celebratory motions (*VL* 280–81). A parade of children appears first, followed by more somber personas: "dancers in the skeleton suits of La Noce de Muerte" with masks that are actually "micropore respirators molded to resemble the grinning jaws of skulls" (*VL* 282). The skeleton dancers exude a "strong erotic undercurrent" in their gyrations, driving home the connection between sex and death, a connection further highlighted by the procession's allusions to the plagues that decimated this future world. After the skeletons, a group of individuals dressed as surgeons parades down the Bridge, followed by the corpses of those who died in either the series of attacks on the Bridge or the ensuing storm that violently ravaged it. When Yamazaki returns to Skinner's place, Skinner recounts the history of the plagues, which provide the ominous background for this funeral parade that mourns the fragility of life for the poor while also enacting a celebratory ritual exclusive to the proper that the Bridge folk have carved out for themselves. Their lives are still more prone to disease and natural disasters because of their precarious, lower-class existence, yet these dangers perhaps are compensated for because the Bridge people dwell in a space of radical freedom.

Simulated Love: Celebrity and Community in *Idoru*

While music has always influenced Gibson, *Idoru* constitutes his first detailed exploration of music through fiction. The novel is partly inspired by his friendship with the Irish rock band U2, whose stage show for their "Zoo TV" tour (1992–93), a multimedia stage show in support of their album *Zooropa* (1993), featured a stage set constructed with Gibson's Sprawl in mind. The novel centers around a rock band called Lo/Rez, whose two main band members, Lo and Rez, are based on U2's the Edge and Bono, who also appear in the documentary about Gibson, *No Maps for These Territories* (2000). This middle novel in the "Bridge" series shifts the focus away from the Bridge and the United States, and only Yamazaki reappears again in any real capacity. Rydell shows up briefly, but Chevette is completely absent. Whereas *Virtual Light* concerns lower-class characters, *Idoru* shifts gears to show us the world of the "Bridge Trilogy" from predominantly upper-class perspectives and to delve even further into the media-saturated society of the spectacle that dominates the globe.

Idoru opens with the introduction of a new character named Colin Laney, who formerly worked for an outfit named Slitscan, a celebrity-focused media organization that collects scandalous information on celebrities in a manner similar to current American magazines such as *People, Us Weekly,* and *Star;* newspaper tabloids such as *The National Enquirer;* and, probably most important, *TMZ,* the television show that broadcasts videos of celebrities caught out on the town, often in embarrassing or scandalous situations. The depiction of Slitscan provides one of the methods that *Idoru* uses to continue and deepen the depiction of our celebrity-obsessed culture. The first several chapters involving Laney take place in a Franz Kafka–themed club called Death Cube K, which features various rooms dedicated to major works by the Czech author: "The Metamorphosis" (1915), "In the Penal Colony" (1919), and *The Trial* (1925). The setting provides an ironic backdrop for Laney's bizarrely casual interview with Keith Alan Blackwell, to whom he recounts his previous time at Slitscan and the reason for his departure. Shinya Yamazaki, now purporting to be "a student of existential sociology," reappears from *Virtual Light* and observes their interaction (*Idoru* 7). The first chapters dedicated to Laney are composed mostly of flashbacks that depict the celebrity culture of the time while also exploring Laney's own peculiar ability to recognize patterns.

The alternating chapters follow a fourteen-year-old girl named Chia Pet McKenzie, whose parents named her after an item (the Chia Pet) seen on a shopping channel. Her name proves appropriate, because Chia becomes obsessed with media spectacle of the band Lo/Rez. The seeming impossibility of a human marrying a hologram with artificial intelligence remains an object of debate and consternation among Lo/Rez's management and his fan club. While the American Lo/Rez fans seem disconcerted by Rez's engagement, Takayuki Tatsumi points out that this marriage prospect constitutes an otaku (the uniquely Japanese term for "fanboys") fantasy: "To Otaku, then, the interspecies marriage of a human pop star with an artificial idol represents the most sophisticated form of man-machine interface. From another perspective, it is the figure of the idol that will make us all members of the Otaku" (*Apache* 133). Aboard her flight, the naïve Chia meets a woman named Maryalice, who persuades her to take an item off the airplane, an event that Chia forgets as she goes about her investigation of Lo/Rez gossip.

Laney's interview with Blackwell revolves around the same rumor. Blackwell has been tasked with hiring Laney for a position with the Lo/Rez management to explore whether someone is manipulating Rez to marry Rei Toei. Laney's special skill involves parsing data collections to discover what he terms "nodal points," major events toward which the data converge in ways perceptible only to Laney. Laney's background with Slitscan and his current job with Blackwell demonstrate how humans have become defined by their data. Slitscan seeks to use celebrity data to destroy careers with scandalous footage or information, a practice that Laney finds profoundly distasteful after he follows a female celebrity's data to its nodal point—her suicide.

Laney's boss at Slitscan, Kathy Torrance, serves as the novel's mouthpiece about the nature of celebrity, and she demarcates those celebrities who are famous for being famous and those who have some enduring charismatic quality; the second category includes Rez, who proves impervious to Slitscan's assaults. Torrance maintains that "Nobody's really famous anymore" because "There's not much fame left, not in the old sense" (*Idoru* 5). Instead of traditional fame, which was presumably based on some special talent, celebrities are created: "We *make* these assholes celebrities. It's a push-me, pull-you routine. They come to us to be created" (*Idoru* 5). This proves true of the Japanese idols from which *Idoru* draws its inspiration—these singers' personalities are constructed as role models for the public, and their lives become texts crafted for public consumption. The seemingly unstoppable trend of "boy bands" in the United States provides a similar paradigm in which the band members' identities are fabricated to resonate with adolescent female fans. Such manufactured, simulacral groups seem to predominate in the future, thus explaining Torrance's hatred of Lo/Rez: "In Kathy Torrance's system of things, the singer had been reserved a special disdain. She had viewed him as a living fossil, an annoying survival from an earlier, less evolved era. He was at once massively and meaninglessly famous, just as he was both massively and meaninglessly wealthy. Kathy thought of celebrity as a subtle fluid, a universal element, like the phlogiston of the ancients, something spread evenly at the creation through the universe, but prone now to accrete, under specific conditions around certain individuals and their careers" (*Idoru* 8). Rez hearkens back to the rock gods of the 1970s, and he refuses to destroy himself, like so many rock stars, or even engage in overly scandalous behavior. Furthermore, his music transcends demographics and appeals to everyone from young girls to older male fans such as Blackwell. In a world of simulation, Rez exists as a singularity of authenticity that persists according to a twentieth-century paradigm of celebrity. Now, he wants to engage in a relationship with a distinctly twenty-first-century celebrity that just might instantiate new evolutionary pathways.

Laney accepts the job with Lo/Rez, and Chia meets with the Japanese chapter of the fan club without really learning anything new. She enlists the help of Masahiko, the otaku brother of her host, who is a member of an online community known as the Walled City. Another interstitial space, the Walled City bases its community on Kowloon Walled City, a Hong Kong military fort that turned into a lawless community similar to that of the Bridge. Kowloon was eventually evacuated and destroyed, and a park has since been erected in its place to demonstrate how the forces of control always reappropriate potentially heterotopian spaces. With the aid of the Walled City and its hackers, Chia and Masahiko begin tracking down the rumors of Rez's engagement, but they soon discover they are being hunted by the Russian mafia, which desires the contraband item in Chia's luggage. The two manage to discover little about Rez's engagement other than an account of his announcement, which has since been mostly hushed up; the club where he made the pronouncement has subsequently closed. Instead, they end up in a "love hotel," where they can access the Internet through private channels without being traced, and they discover that Chia's luggage contains a nanotech assembler capable of reshaping material into any form, a tool that it is illegal for private individuals to possess.

Meanwhile, Laney proves incapable of finding any patterns in the data surrounding Rez because all his transactions are mediated by others. Since he has people who take care of everything for him, none of the data carry any of the unique patterns that converge around individuals. They decide to increase the complexity level of the data by incorporating fan data into the manifold that

Laney scans, hoping to add personality to the data that will allow him to discern unique patterns. Laney finally meets Rez and Rei Toei at another uniquely retrofitted space, this one called "The Western World," a kind of secret club/restaurant. The club was built after the quake that decimated Japan and killed eighty-six thousand people. It is located above two floors of office space in a building that has been "declared structurally unsound" and "sealed by emergency workers at the ground floor," but a climb up "eleven flights of mildly fissured concrete stairs" brings the adventurous partygoer to this secret space that has "become a benchmark in Tokyo's psychic history, an open secret, an urban legend" (*Idoru* 174–75). Like the Bridge or the Walled City, the ironically named Western World inscribes a place off the grid that has been allowed to exist even though it does not fit into the urban planning framework.

Rei Toei's presence both fascinates and unnerves Laney because she represents a hypercompressed collection of data that continually enlarges and mutates along with her experiences. For her to be present somewhere, she must be accompanied by a handler who manages the projection of her hologram. Suddenly their dinner gets interrupted by an attack on Rez, which results in their all fleeing the scene. Soon, thanks to a general call for help, they learn of Chia and Masahiko, who are now being held captive in the love hotel by Maryalice and her boyfriend, Eddie. Eventually, they all arrive at the love hotel, where Rez convinces them to give him the nanotech assembler, which he seems to believe will aid his plans to wed Rei Toei. The novel ends with the news that Rez and Rei Toei are building an island home together, demonstrating how the virtual has begun to commingle with the actual, a theme that is more fully developed in the final novel of the trilogy.

Cardboard Cities and Actualized AIs: Singularities in *All Tomorrow's Parties*

Gibson's essay "My Obsession" provides an interesting prologue to *All Tomorrow's Parties,* since the two texts were both released in 1999. One of several pieces that Gibson wrote for *Wired* magazine in the 1990s, "My Obsession" details Gibson's early experiences with eBay and provides a fascinating analysis of our society's obsession with "valuable stuff." Gibson's personal tale reveals how eBay constitutes "our current collective unconscious," as Jameson suggests, because it taps into our memories and commodifies them ("Fear" 386). For Gibson, the object of obsession is vintage watches, which resonate with memories of his father and a lost watch he was never able to reclaim. Gibson first explains how he often survived financially in the 1970s by being a talented "picker," someone able to find desirable merchandise among the chaotic manifold of thrift shops. Gibson believes that such major treasure finds are no longer possible because "The market has been rationalized. We have become a nation, a world, of pickers" (*DTPF* 134). He argues that there are several reasons for this: "the cult of nostalgia" and "the democratization of connoisseurship," both of which are driven by eBay, which never judges a person's taste in collectibles but merely offers a space for their buying and selling: "Whether one collects Warhol prints or Beanie Babies becomes, well, a matter of taste" (*DTPF* 135). Gibson concludes his piece with an image of an actual bazaar in Istanbul, where he purchases a jewel to make a necklace for his then future wife, and he ends with an important line: "But I'm glad we still have a place for things to change hands. Even here, in this territory the map became" (*DTPF* 151). Gibson's essay concerns how the virtual territory has replaced the need for physical spaces of exchange, which proves somewhat ironic considering the fact that *All Tomorrow's Parties* features an antique collectibles shop that specializes in vintage watches and other mechanical or electronic items. This depiction of how the territory of cyberspace has eclipsed the map that it emulates also conditions any reading of *All Tomorrow's Parties* because the novel concerns the attempt to create a place not inscribed on the maps of control, a physical space not connected to the electronic grid or the influence of governmental rule.

Taking its title from a Velvet Underground song, *All Tomorrow's Parties* returns to the world of the Bridge and brings together characters from the first two novels of the trilogy. Since we last saw them, Rydell and Chevette have developed a relationship and then called it quits, Rei Toei has disappeared, and Colin Laney has gone off the grid and begun living in a cardboard box city, where he constantly tracks the data patterns surrounding a public relations man named Cody Harwood. Laney believes that the world is converging toward a massive nodal point, the likes of which has not been seen since 1911 (a date that the novel never explains). Chevette and Rydell end up being inexorably drawn back to San Francisco, where their paths once again converge later in the novel. Rydell resigns from his job as a Lucky Dragon convenience store security guard to begin working for Colin Laney, and he accepts an offer to drive a car to San Francisco with musician and professional drunkard Buell Creedmore. Chevette, on the other hand, believes that she spots her abusive ex-boyfriend on a video camera and decides to take a trip with her media studies friend Tessa, who is filming a documentary on interstitial spaces and wants Chevette to serve as a guide for a segment on the Bridge. Another intermittent storyline centers on a young mute boy named Silencio, who harbors a fascination with watches and has an uncanny ability to ferret out information about them online, and Fontaine, a pawnshop owner who discovers the young boy cowering in his shop one morning and gives him shelter. Finally, there is the shadowy assassin Konrad, whose motives and alliances shift throughout the novel as he follows his darkly Taoist philosophy of life.

The novel's plotting proves much more complicated than that of the previous two novels in the trilogy, but, despite their infrequent appearances, Colin Laney and Rei Toei provide the driving forces as all the characters converge toward Laney's predicted nodal point. The novel provides more background on Laney and his special ability, which developed after he was given an experimental drug called 5-SB. The drug has caused Laney to obsess over the character of Cody Harwood, who has voluntarily administered 5-SB to himself in order to perceive and manipulate forthcoming nodal points. With the aid of the Walled City, Laney works through the other characters to prevent Harwood from achieving his goal of turning historical foreknowledge to his advantage.

While the powerful and wealthy become insidious manipulators who desire to alter the flow of history, the marginalized seek to use alternative, heterotopian spaces for subversive practices. The forces of control constantly try to reappropriate such spaces, as evidenced by the urban-planning initiatives mentioned in *Virtual Light* and brought to light again in *All Tomorrow's Parties.* Chevette immediately gets a taste of this reappropriation when she returns to the Bridge only to find that Lucky Dragon has set up a franchise location at the entrance, thus commodifying the Bridge, which has increasingly become a tourist destination. Although Harwood sets the Bridge on fire, his plans are foiled when Rei Toei and her allies help urge Silencio to use his savantlike abilities to track down the source of Harwood's online presence and shut him down, rendering him incapable of influencing the coming nodal point. The nodal point occurs after nanofax machines have been installed in every Lucky Dragon around the world. The nanofax machines use nanotechnology to copy an object and then reproduce it at any point in the world that also has a nanofax. While the machine's ability seems impressive, its true power does not become apparent until Rei Toei virtually accesses the machines and copies herself, thus allowing her to cross over into the physical world. The nodal point occurs when all of the nanofax machines in the world simultaneously manifest a nude version of Rei Toei, who promptly walks off into the night. *All Tomorrow's Parties* ends before we see the effects of this nodal point; however, its implications prove virtually infinite as it provides a way of literally hacking and programming reality, of crossing the boundary between the virtual and the actual.

Toward a Deterritorialization of Control . . .

In *Anti-Oedipus,* Deleuze and Guattari develop the concept of deterritorialization as a process that makes the world's organization start "coming undone" and that can lead to the creation of new kinds of spaces: "the flows cross the threshold of deterritorialization and produce the new land—not at all, but a simple 'finding,' a 'finished design,' where the person who escapes causes other escapes, and marks out the land while deterritorializing itself" (322). Gibson's interstial spaces participate precisely in this unplugging from organizational structures. Gibson's interest in interstitial spaces can be traced all the way back to Nighttown in "Johnny Mnemonic," and the "Bridge Trilogy" focuses on different attempts to construct spaces of freedom outside the reach of control. However, as corporate forces such as Lucky Dragon and Cody Harwood indicate, control and capital cannot allow any spaces to escape commodification and territorialization. While spaces such as the Bridge and the Walled City temporarily deterritorialize the control grid and reterritorialize it according to utopian paradigms of freedom, they constantly run the risk of being discovered or becoming too popular and consequently suffering reterritorialization by the forces of control. Gibson's explorations of control and the desire for radical freedom began in the future of the Sprawl, and the "Bridge Trilogy" brings them closer to home. As we will see, the "Bigend Trilogy" examines how control has instantiated itself in our real world and how subjects seek freedom and self-actualization only to constantly discover the agents and gridlines of control lying in wait, for the advent of the Internet and GPS technology render the interstitial a type of space that increasingly borders on extinction.

CHAPTER 5

Twenty-First-Century Singularities

The Future's End in Gibson's "Bigend Trilogy"

While the "Bridge Trilogy" brought Gibson's fiction closer to the present, his aesthetic approach changed even more profoundly with his next series of novels. Generally referred to as the "Bigend Trilogy" because of the recurring advertising executive of the same name (it is sometimes called the "Blue Ant Trilogy"), the novels occur within the recent past, and Gibson uses each novel to deal with contemporary historical events in the United States. Whereas the "Bridge Trilogy" developed the concept of singularities (or nodal points, as Colin Laney terms them), the "Bigend Trilogy" focuses on actual singularities that have reshaped global civilization in the twenty-first century. *Pattern Recognition* (2003), *Spook Country* (2007), and *Zero History* (2010) each examines characters that interact with a global society in the wake of a particularly traumatizing singularity. The novels still almost inexplicably maintain a science fiction feel despite having eschewed all the common trappings and tropes of science fiction. In essence, they demonstrate how science fiction is perhaps no longer necessary in the fully postmodern world because our lives have become the stuff of science fiction.

Virtual Existentialism: *Pattern Recognition* and the Quest for Meaning after 9/11

Many critics have commented on the connection between the protagonists of *Neuromancer* and *Pattern Recognition:* Henry "Case" Dorsett and Cayce Pollard. Gibson ensures that we know "Cayce" is homophonic with "Case." Certain critics have even gone so far as to posit that *Pattern Recognition* constitutes a rewriting of *Neuromancer* in a realistic, nonscience-fictional milieu.

However, *Pattern Recognition*'s resonances with his early works encompass more than just *Neuromancer*, for the book includes the quest for a mysterious artist from *Count Zero* as well as a fascination with singularities carried over from the "Bridge Trilogy." The novel concerns Cayce Pollard, who is hired by Hubertus Bigend, the CEO of the Blue Ant Corporation, to hunt down the creator of a series of mysterious film clips that have been disseminated virally via the Internet. Bigend provides the unifying persona for this trilogy, and he duplicates the earlier characters of Virek and Cody Harwood in many ways. Each book in the trilogy corresponds to a particular singularity in the first decade of the twenty-first century, and *Pattern Recognition* was one of the first novels to focus, albeit subtly, on the effects of the September 11 attacks.[1]

Pattern Recognition revolves around Cayce's quest for the "Footage," a series of peculiar film clips that have been uploaded to the Internet and spread virally without any reference to their origin or purpose. Released in 2003, *Pattern Recognition* appeared two years before the advent, in 2005, of YouTube, which revolutionized video sharing. In 2003 it still required some significant effort for users to find and download videos; downloading itself has become somewhat passé as streaming media have steadily overtaken not just physical media but downloadable media as well. The followers of the Footage, or "Footageheads," as they call themselves, discuss the Footage via a forum titled Fetish:Footage:Forum, a place where Footage otaku can congregate. The name "Fetish:Footage:Forum" (or "F:F:F" for short) signals that the forum is probably a Usenet newsgroup. Newsgroups once provided one of the major means of discussion and data dissemination for Internet users; however, their use has steadily declined as Web forums and social media sites such as Facebook and Twitter have grown in popularity. Despite the now somewhat antiquated depiction of viral videos and newsgroups, *Pattern Recognition* still manages to provide an insightful examination of how virtual channels permit users to form digital social bonds and to find meaning as deep as (or perhaps even deeper) than the meaning they find in so-called real, physical interactions.

The title *Pattern Recognition* resonates in multiple ways that deserve mentioning. For starters, the term "pattern recognition" refers to machine learning, an important part of artificial-intelligence design that focuses on how machines can parse data to find patterns and learn from them. Pattern recognition is also closely related to the process of data mining, in which computers try to discern understandable structures among given data sets. The simplest way to understand how these closely allied branches of computer science have directly affected us is to consider a major commercial website such as Amazon, which keeps track not only of recent purchases but of every item that users search for or look at during their visits to the store's site. Then Amazon can often uncannily predict other items that you might like to buy and display them for your perusal on your own "unique" version of the homepage when you revisit the site. Such pattern recognition becomes increasingly complex and exact as sites, heuristics, and algorithms become more refined. The title also has other important meanings. As Lee Konstantinou points out, pattern recognition also recalls Marshall McLuhan's claims about the digital world. As McLuhan states, "Electric circuitry profoundly involves men with one another. Information pours upon us, instantaneously and continuously. As soon as information is acquired, it is very rapidly replaced by still newer information. Our electrically configured world has been forced to move from the habit of data classification to the mode of pattern recognition" (63). Data assaults us so ubiquitously and perniciously that it proves impossible to categorize all of it, and our faculties (as Kant would call them) must instead reattune themselves to function like a computer—that is, to recognize patterns among the increasingly chaotic manifold that is the society of the spectacle.

Pattern recognition also refers to Cayce Pollard's line of work—coolhunting. As her Google search results indicate, "Google Cayce and you will find 'coolhunter,' and if you look closely you may see it suggested that she is a 'sensitive' of some kind, a dowser in the world of global marketing. Though the truth . . . is closer to an allergy, a morbid and sometimes violent reaction to the semiotics of the marketplace" (*PR* 2). Cayce's profession as a coolhunter means that various corporations hire her to decide whether their new products or logos will connect with audiences. The images of advertising have buried themselves so deeply in Cayce's psyche that she has even developed an allergy to logos, particularly Bibendum (the Michelin Man), and she can wear only nondescript clothes with the labels cut off. In essence, Cayce's mind functions like a computer: it extrapolates from given trends to determine what will be considered "cool" before anyone else knows it. However, Cayce also engages in another form of pattern recognition. She and the United States as a whole are still searching for patterns and meaning in the wake of 9/11. In essence, one of the major themes of the novel is the country's existential quest for meaning after the September 11 attacks. Jean Baudrillard characterizes the attacks as "the absolute event" that "unite[d] within itself all the events that had never taken place" (*Spirit* 4). It serves as the absolute event because it had been presaged in various ways by the media and our society, with its focus on the spectacle. Slavoj Žižek argues that the attacks unfolded according to the paradigm established in American disaster films: "That is the rationale of the often-mentioned association of the attacks with Hollywood disaster movies: the unthinkable which happened was an object of fantasy, so that, in a way, America got what it fantasized about" (16). Paul Virilio, on the other hand, contends that the media spectacle of the attacks was conditioned by the rise of reality television: "Let us make no mistake about it, the modernity of 'Big Brother' and its clones is the direct successor to the multimedia presentation of the Gulf and Kosovo conflicts . . . an image strategy which preceded the perfectly orchestrated image strategy of the terrorist attacks of September 2001" (*Ground Zero* 42). Gibson taps into the trauma of 9/11 and the American attempt to process it by means of Cayce's family. Her father, Win Pollard, a former CIA employee, disappeared on the day of the attacks, and Cayce has yet to make peace with this fact. Her mother has even turned to EVP (Electronic Voice Phenomena) as a means of potentially communicating with her husband beyond the grave.[2] With this trauma and existential angst in her background, Cayce accepts the offer from Hubertus Bigend of the Blue Ant advertising agency.

Cayce's quest for meaning and closure parallels the nation's existential angst in the wake of the September 11 attacks, but it also gestures toward a larger epistemological crisis in the postmodern era, one that ineffectively tries to define our present moment in history. The novel argues that the twenty-first century exists beyond such stable definitions as past, present, and future. Bigend explains to Cayce that we no longer have a future:

> We have no idea, now, of who, or what the inhabitants of our future might be. In that sense, we have no future. Not in the sense that your grandparents had a future, or thought they did. Fully imagined futures were the luxury of another day, one in which 'now' was of some greater duration. For us, of course, things can change so abruptly, so violently, so profoundly, that futures like our grandparents' have insufficient 'now' to stand on. We have no future because our present is too volatile. . . . We have only risk management. The spinning of the given moment's scenarios. Pattern Recognition. (*PR* 58–59)

The novel centers on the desire of characters such as Cayce Pollard to find meaning in a world where estrangement, absurd horror, and dizzying difference threaten to crush them from all sides. *Pattern Recognition* concerns the fragmented postmodern subjects' quest to find meaning and value in their lives. Ultimately, Cayce gets a sense of how existential value can still be found in the postmodern world through her quest for the Footage's filmmaker.

The Footageheads' debates over the nature and meaning of the Footage parallel this postmodern desire for coherent meaning. Uploaded virally on the Internet, the Footage consists of different film fragments, short clips featuring the same couple and bearing no identifying features as to location or time period. Since the Footage proves so fragmentary, the Footageheads have proposed various theories about the nature of the work as a whole. The Footageheads have broken down into two basic theoretical camps: the Completists and the Progressives. The Completists believe that the fragments represent pieces of a finished work that are slowly being disseminated. The Progressives, on the other hand, led by Cayce's virtual friend Parkaboy, argue that the clips constitute pieces of a work in progress that are being rolled out as they are completed. Separate from these discussions, the Footageheads also debate the number of people responsible for the Footage—is it the product of an entire film crew or the work of a lone "Garage Kubrick" producing all of the Footage by him/herself? (*PR* 50) Cayce seeks out the source of the Footage almost as if she were searching for a deity to explain the nature of existence.

On her quest, she learns that the virtual can cross over into the actual and that seemingly real appearances cannot always be trusted. She develops a close relationship with Parkaboy, and the two learn that one particular clip of Footage contains a steganographically concealed watermark, a watermark concealed by patterns of information that can be decoded only with the appropriate key. To uncover more information on this watermark, Parkaboy and some friends begin crafting a fake Japanese female named Keiko to ferret out information from otaku websites. To complete their deception, they create a Photoshopped image of Keiko from a friend named Judy, and they use this image to gather information from a Footage otaku named Taki:

> What we did to up the wattage for Taki, aiming to maximize libidinal disturbance, we shot this long tall Judy then reduced her by at least a third, in Photoshop. Cut'n'pasted her into Musashi's kid's sister's dorm room at Cal. Darryl did the costuming himself, and then we decided to try enlarging the eyes a few clicks. That made all the difference. Judy's epicanthic folds are long gone, the way of the modest bust nature intended for her (actually we've got her wrapped in Ace bandage for the shot, but nothing too tight) and the resulting big round eyes are pure Anime Magic. (*PR* 132)

A pure simulacrum, the image of Keiko taps into the distinction among the virtual, the real, and the actual, which is crucial to understanding the society of the spectacle and the computerization of society.

Building upon the French philosopher Henri Bergson's ideas from *Time and Free Will* (1889) and *Matter and Memory* (1896), Gilles Deleuze clarifies the difference between the "possible" and the "virtual": "From a certain point of view, in fact, the possible is the opposite of the real, it is opposed to the real; but, in quite a different opposition, the virtual is opposed to the actual. We must take this terminology seriously: The possible has no reality (although it may have an actuality): conversely, the virtual is not actual, but *as such possesses a reality*" (*Bergsonism* 96). Therefore, the virtual images of the screen may not have a material body, but they exist in reality nonetheless, and the virtual has the potential to give birth to actualizations founded in the virtual's possibilities of difference. Deleuze later connects this to the foundational nature of our lives and identities: "A life contains only virtuals. It is made up of virtualities, events, singularities. What we call virtual is not something that lacks reality but something that is engaged in a process of actualization following the plane that gives it its particular reality" (*Immanence* 31). The virtual harbors the potential differences that can be actualized to impact our lives profoundly. Hence, an image can appear to just be an image while also containing further information within the data that comprises the image, the image can harbor an entirely new identity, or the image can proffer some kind of existential meaning that reality itself seems to lack.

Eventually, Cayce receives a Russian e-mail address and travels to Russia to meet the actual filmmaker. Stella, the sister of the Footage's creator, introduces her to Nora, the brain-damaged *auteur* behind the film clips. Nora received her injury during an assassination bombing that killed her parents, thus aligning her with Cayce's own situation with her father. Nora recalls the semi-autistic artificial intelligence from the end of *Count Zero,* which created its boxes without any real intention or knowledge of its actions. Nora takes footage from security cameras and edits it down to create the Footage clips (another example of *bricolage* as art), which her sister then posts in obscure locations on the Internet. Thus, Cayce's quest ends with a creator who cannot answer her questions and proof that none of the Footagehead theories were valid. There is no overarching film or totalizing meaning: there is "only the wound speaking wordlessly in the dark" (*PR* 316). This absence of meaning is also evidenced when Cayce receives data about her father and his disappearance. The Russians have allowed the dissemination of the video clips to probe for holes in their security network, and they have been spying on Cayce's progress toward finding the filmmaker. In return, they give her their files on CIA operative Win Pollard and his mysterious disappearance. The files provide little comfort or knowledge to Cayce, but the novel's hopeful ending and Cayce's later reappearance in *Zero History* reveal that she finds meaning and identity in her marriage to Parkaboy, her children, and a new occupation.

New Paradigms of Control: GPS and Paranoia in *Spook Country*

Spook Country is Gibson's spy novel, and it returns to Gibson's signature rotating chapter style, following three different main characters as it explores the nature of espionage in the era of the Patriot Act and the Iraq War. First, we meet Hollis Henry, a former member of a 1990s alternative band called the Curfew, who has recently been hired by Hubertus Bigend to write a magazine article for a start-up magazine called *Node,* a European response to *Wired,* the American tech magazine for which Gibson wrote several articles in the 1990s. Hollis's original assignment revolves around an artist named Alberto Corrales, a practitioner of locative art, an emergent form of art that relies upon GPS coordinates and virtual-reality goggles. Corrales creates artworks that users can see at particular GPS coordinates using VR equipment. At present, Corrales remains fascinated with re-creating celebrity deaths at the actual locations where they occurred. Hollis first experiences the technology by witnessing the corpse of River Phoenix lying in front of the Viper Room on Sunset Boulevard in Hollywood. After much prying and persuasion, Corrales introduces her to Bobby Chombo, the computer expert who performs the networking and GPS manipulation that enable Corrales to create his "art." A complete paranoid, which the novel suggests is perhaps not unwarranted, Chombo lives in a massive warehouse structure that he marks off with gridlines. He never sleeps in the same square twice because of his obsession with GPS coordinates.

Chapter 2 introduces Tito, a Chinese Cuban "illegal facilitator" who represents part of a family of facilitators who have engaged in espionage dating back to the CIA's involvement in Cuba during the 1960s. Chapter 3 switches to the characters of Milgrim and Brown. A hyperconservative spy with a Fox News addiction, Brown tails Tito and his bunch as they trade information using iPods; as always, Gibson remains fascinated with alternate uses for technology. Capable of Russian translation, Milgrim is also addicted to benzodiazepines (a class of drugs generally used as sedatives, muscle relaxants, and anticonvulsants), and Brown uses his addiction to keep him as a kind of slave. The novel becomes much more overtly political than any of Gibson's previous or subsequent works as it all but openly condemns the handling of the Iraq War and the Bush administration's passage of the Patriot Act. In fact, the novel suggests that "America had developed Stockholm syndrome toward its own government, post 9/11" (*Spook* 310). Stockholm syndrome refers to the psychological condition in which kidnapping victims and hostages begin to identify with, sympathize with, and perhaps even help their captors. Thus, the novel suggests that the government used 9/11 to hold the United States hostage and to convince Americans that the oppressive Patriot Act and the wars in Afghanistan and Iraq were actually in the country's best interest. This paranoia associated with the excessive legalization of spying under the Patriot Act led to a McCarthyesque brand of fearmongering that claimed any person on the street might be a "terrorist." This paranoia is epitomized in the novel by Milgrim, who has "internalized the watchers" in a truly Foucaultian sense, and by Bobby Chombo, who has also internalized power in his fear of the GPS gridlines and the forces of control that they imply.

Like most of Gibson's previous novels, *Spook Country* concerns an emergent technology—locative art. While the technology seems like a curiosity piece at first, a clever outgrowth of GPS technology and virtual reality, the novel later demonstrates the actual ramifications of the technology when Hollis visits a room that has been annotated using locative art. Every item in the room has the artist's comments, hyperlinks, and other data that guide the user outward from the physical environment. Like the nanofax in *All Tomorrow's Parties,* locative art demonstrates how the virtual begins to actualize itself and directly affect the physical realm. Cyberspace, as Hollis's friend Odile explains, has started to evert, to spread outward and craft itself a physical body, leading to an even more frightening consolidation of global control but also opening up potential spaces of subversion for individuals such as Bobby Chombo who know how to manipulate the system.

Bigend's fascination with locative art soon shifts, and Hollis becomes embroiled in full-fledged espionage as she and various other characters attempt to track down a secret cargo container. The search for the secret cargo introduces some major new characters, including the Old Man, an unnamed former CIA agent who has gone rogue and who uses his abilities to frustrate war profiteers, and Garreth, his daredevil base-jumping driver, who performs jobs for the Old Man. Tito and his family also work for the Old Man, who has ties with them stretching back to Cuba. While he never receives a name, the novel strongly suggests that the Old Man is really Win Pollard, Cayce's missing father from *Pattern Recognition,* and that 9/11 and the events following it caused him to lose faith in the United States and its intelligence community. With the aid of Milgrim, Brown attempts to track down the Old Man and the shipping container as well.

Bigend's interest in the container's contents and locative art seems somewhat obscure at times, but he explains his overall motives to Hollis: "I've learned to value anomalous phenomena. Very peculiar things that people do, often secretly, have come to interest me in a certain way. I spend a lot of money, often, trying to understand those things" (*Spook* 105). He then reveals that the discovery of the Footage's origins led to a lucrative program known as Trope Slope in which advertisements are inserted into old films. Bigend's interest in "anomalous phenomena" constitutes part of his larger plan, which is revealed in *Zero History,* to understand the order flow and to be able to predict fluctuations in the stock market a few minutes in advance. Hence, Bigend becomes the emblem of control because he does not prescribe subject behavior but catalogues it in order to make predictions and exert his power. The Old Man struggles against just such opportunists, as is evidenced when he reveals that the shipping container actually contains millions of U.S. dollars that have been illegally diverted from the Iraq recovery fund. The Old Man does not want the money for himself but instead uses his motley crew of individuals to irradiate the money, making it impossible to launder or smuggle easily. The Old Man represents the forces of control turned against themselves, but *Zero History* suggests that such efforts might be in vain, as control continually adapts to subversive subject behavior in order to provide the continual illusion of freedom without jeopardizing an iota of control's power. As Deleuze points out in "What Is the Creative Act?," the society of control operates through the illusion of freedom: "Control is not discipline. You do not confine people with a highway. But by making highways, you multiply the means of control. I am not saying this is the only aim of highways, but people can travel infinitely and 'freely' without being confined while being perfectly controlled" (322). The Internet (or the "information superhighway," as the cliché once went) allows means of control to proliferate even more wildly as the subject constantly provides new streams of data, all of which can be used to better control him or her.

The End of the History: *Zero History* and the Death of the Future

Gibson's final entry in the "Bigend Trilogy," *Zero History,* features a setup similar to that in the previous two novels: Bigend hires Hollis to track down the creator of a secret brand of clothing called Gabriel Hounds, extremely well-made yet simple articles of clothing that are disseminated via infrequent and secret drops around the world. Alongside Hollis, the novel also features the return of several characters from *Spook Country:* Milgrim, Heidi (Hollis's bandmate), Garreth (the former employee of the old man and Hollis's former boyfriend), Bobby Chombo, and Cayce Pollard. Some time has passed between the events recounted in *Spook Country* and those described in *Zero History.* Hollis developed a serious relationship with base-jumper Garreth and then broke up with him, and she also lost a lot of money during the global financial crisis of 2007 and 2008. Bigend paid for Milgrim to go into rehabilitation and be cured of his benzo addiction, but he still requires placebos to keep himself in check. Bigend employs both Hollis and Milgrim in his pursuit of Gabriel Hounds clothing, which has been released in a viral pattern similar to the Footage in *Pattern Recognition,* and the Gabriel Hounds design represents a return to real quality as opposed to the simulacral surface of most fashion. Most designer styles, as *Pattern Recognition* says of brands such as Tommy Hilfiger, constitute nothing more than "simulacra of simulacra of simulacra" (*PR* 18). The viral dissemination of the Gabriel Hounds line demonstrates how virtual patterns can actualize themselves in radical forms of difference.

The novel's title refers to the concept that we no longer have a history or any idea of the future, an idea that can be traced directly from Hegel to Marx to Fukuyama and beyond. More explicitly, the title alludes to the character of Milgrim, whose ten-year addiction has caused him to miss all of the major events of the past decade. He does not even have a credit history, one of the primary methods used to judge a person's value and identity in the era of global corporations and control. The Gabriel Hounds brand actually seeks to achieve a similar state of ahistoricity in which time and current trends fail to influence true quality and style: "It's about atemporality. About opting out of the industrialization of novelty. It's about a deeper code" (*Zero* 116). Bigend purports to be interested in Gabriel Hounds because he believes the brand will enable him to secure military uniform contracts, and military uniforms often directly impact fashion styles more generally. However, Bigend's true purpose aims at a much larger and sinister goal, and it reaches back through the investigations of the previous two novels. He also desires to step outside history in his quest to discover the order flow, a radical form of pattern recognition that will enable him to predict market fluctuations.

Bigend does not explain his ultimate plans until the novel's final pages, long after the creator of Gabriel Hounds has been revealed as Cayce Pollard. Hollis finally meets the creator at a "pop-up" event meant to initiate the process of taking Gabriel Hounds public—the exhibit or sale constitutes a pop-up because, like a pop-up ad on a computer, it has appeared spontaneously, another example of how computer technology affects physical reality. The novel never uses Cayce's name but ensures that the reader of both novels recognizes her by alluding to the story from *Pattern Recognition*. The reader discovers through Cayce's conversation that she remains happily married to Parkaboy and has children with him. She has found purpose in her life through her marriage, her children, and her clothing line, which was inspired by her allergy to simulacral styles and corporate branding. Hollis discovers the origin of Gabriel Hounds, but she decides to keep Cayce's secret because the characters all determine that Bigend is actually pursuing something potentially villainous and begin working against him.

While the novel does not explicate how Bigend's previous searches relate to the order flow, it becomes apparent that he has been researching viral phenomena and aberrant human behavior to help him perfect the algorithms necessary to calculate the order flow. The novel reveals that Bigend actually hires individuals who will go rogue or turn against him because their actions teach him about major aberrations in subject behavior. For Bigend, "stasis is the real enemy. . . . Stability's the beginning of the end. We only walk by continually beginning to fall forward" (*Zero* 177). By valuing "anomalous phenomena," as he terms them in *Spook Country,* Bigend manages to focus on change and difference, which prove essential to understanding the flux of something as complicated as human behavior and its relation to stock market values. Bigend achieves the ultimate goal of capitalism: he utilizes technology to commodify the most amorphous of objects—human behavior. He can now use his knowledge and technology to manipulate and profit from human emotions and desires; he has become control itself in his ability not only to collect information but to predict and hence influence human society on a global level.

Dystopia Now

The very fact that Gibson set his most recent novels in the present makes an unspoken argument about how our world has become its own kind of science fiction. The dystopias depicted by classic sci-fi authors or even by the early Gibson never occurred, but the "Bigend Trilogy" contends that dystopia has arrived in a subtler and perhaps more sinister fashion. Big Brother does not distribute posters all over town but is present in every circuit and connection of the Internet. The three novels examine how global computer networks and GPS technology have instantiated Lyotard's "hegemony of computers" on a physical level. Space itself has become information, as have the subject's most mundane social interactions online. The computer offers freedom, as Timothy Leary believed, but it also introduces a profound new channel of control into our households and even our pockets as cell-phone technology has progressed.

CHAPTER 6

Engaging with Difference

William Gibson's Genre and Media Explorations

For the most part, Gibson's literary output divides itself neatly into four stages from pre-*Neuromancer* stories through his three completed trilogies, but he has also produced a variety of other works that do not fit neatly into these categories. Aside from his previously discussed works, Gibson has also published a profoundly experimental multimedia poem, a stand-alone collaborative steampunk novel, several uncollected stories, a handful of screenplays for films and television episodes, and numerous works of nonfiction. This chapter does not seek to discuss all of these works. While Gibson recently published a fascinating collection of his nonfiction pieces called *Distrust That Particular Flavor,* (2012), his uncollected essays, introductions, reviews, interviews, and other works of nonfiction could easily fill several more volumes, and this does not even count his regular blog entries or his Twitter postings, which could also be considered part of his body of work.

Steam-Powered Victorians: Alternate Modes of Control in *The Difference Engine*

As a genre, steampunk often offers the depthless pastiche that Jameson finds so toothless; it merges elements of different genres (typically the Victorian novel and science fiction) but in a way that seldom opens itself up to critical reflection. Generally, steampunk works feature alternative histories that imagine a society in which steam power produced marvelous innovations in society. Steampunk stories typically take place in the nineteenth century (often in Victorian England or the American Wild West), but sometimes they concern other worlds where technology developed along lines different from those it took in our own. Some of the earliest influences on the genre include the nineteenth-century sci-fi writers themselves (Jules Verne, H. G. Wells, and Mary Shelley) and early twentieth-century examples such as Fritz Lang's *Metropolis* and L. Frank Baum's Tik-Tok character, a clockwork man (often considered one of the first robots in literature) who first appears in *Ozma of Oz* (1907). While vapid steampunk predominates, respectable and thought-provoking examples of the genre do exist from creators in various media: Hayao Miyazaki's anime adventures *Castle in the Sky* (1986) and *Howl's Moving Castle* (2004), Jean-Pierre Jeunet and Marc Caro's *The City of Lost Children* (1994), China Miéville's *Perdido Street Station* (2000), and Katsuhiro Otomo's *Steamboy* (2004) all engage in intelligent, artful uses of the genre. However, Sterling and Gibson's *The Difference Engine* remains one of the most highly acclaimed and influential steampunk novels.

The novel takes its title from the device known as a difference engine, "the mechanical computers or 'engines' designed by Charles Babbage in the early nineteenth century" that were never actually realized (*WGLC* 44). The novel imagines that these devices were not only successfully constructed but immediately adopted by all levels of society, including the police and the government, thus causing a computerization of the Victorian era. As Tom Henthorne points out, *The Difference Engine* is a counterfactual novel but one that incorporates both historical and fictional characters. To follow along with its theme of computerization, Sterling and Gibson divide the novel into iterations instead of parts or chapters, culminating in a final section, titled "Modus." Like most of Gibson's novels, *The Difference Engine* features a revolving cast of three main characters: the courtesan Sybil Gerard, the paleontologist Edward Mallory, and the travel writer Laurence Oliphant. Also, like most Gibson novels, the three characters' lives intersect because of an object they are seeking: a set of computer punch cards that supposedly contain a groundbreaking computer program. The characters' stories unfold in a Great Britain that now dominates the world because of its steam power and computer engines, and the Romantic poet Lord Byron has gained power as prime minister on the basis of a platform of radical technocracy. Britain has used its computers and its steam-powered military to rise to prominence as a world power, and it has installed a kind of steam-driven society of control in its own land, using the engines that now collect data on the populace. The novel also deals with the ecological fallout of such technology as London begins to fall prey to the Stink, an environmental disaster brought on by pollution from British technology. The novel finally reveals that the elusive program called the "Modus" was written by Ada Lovelace (Lord Byron's daughter) and contains the proofs for two important theorems, which in our world became known as Gödel's Incompleteness Theorem after they were proven by the mathematician Kurt Gödel in 1931. Lovelace gives a lecture on the theorems in the novel's final section. The novel proves provocative because it takes the themes from Gibson and Sterling's cyberpunk works and transports them to an alternative past, a past that becomes dystopian in a way that resembles cyberpunk future worlds. Pollution and control both run rampant, but individuals can also still use their own abilities to blaze new paths for technology and identity.

Stylistic Experimentations: Gibson's Uncollected Short Fiction

The short piece "Academy Leader" was composed for Michael L. Benedikt's 1991 collection *Cyberspace: First Steps,* which features essays that explore the implications of cyberspace for various fields such as philosophy, communications, and sexuality studies. Gibson's contribution reads like an homage to William S. Burroughs in which Gibson attempts to ape his cut-up method. The piece opens with a disorienting series of images and a reference to Inspector Lee from Burroughs's "Nova Trilogy." Then, Gibson proceeds to give us the origins of the word "cyberspace," which he has received so much acclaim for coining: "Just a chance operator in the gasoline crack of history, officer. . . . Assembled word *cyberspace* from small and readily available components of language. Neologic spasm: the primal act of pop poetics. Preceded any concept whatever. Slick and hollow–awaiting received meaning. All I did: folded words as taught. Now other words accrete in the interstices" ("Academy" 27). This seemingly garbled passage actually contains the story's kernel of meaning: it concerns Gibson's coining of the term as well as the manner in which diverse meanings can accrue to a word. In an act of *bricolage,* Gibson took the ready components of language and folded them together to suit his purpose, but the initial use of the word was "hollow," so readers could readily fill it with their own interpretations, thus leading to the concept's intense influence and ultimate elevation to cliché status.

The story proceeds to catalogue the potential commercial aspects of virtual reality as well as its capacity for "private fantasy" ("Academy" 28). Bits of a story about a young woman experiencing Kyoto through virtual-reality glasses and gloves are cut into discussions of how communication technologies never die out; the street simply finds new uses for them, just as Gibson found inspired redefinitions of the words "cyber" and "space." The piece ends with a sentence in quotation marks, although no speaker is identified: "The targeted numerals of the ACADEMY LEADER were hypnogic sigils preceding the dreamstate of film" ("Academy" 29). The story culminates with this sentence because again it is densely packed with words that can be interpreted in any number of ways. Its invocation of the "dreamstate of film" proves significant because film itself once seemed like a virtual reality to the viewers of the early Lumière Brothers films, which supposedly caused viewers to flee from the onscreen train. Film has persisted as a technology despite the advent of digital technologies and computer animation. Of course, the genre has morphed drastically because of advances in digital film and computer graphics; some films create entire virtual realities instead of filming in real-world locations.[1] However, the final sentence proves even more important because Gibson actually identifies its origin in his piece "African Thumb Piano," his 2011 introduction to his collection *Distrust That Particular Flavor.* In that essay, he mentions a version of the sentence as being the first sentence he managed to write in his quest to teach himself to write fiction. Thus, "Academy Leader" comes back full circle at the end to provide an image of the creative process and the ways in which writers imbue works with particular images and meanings while readers may subsequently derive rather different intents from the words.

Originally published in the December 1, 1991, issue of *Washington Book World,* William Gibson's "Cyber-Claus" blends together Christmas mythology and cyberpunk clichés in a way that lampoons both.[2] The story proves somewhat slight: an abbreviated, paranoid, cyberpunk rewrite of Clement Clarke Moore's poem "A Visit from St. Nicolas" (1823; more popularly known today as "'Twas the Night before Christmas") that pokes fun at genre expectations. The story proves to be classic Gibson with its constant evocation of both fashion labels and references to old movies, such as George Pal's adaptation of H. G. Wells's *The War of the Worlds* (1953). The story basically announces its intention when the narrator states, "Now that literally everything was digital, History and Image were no more than Silly Putty in the hands of anyone with a BFA and a backer in Singapore. But that was just the nature of Postmodernity, and, frankly, it suited me right down to the ground." The story imagines a seemingly super-wealthy character who awakens from an induced state of sleep to discover that his security systems have discovered bizarre "bio-activity" on the roof of his house. Communicating with his home security system, the narrator envisages the drones that have been dispatched to deal with the threat but nonetheless arms himself with a Honda gun that fires gel ammunition as the threat begins to descend the chimney and the story ends. The story uses pastiche as Gibson intertwines cyberpunk imagery and traditional Christmas tales to serve a comedic purpose and to simultaneously comment upon how paranoia, hypercommercialism, and surveillance could perhaps rob society of its childhood wonder. "Cyber-Claus" thus playfully imagines how the conflicts between tradition and constant digital innovation might play out in a manner similar to *Futurama*'s reimagining of Santa Claus and Christmas.[3]

Gibson's short story "Doing Television" appeared in two different versions under two distinct titles. "Doing Television" originally appeared in *Tesseracts*[3] (1990), an anthology of Canadian speculative fiction, and later appeared in a slightly longer version titled "Darwin" in the magazines *The Face* and *Spin* in 1990. My discussion refers to the original "Doing Television" version of the story. The story takes place in a universe that seems rather similar to that of the "Bridge Trilogy" in certain ways but is not directly connected to those works. The story concerns a family in a hotel room battered by the Santa Ana winds in a future in which climate change has become a deadly reality. Fortunately, in this future, television offers even more profound escapes from reality than its cathode-ray tube or even ultra-HD flat-screen ancestors could promise. The virtual reality in "Doing Television" resembles the version presented in the "Bridge Trilogy" more than that seen in the Sprawl novels: the user puts on a vest, gloves, and glasses that allow them to interact with programs as diverse as "Gladiator Skull" and "Natureland" ("Television" 392). A third-person limited omniscient story, "Doing Television" focuses on the consciousness of Kelsey, whose brother Trev hogs the television with his constant desire for violent stimulation. Kelsey prefers the calmer, more picturesque experiences such as "Natureland." Like the "Bridge Trilogy," the story occurs in a world in which the power of nation-states has waned in the presence of corporation control: "Kelsey isn't sure what countries are. Lines on a map. Colors. A concept dim as aristocracy. Kelsey has two passports, one issued by the United States of America, the other by her mother's company" ("Television" 393). Her mother's two passports demonstrate how the corporate has become as powerful as, if not more powerful than, the nation-state. The family is moving to the Darwin Free Trade zone, and the story ends with Kelsey's wish to be there: "She wishes she were already in Darwin, walking the miles of mall. Like every mall anywhere. Like doing television" ("Television" 394). This final equivalence of malls and television criticizes the uniformity that comes along with corporatization; as corporations expand, they absorb small businesses, leading to ubiquitous uniformity. Television adds to this phenomenon because it provides the media branch of corporations. In addition, since it now provides a virtual reality, it has replaced users' actual physical experiences with uniform patterned behavior.[4] Therefore, whether they are walking through a mall or "doing television," their existence plays out within standardized formats established by the corporations.

Gibson's most recent short story, "Dougal Discarnate," recalls his early Mervyn Kihn story "Hippie Hat Brain Parasite" because it also features a fictionalized version of Gibson who experiences paranormal phenomena and makes reference to mystical conspiracy theories such as ley lines. The story takes place in Kitsilano (or "Kits"), the neighborhood where Gibson lives in

Vancouver. The story opens in the 1980s, when Gibson meets a disembodied man named "Dougal," who separated permanently from his body during an extreme acid trip in 1972; a Quicksilver Messenger Service jam provided the impetus for his discarnation.[5] However, this lack of consciousness did not hinder his body from attending Langara College in Vancouver and "becom[ing[an accountant" ("Dougal" 232). In a kind of parody of ghost stories, the character Bill becomes friends with Dougal, who shares his love of bad sci-fi films. The pair both despise *Star Trek* and *Star Wars* while finding Tarkovsky's *Stalker* too boring to stay awake: "But really what we both wanted was Mick Jagger driving around some half-assed dystopian L.A. in a six-wheeled armoured car, painted red" ("Dougal" 237). In this sentence, Gibson becomes somewhat self-reflexive, and he begins gesturing toward the story's theme, which concerns real-world utopias and dystopias. In the passage just quoted, Gibson alludes to the mostly forgotten early 1990s sci-fi film *Freejack* (1992), which stars Emilio Estevez, Mick Jagger, Rene Russo, and Anthony Hopkins. This reference proves ironic because the film represents part of Hollywood's co-opting of cyberpunk themes, which were subsequently watered down and rendered absurd. The allusion also allows Gibson to set up his ideas about utopianism/dystopianism.

The narrator explains that "[t]he dystopian movie thing . . . was actually about Kits. A mirror. Inversion. Utopias are by definition unreal. Dystopias are merely relatively unpleasant. One person's raging dystopia is another's hot immigration opportunity. But there's something about living in such a thoroughly, however relatively, non-dystopian place" ("Dougal" 237). Here, Gibson sets up Vancouver not as a utopia, which proves impossible, but as a space tending toward the utopian, which he opposes to New York before "the regooding," referring to the massive clean-up of New York that took place during the 1990s ("Dougal" 237). As the narrator states, before the 1990s, "If you were ready to put up with some relatively serious dystopia, you could live there, then. It wasn't about having enough money. It was about wanting something else badly enough, the secret semi-utopian flipside, the freedom of the splendidly broken metropolis" ("Dougal" 238). Here, Gibson begins playing with the notion of utopia as a term relative to the spectator's desires; even the seemingly dystopian New York of the 1970s and '80s could be utopian if it aligned correctly with an individual's wants or passions. The same holds true for Dougal, who starts heading down a dystopian path before finding his own utopia. Dougal starts "doing television" in his own unique way—he learns that he can get high by positioning himself behind old cathode-ray televisions. The beams from the electron gun and the electromagnets inside apparently alter his wavelength enough to make him high in a truly discarnate way. Dougal begins wallowing in self-pity and television abuse until he meets the discarnate spirit of an

Okinawan woman who "introduced [him] to the ins and outs of one particular kind of Okinawan shamanism, one centered around congress with discarnate entities" ("Dougal" 240). He finds satisfaction in Okinawa because, for him, the woman's presence makes it utopian, and the story suggests that Gibson's life with Deborah has done the same for him in Vancouver.

Real Utopias and Dystopias: Comments on Selected Works of Nonfiction

Gibson has published a wide variety of nonfiction works, but two pieces from the 1990s in particular demonstrate how he can deploy nonfiction to critically engage with the same concepts that permeate his fictional works. While Gibson's fictional works have frequently dealt with the idea of retrofitting and simulacra, "Disneyland with the Death Penalty," his 1993 essay for *Wired* magazine, examines how the island city-state of Singapore has erected its retrofitted, simulacral edifice of financial superiority atop the remnants of British imperialism. A city devoid of litter, Singapore in Gibson's eyes is a "relentlessly G-rated experience, micromanaged by a state that has the look and feel of a large corporation . . . an affluent microcosm whose citizens inhabit something that feels like, well, Disneyland. Disneyland with the death penalty" (*DTPF* 72). An immaculately clean city in which everything works like clockwork and everyone conforms for the greater good, Singapore allows Gibson to meditate on how totalitarianism can exist behind the façade of a smiley-face button. Exhibiting the attitude of someone raised on counterculture, Gibson seeks out any traces of difference or revolt. However, he finds a populace that seems like it was churned out of the pods from *Invasion of the Body Snatchers:* "Young, for the most part, and clad in computer-weathered cottons from the local Gap clone, they're a handsome populace; they look good in their shorts and Reeboks and Matsuda shades" (*DTPF* 75). When he spots one young man in a t-shirt with Rastafarian colors, Gibson wonders if he is incredibly brave or just suicidal, and he never spots "a single 'bad' girl in Singapore" (*DTPF* 75). This absence of bad behavior makes Gibson uneasy, so he purposefully goes in search of it in his interactions with the people of Singapore.

He does once spot "two young Malayan men" sporting "heavy metal black," one of whom, as mentioned, wears a "t-shirt [that] was embroidered with the Rastafarian colors" (*DTPF* 75). Since this is the only instance of nonconformity that Gibson witnesses, he assumes that "its owner must have balls the size of durian fruit, or else be flat-out suicidal, or possibly both" (*DTPF* 75). Either way, the absence of other "deviant" individuals haunts Gibson (a child of the '60s and a fan of punk music), so he goes on a quest for nonconformity in the usual places. First, he drops into a music shop and asks if it sells Shonen Knife albums.[6] The music-store owner curtly responds, "Sir, this is a music shop," perhaps believing Gibson to be asking about cutlery or a kind of weapon. Gibson characterizes the music selection as a "stock [that] had been vetted by Mormon missionaries" (*DTPF* 76). He comes to the conclusion that "it really does seem like 1956 in Singapore; the war (or economic struggle, in this case) has been won, an expanded middle class enjoys great prosperity, enormous public works have successfully been undertaken, even more ambitious projects are under way, and a deeply paternalistic government is prepared, at any cost, to hold at bay the triple threat of communism, pornography, and drugs" (*DTPF* 77). It is important here to note that Singapore is not communist like its neighbors China and North Korea but instead profoundly capitalist; it signifies capitalism taken to its absolutely totalitarian conclusion in which everything works like an assembly line in service of the common goods of profit and efficiency. Individualistic desire, as represented by pornography, drugs, and dangerous media, must be squelched in favor of the whole's common good.

Gibson continues to seek "the wrong side of the tracks" or "parts [of the city] that have broken down and fallen apart, revealing the underlying social mechanism" (*DTPF* 77–78). Singapore has even replaced its seemingly irrepressible sex district with a subway station that exhibits "all the sexual potential of Frontierland" (*DTPF* 79). However, the "heterosexual handjob business," as Gibson terms it, has fared better since most shopping centers feature a "health center" potentially "located between a Reebok outlet and a Rolex dealer" where heterosexual males can exorcise those "nagging erections" that might prove counterproductive (*DTPF* 80). Gibson discovers that the city's two passions are shopping and eating—consumerism distilled to its most basic functions. While the malls all feature the same shops (a fact that is now true in the United States as well), Gibson does find the food to be amazing: "The food in Singapore, particularly in the endless variety of street snacks in the hawker centers, is something to write home about" (*DTPF* 82). Furthermore, the stringent health inspectors ensure that all food is safe, thus alleviating some of the concerns of international travelers. Everything is safe, unless you break the law, as Gibson witnesses when he sees two separate cases of men trying to transport illegal drugs through the country. One man receives the death penalty for importing 4.32 kilograms of heroin, and the other receives the death penalty for a mere two pounds of cannabis. The cleanliness and safety of the city comes with a zero-tolerance policy. While Gibson admits to finding the city boring, offering "the same ennui that lies in wait at any theme park," he also seems to start feeling nervous as an outsider with nonconformist attitudes. As if he is fleeing a degenerating scene, Gibson announces to his mirror, "My ass . . . is out of here" (*DTPF* 87).

The final section of the essay proves rather humorous as Gibson, feeling guilty and like a criminal despite having done nothing wrong, attempts to slink out of the country in the wee hours of the morning. Catching a cab at 4 A.M., Gibson learns there are times when people break the laws; the taxi driver runs every red light, responding, "Too early policeman . . . " (*DTPF* 87). At Changi airport, Gibson admits that he "must've been starting to lose it" because he sees a piece of litter and begins to rabidly take pictures of it despite the police officers with machine guns (*DTPF* 87–88). After receiving angry looks and watching the guards remove the piece of trash, Gibson says, "I avoided eye contact, straightened my tie, and assumed the position" to board his flight to Hong Kong. Once in the air, Gibson ends the piece by stating, "I loosened my tie, clearing Singapore airspace" (*DTPF* 88). While Gibson's nonconformist attitude chafes against the forced conformity the simultaneously admiring the country's staggering accomplishments in public health, environmental protection, and information technology, which seem impossible in more democratic frameworks. Ironically, Gibson also notes in the afterword appended to the essay in *Distrust That Particular Flavor* that Singapore reacted to the piece by banning *Wired* magazine. He explains that Singapore's totalitarian extremes have softened somewhat since the essay was written. In a final bit of rare political commentary, Gibson subtly juxtaposes Singapore's totalitarianism with the current state of affairs in the United States: "Though at least it [Singapore] was upfront about it [totalitarianism], I would add today, from the perspective of a harsher era" (89). Here, Gibson is no doubt drawing a comparison with the increased levels of control and surveillance in the post-9/11 United States.

Gibson's 1997 essay (or perhaps short story) "Thirteen Views of a Cardboard City" provides an interesting parallel to "Disneyland with the Death Penalty." First printed in 1997 by *New Worlds*, a classic British sci-fi magazine, "Thirteen Views" was later reprinted in James Patrick Kelly and John Kessel's anthology *Rewired: The Post-Cyberpunk Anthology* (2007). The story has no plot but, as suggested by its title, instead features descriptions of thirteen different camera shots of a cardboard city erected by homeless people in a Tokyo subway station. This series of snapshots recalls the camera-eye narratives used by previous authors such as John Dos Passos, in his *U.S.A Trilogy* (*The 42nd Parallel* [1930], *1919* [1932], and *The Big Money* [1936]), and William S. Burroughs in various works, particularly *The Wild Boys: A Book of the Dead* (1971), in which Burroughs conveys the postapocalyptic action from the viewpoint of camera angles. However, here it is merely snapshots instead of moving camera images—we are presented with tableaux of this environment from which we must deduce meaning. The story definitely provides some of the impetus for the cardboard city from *All Tomorrow's Parties* in which Laney has taken up residence after Rei Toei's disappearance; however, the connections between the two works are minimal enough to warrant a separate reading of the story.

Surprisingly, the cardboard city of the pictures is not dirty or filled with garbage but instead has been meticulously organized by its residents. Another example of interstitial space in Gibson's writing, this real-world example consists of people once again scavenging and making use of old things, engaging in the act of *bricolage* on a daily basis to allow them to survive and to have enough comforts to provide them with a sense of identity. The story never features any characters; we see only the objects of the people and never the people themselves. While the story takes the detached, emotionless tone of a machine (the camera), the images nevertheless manage to provoke profound emotions as we move from area to area and meditate on the objects there. Murals predominate on many boxes, bringing a sense of artistry, uniqueness, and identity to otherwise squalorly and mass-produced dwelling spaces. As the photographs variously depict cooking apparatuses, sleeping spaces, and even old radios, they eventually show a series of children's toys, driving home the human cost of the situation while simultaneously demonstrating how love still blossoms even here.

Finally, the camera depicts a box obviously used for an office, thus demonstrating that the cardboard city's denizens have not given up but still strive to rise above their situation. The story drives this point home in the final "view" of the story; a close-up of a shelf, upon which sit three photographs. Finally, in these photographs, we get images of one of the citizens of the cardboard city even though it is only an image of an image. The narrator begins to speculate about how long the man has lived here with his cat and his guitar, and the camera doll[ies] back here to reveal a "filofax" containing "Names. Numbers. Held as though they might be a map, a map back out of the underground" (*DTPF* 128). Here, the story ends on an optimistic tone, depicting a human spirit that refuses to submit to its surroundings. Even more profoundly, the story's comparison of the cardboard boxes to more traditional living spaces suggests that we all live in boxes of one size or another, spaces that constrain us and organize our lives according to our socioeconomic status. The more affluent have apartments, condos, and houses of increasing scale, while the truly marginalized may have to create their own spaces. No matter what the size or state of the space we inhabit, Gibson's story hauntingly suggests that identity, desire, and drive can persist no matter what our status.

Cinematic Experimentations: Gibson's Forays into Screenwriting

Gibson's screenplay for *Alien*[3] opens with the same situation depicted in the close of James Cameron's *Aliens*. *Aliens* ends with the apparent destruction of all the xenomorphs on LV-416 and the escape of four characters aboard the Sulaco: Ripley, the young girl Newt, a wounded Corporal Hicks, and the severely damaged android Bishop. At the beginning, the quartet remain in hypersleep, the same state that both opens and closes *Alien* and *Aliens*. The military dropship, called the Sulaco, has strayed into an illegal area, resulting in a military interceptor craft attaching itself to the Sulaco and boarding it. The marines soon discover an alien egg nestled in Bishop's cryotube, and a pitched battle ensues that drenches Ripley's cryotube with the aliens' corrosively acidic blood, thus causing her to not appear in the script. Gibson had been told to remove Ripley's character from the script because Sigourney Weaver had not agreed to return to the franchise. Instead, Gibson's screenplay focuses on Hicks and Bishop as well as some other new characters they meet.[7]

Newt and Hicks reawaken on a space station called Anchorpoint, where Bishop receives a rebuild as well. Newt leaves shortly after their arrival to live with her grandparents back on Earth, and Hicks begins to hear rumors that the Weyland-Yutani corporation (the corporate villain of the films) has reserved xenomorph materials to create new biological weapons. The Weyland-Yutani genetic engineers experiment with the alien DNA, which has the ability to cannibalize and then fuse with its host DNA, leading to different hybrid forms of the alien as implied by the term "xenomorph." Soon, their experiments go awry, and the genetic manipulation allows the alien species to spread like an airborne virus. Instead of the typical chest-burster birth made famous in *Alien*, these new aliens unnoticeably alter their human hosts' internal structure and then, once gestation is completed, rip off the human flesh to reveal full-grown alien warriors.

After countless causalities, Bishop and Hicks triumph over the aliens through a series of darkly lit action scenes. The screenplay ends with Bishop suggesting that the human race must pursue its common enemy to its source and exterminate it. The studio believed that Gibson's screenplay was weak, and numerous writers submitted further scripts before the final version was settled on for the film. As Gibson explains on his blog, "It became the first of some thirty drafts, by a great many screenwriters, and none of mine was used (except for the idea, perhaps, of a bar-code tattoo)" (9/1/2003). However, the idea that the DNA fuses with the hosts to create a new DNA appears in both cuts of the action film. The theatrical version features the alien gestating in a dog, and the special edition cut, usually considered to be superior, has it grow inside an ox, which causes the alien to emerge in a more quadrupedal form than was the case in the previous two films in which it had gestated in human hosts. Furthermore, the scenes of scientists experimenting with the xenomorph's DNA presage the scenes in Jean-Pierre Jeunet's *Alien: Resurrection* (1997), and the idea that the xenomorphs are the result of an ancient arms race is similar to the revelations in Ridley Scott's pseudo-prequel *Prometheus* (2012), a film that ends with a human and an android character pursuing the aliens to their home world in the manner suggested by Bishop in Gibson's screenplay. In summation, while little if anything of Gibson's screenplay appears onscreen in *Alien³*, Gibson certainly exerted his own influence on this classic science fiction franchise.

"Johnny Mnemonic" remains the only one of his stories that Gibson managed to successfully develop into a screenplay and feature film, which was directed by his friend Robert Longo. Longo's claim to fame was directing videos for the alternative band R.E.M.'s classic "The One I Love" and the new wave band New Order's equally iconic "Bizarre Love Triangle." *Johnny Mnemonic* constitutes his only feature film and the last entry in his filmography.[8] Gibson worked closely with the production, but re-edits from the production company resulted in a film that is more often panned than lauded. Generally, the Japanese "Director's Cut" of the film receives higher praise than the American release (*WGW* 91–95). As released, the film felt severely flawed in 1995 and seems even more so today, but a large part of the film's problem resides in the casting of Keanu Reeves in the title role and the addition of rather uncharacteristic, bombastic speeches for the character, who now has a penchant for expensive clothes, swanky hotels, constant room service, and exorbitantly priced prostitutes. The rest of the cast outshines Reeves, but the film still feels a little silly. For the purposes of this discussion, I focus almost exclusively on Gibson's published manuscript with only passing references to the film; Gibson published the screenplay partly to demonstrate his and Longo's intentions for the film before the studio got its hands on it. Gibson's screenplay provides an interesting look at an attempt to cross over from one medium to another, but it proves somewhat flawed as well.

Gibson both adds and alters numerous elements for the *Johnny Mnemonic* screenplay. Most important, the screenplay explains the information that Johnny is carrying in his head. In the future depicted in the film, a ravaging disease has decimated large portions of the populace. Brought on by exposure to ubiquitous electronics, Nerve Attenuation Syndrome (N.A.S.) causes those infected to undergo the "black shakes," a neurological degeneration that ends in death. Furthermore, Molly Millions disappears from the plot and is replaced by Jane, a bodyguard character who serves as a deus ex machina savior for Johnny. Johnny himself has become little more than a stereotypical, two-dimensional action hero in his own right. The screenplay also introduces two other major characters: Takahashi and the Street Preacher. The screenplay turns the Yakuza assassin into Shinji, who is only a lackey for the Newark Yakuza boss Takahashi (played by the great Japanese actor and director Takeshi Kitano, also known as "Beat Takeshi"), whose daughter recently died of N.A.S. A major subplot of the screenplay revolves around Takahashi's search for Johnny and his simultaneous attempt to deal with his grief. He repeatedly receives bizarre transmissions from an entity within the matrix that appears in the form of an angelic face.

Gibson's screenplay sets the stage with establishing shots of riots and violence to shape the dystopian tone of this future. The script adds a bit more to Johnny's background. He has had part of his childhood erased to make room for the wetware that allows him to store data in his brain, suggesting that Johnny has chosen his job to fill some lack from his childhood. The deal between Johnny and the members of the Vietnamese group with whom he meets in a Beijing hotel quickly goes south when the Yakuza attack. Johnny finishes transferring the data into his head, but it requires twice his storage capacity (the "exorbitant" limit of 320 gigabytes seriously dates it now). The keys to unlocking the data are three random images chosen from television. Johnny escapes as Shinji's crew kills the Vietnamese group and discovers the data's destination in Newark.

With an overload of data in his head that will lead to seepage, his death, and the possible corruption of the data, Johnny arrives in Newark, which is part of the Sprawl that stretches from Atlanta to Boston. Once there, Johnny contacts his agent Ralfi (played by the horror and independent cinema icon Udo Kier) and begins to suspect he has been set up. Ralfi turns on Johnny and attempts to decapitate him in order to deliver his head to the parties that seek it, but Jane saves him for the promise of money to become his bodyguard. She and Johnny escape, but both are suffering from severe health problems as Johnny's seepage begins to take hold and Jane's N.A.S. starts to diminish her stature as an implant-enhanced bodyguard.

Meanwhile, Shinji has disappointed his boss Takahashi, so Takahashi hires another new character in the screenplay: the Street Preacher. While his background never receives full explication, the Street Preacher has rebuilt himself with various wetware implants to the point that he is both almost indestructible and barely human anymore. A supposedly religious leader, the Street Preacher can be hired as an assassin, and he uses his earnings to support his implant addiction. His role feels comical as he delivers lines that blend Christian scripture with homicidal intent. Unlike the short story, the Street Preacher steadily eclipses Shinji (the Yakuza assassin who never receives a name in the short story) as the chief villain of the screenplay; the same goes for the film, in which Dolph Lundgren, most famous for his role in *Rocky IV* (1985), portrays the character.[9] While trying to evade both the Street Preacher and the Yakuza, Johnny and Jane receive assistance from Spider (played by the punk music icon Henry Rollins),[10] an underground medical specialist of sorts who treats the marginalized victims suffering from N.A.S. While trying to help the pair, the Street Preacher finds them and kills Spider, who directs them to Jones for assistance.

The two arrive at the headquarters of the Lo Tek resistance, which seeks to undermine the global control grid and to fight back against the corporations. Its base of operations, called "Heaven," is located on an abandoned bridge, which presages the Bridge novels. It has been outfitted as a defensive fortress, with Volkswagen Beetles that have been retrofitted to drop like gigantic junk bombs on any would-be assailants. Once in Heaven, they meet J-Bomb (played by the rapper/actor Ice-T) and Jones (the wetwired junkie dolphin from the short story), who determine that Johnny's digital cargo is more important than he imagined; he carries the cure for N.A.S., which the pharmaceutical company Pharmakon has developed but wants to suppress because it can earn more money treating the disease than curing it. The name "Pharmakon" alludes to Plato's *Phaedrus,* in which King Thamus suffers from memory loss, so the Egyptian god Thoth presents him with writing as a cure (*pharmakon*), but Thamus refuses it, seeing it as a technology that will only lead to forgetfulness instead of true memory. The *pharmakon* becomes an emblem for that which is simultaneously curative and poisonous at the same time. Thus, the story depicts pharmaceutical corporations (and all corporations by extrapolation) as entities that serve as both the means of the human race's survival and the source of its enslavement and control. For Derrida, the *pharmakon* constitutes a perfect example of how meanings proliferate: "The *pharmakon* is the movement, the locus, and the play: (the production of) difference" (*Dissemination* 125). Derrida contends that the *pharmakon* provides the perfect example of how a word not only contains multiple meanings but can actually contain diametrically opposed meanings. Similarly, Pharmakon puts forward one face that positions itself as working for the betterment of humankind, but, like the society of control itself, the corporation proves Janus-faced as it offers freedom from the disease while actually fostering the illness. Ultimately, *Johnny Mnemonic* ends with a truly revolutionary moment in which the forces of control are turned against themselves as the Lo Teks successfully download the files from Johnny's brain and disseminate them to the world.

In addition to his film screenplays, Gibson also worked on two different episodes of Chris Carter's critically acclaimed sci-fi/horror series *The X-Files* (1993–2002), which follows FBI agents Fox Mulder and Dana Scully as they investigate alien visitations and other paranormal phenomena. Co-written with fellow cyberpunk Tom Maddox, the episode "Kill Switch" was first broadcast on February 15, 1998, during Season 5 of the series.[11] The story opens with a massive shoot-out in a diner after a series of identical phone calls has drawn a variety of different gang assassins to the location. In the aftermath, Mulder and Scully discover the corpse of Donald Gelman, "a Silicon Valley folk hero," as Mulder calls him, who did research into artificial intelligence before his disappearance. The two recover a CD-ROM from his laptop that contains a single song: the 1950s R&B hit "Twilight Time" by the Platters. However, a visit to the Lone Gunmen (a trio of recurring characters who are both extreme conspiracy theorists and computer hackers) reveals that the disk actually contains encrypted data.[12] After investigating Gelman's e-mail, Mulder and Scully discover a code that leads them to a shipping container, where they meet the Invisigoth, an almost gut-wrenchingly stereotypical goth/cyberpunk female hacker who explains that the site is being targeted by a Department of Defense satellite. A hacker legend as well as Gelman's protégé, the Invisigoth reveals that Gelman had successfully created a sentient AI that escaped into the Internet and can now track and eliminate potential threats using government laser satellites. The episode connects the satellites to GPS, at the time still used only by the military, as well as to the Reagan-era Strategic Defense Initiative (aka "Star Wars"). The Invisigoth also discloses that she and Gelman had a plan to upload their consciousnesses to the Internet in true cyberpunk style. Eventually, Mulder discovers the trailer where a dedicated server and T3 line serve as the AI's homebase. The episode takes a somewhat idiotic turn as Mulder gets trapped in a virtual-reality world and must be saved by Scully, who uses video-game karate powers to defeat evil nurses. Finally they manage to upload the kill-switch command from the CD-ROM that destroys the trailer and server just as the Invisigoth enters the facility and potentially uploads herself to the Internet. While it seems rather dated and cheesy today, the episode still manages to be an entertaining imagination of how cyberpunk story lines could occur in the present of the 1990s.

Unfortunately, Gibson's follow-up *X-Files* episode, "First Person Shooter," also coauthored with Tom Maddox, proved much less satisfactory. Based on the first-person-shooter video games that became increasingly popular in the late 1990s, "First-Person Shooter" was first broadcast on February 27, 2000, as part of Season 7. First-person-shooter games first began to gain popularity with id Software's *Wolfenstein 3D* (1992), which focused on killing Nazis from a first-person point of view. However, it was id Software's follow-up *Doom* (1993), which featured much smoother graphics, that turned the genre into a sensation that continues even to this day. Further releases such as *Quake* (1996), *Unreal* (1998), and *Half-Life* (1998) introduced multiplayer capabilities into the first-person-shooter paradigm and effectively set a standard that still influences the video-game industry. Despite its potentially interesting subject matter, the episode brought *The X-Files* to an all-time low and is often considered one of the worst episodes. The story concerns a game that blends paintball/laser-tag-style games with virtual reality. The characters enter a space with real "armor" and "guns" and engage with projected, virtual enemies. However, a "superhot" female assassin who was not programmed into the game begins to kill players in a very real fashion using antique weaponry. This episode also features the Lone Gunmen because Gibson and Maddox were fans of the trio, and series creator Chris Carter directed the episode, but the content only goes from bad to worse as the male characters devolve into Neanderthals with the testosterone levels of teenagers and alternate between slobbering over the porn-star/stripper who had her body scanned for the game and wanting to wantonly blow stuff up. Somehow, the episode manages to be sexist and insulting to both male and female audience members, and it further deteriorates as Mulder and Scully inexplicably get trapped in the game and cut off from reality. A failed attempt to explore the culture of video gaming, "First Person Shooter" proves that Gibson was right to devote his energies to the world of fiction.

Toward a New Artistic Medium: Memory and Technology in *Agrippa: A Book of the Dead*

A collaborative work between Gibson and the artist Dennis Ashbaugh together with their publisher, Kevin Begos, Jr., *Agrippa: A Book of the Dead* (1992) proved to be Gibson's most original and innovative work in many ways as it appeared as a multimedia, digital text that commented simultaneously on the new avenues that technology opens up for art and the effect of such technology upon human memory. *Agrippa* appeared as a true hypertext: its $2,000 deluxe edition came in the form of an artist's book that featured alternating pages of artwork and a code that appears to be DNA, with its repeating letters G, T, A, and C. The book was released in a distressed-looking case and wrapped in a shroud, thus immediately setting up the book's theme of history and memory. The genetic codes of the text also draw a connection to the genetic information that is passed down from one generation to the next. Finally, the book contained a 3.5-inch floppy disk, the standard of the time, which stored a three-hundred-line poem by William Gibson. After running the poem, the disk was programmed to encrypt itself and become unreadable after one use.[13]

Gibson's poem concerns a photo album of his father's, which is tied with a ribbon and tattered like the *Agrippa* book itself. A surprisingly powerful, structured, and lyrical poem written by someone known mostly for his science fiction, *Agrippa* concerns the nature of memory and the mechanisms that technology provides for preserving it. The poem unfolds mostly as a series of stanzas focused on the photographs that Gibson finds within the book, largely rural photos set in Wheeling, West Virginia, and Wytheville, Virginia. The juxtaposition of the poem's predominantly rural content and its cutting-edge distribution format offers an interesting insight into the far-reaching impact of technology. The photographs lead into autobiographical reflections and remembrances in stream-of-consciousness style. The poem centers on the notion of "the mechanism," which is equated both with the old-timey box camera that captured the images and with the pistols that Gibson shot as a young boy and a man. The mechanisms are diametrically opposed in that one takes life while the other has the power to preserve images of it. Similarly, the floppy disk that stores the poem represents another mechanism capable of preserving knowledge and memory or perhaps even life itself, if certain sci-fi predictions of the future are to be believed.

The work's equation of technology and memory revolves around the human mechanism and its flawed ability to preserve experience accurately. Much like the floppy disk that encrypts itself after one use, experience cannot be re-created except by the faulty human hardware of memory. Like the photograph, the computer and data storage offer powerful new ways of preserving experience and knowledge. Ultimately, Gibson's *Agrippa* proves so profound because it melds poetry, one of the oldest forms of literature, with abstract art, encryption, and data storage to create a truly hybrid and multimedia work of art. It gestures toward the future possibilities of hypertext art while simultaneously demonstrating how even multimedia art still deals with many of the same old universal literary themes, such as memory, death, and identity. Although some of Gibson's excursions into media other than fiction have proved flawed, *Agrippa* demonstrates that Gibson has the ability to direct his skills into new avenues, and he has suggested in interviews that he might return to the world of screenwriting or even publish a graphic novel.

Conclusion

Retrofitting Cyberpunk—
Gibson's Continuing Influence

While cyberpunk may have "died" in the late 1980s, the genre's central themes and many of its trappings have lived on in provocative ways that twist the old genre and continue to make it profoundly relevant. Whether or not cyberpunk is dead remains an issue for debate, but the editors James Patrick Kelly and John Kessel (both cyberpunk authors themselves) have taken it upon themselves to label a post-cyberpunk genre that has (like postmodernism) become self-conscious and aware of its own traits. Consequently, it starts to play with these characteristics as Gibson himself does in his "Bridge Trilogy." Many of these authors are the original cyberpunks themselves, such as Gibson and Sterling, but there is also a new breed of authors, such as Neal Stephenson, Jonathan Lethem, Cory Doctorow, Paolo Bacigalupi, and Charles Stross. Probably the most famous of these authors, Neal Stephenson achieved success and critical acclaim with the publication of *Snow Crash* (1992), a novel that brings a thoroughly Pynchonian sense of humor to a future in which the virtual world proves as important as the real one. The readers experience this world through Hiro Protagonist, a pizza delivery guy who lives out his real life as a hacker and virtual samurai. In the novel, the Sumerian language acts as the firmware programming code for the brain and therefore can be used to hack human brains on a fundamental level. Stephenson's follow-up to *Snow Crash, The Diamond Age: Or, a Young Lady's Illustrated Primer* (1995), explores cyberpunk themes but focuses more on nanotechnology. The novel also begins to more fully depict Stephenson's obsession with the history of mathematics and its relation to computers, particularly the work of Alan Turing, who himself appears in Stephenson's subsequent novel *Cryptonomicon* (1999). *Cryptonomicon* blends historical fiction with realistic depictions of the present while still exploring themes crucial to cyberpunk, such as information, encryption, and the computerization of society and the human.

Gun, with Occasional Music (1994), one of Jonathan Lethem's cyberpunk works, returns to cyberpunk's hard-boiled roots, but it also adds a satirical, self-conscious edge that marks it as a distinctly "post-cyberpunk" work. The Canadian author Cory Doctorow's *Down and Out in the Magic Kingdom* (2003) immerses the reader in a truly bizarre future version of Disneyworld in which two groups war against each other over how to provide visitors with the most satisfying experience that simultaneously conforms to the ideals of Disney himself. The struggle centers on whether older animatronics or holographic attractions are superior. The novel therefore centers on a debate about different levels of simulacra. Paolo Bacigalupi's *The Windup Girl* (2009) generally receives the label of "biopunk," a nascent real-world movement that believes everyone should have open access to genetic information. The novel details a future in which corporations have thoroughly appropriated agriculture by patenting various strains of crops, thereby completely controlling access to their growth and distribution. This genetic modification extends to humans as well, as evidenced by Emiko, "the windup girl" of the title, who was designed to be a slave that obeys the commands of her master. Distinct from the other cyberpunk authors, the prolific author Charles Stross writes novels that often blend cyberpunk elements with hard science fiction and space-opera aesthetics, resulting in novels such as *Singularity Sky* (2003), *Accelerando* (2005), and *Saturn's Children* (2008).

As we noted in the Introduction, cyberpunk arose in Japan around the same time as it did in the United States and Canada, and the circuit of influence has continued to be reciprocal among the three countries. Thus, Japan saw the release of numerous works of important cyberpunk that were undoubtedly influenced by Gibson and his peers. Two of the most influential works of cyberpunk manga from the 1990s are Masamune Shirow's *Ghost in the Shell* (1989–90) and Yukito Kishiro's *Battle Angel Alita* (1990–95) series. While *Ghost in the Shell* follows a special cyborg police force as it tracks down a rogue AI that seeks to liberate itself into the Internet, *Battle Angel Alita* tells the story of a battered android tossed out of a floating upper-class world into the *gomi*-infested surface of the Earth below. During the same time period, the filmmaker Shozin Fukui also directed two important avant-garde cyberpunk films, *964 Pinocchio* (1991) and *Rubber's Lover* (1996). These manga series (together with the animes based on them) and films brought cyberpunk into the 1990s in Japan, and the subgenre has prospered in films such as Takashi Miike's *Full Metal Yakuza* (1997), Yūdai Yamaguchi and Jun'ichi Yamamoto's *Meatball Machine* (2005), and Yoshihiro Nishimura's *Tokyo Gore Police* (2008). Beyond Japan, the experimental Taiwanese artist Shu Lea Cheang's *I.K.U.* (2001) broke new ground for the cyberpunk genre. With a title based on the Japanese slang for "I'm coming," *I.K.U.* is a surrealistic sci-fi porn film about cyborgs who collect orgasm data from the various users they encounter.

Most famously, the *Matrix* trilogy brought cyberpunk back to fame and attention in the late 1990s and early 2000s. Derivative of numerous famous sci-fi works, the films undoubtedly take the term "the matrix" from Gibson's works, but the films' simulated reality serves not as a communication medium but as a prison that keeps humans in a subdued, unconscious state while their bodies are used to generate energy for the sentient computers, robots, and machines that rule the physical world. The films depict the rise of the resistance to the machines and explore the thin line between reality and simulation in true cyberpunk style. One can still feel the influence of Gibson resonating in seemingly noncyberpunk works such as Spike Jonze's recent Oscar-nominated sci-fi drama *Her* (2013), a rather convincing depiction of artificially intelligent operating systems that so perfectly pass the Turing Test that individuals begin to fall in love with their computers. A film only barely extrapolated from the present, *Her* depicts a man who communicates with his computer via an earpiece and soon finds himself going on dates and having "sex" with her before she and the other AIs eventually liberate themselves and join together in a style reminiscent of *Neuromancer*.

Gibson's most recent novel, *The Peripheral* (2014), embarks into exciting new territory and features possibly his most intricate narrative to date. *The Peripheral* continues to demonstrate Gibson's fascination with the nature of history, which was a major theme in the "Bigend" novels, but it expands this interest to include time itself. The novel provides Gibson's own unique take on the classic sci-fi topics of time travel, post-apocalyptic worlds, and parallel dimensions. The novel takes Gibson's alternating chapter structure to new levels of complexity as the narrative is divided not just between different characters but also between different futures. One narrative strand takes place a few decades from the present while the other unfolds in the next century after a cataclysmic environmental disaster decimated 80% of the human population. But the two narratives are not just separated temporally; the earlier narrative actually constitutes a parallel time stream that has been altered by contact from the future. Against this mind-bending backdrop, Gibson imagines how the current technologies of drones, robots, nanotechnology, 3D printing, and virtual-presence devices will evolve in startling new ways that will enable a person to guide a cyborg body in a different time stream. While the novel still feels distinctly Gibsonian, it marks a new aesthetic break in his body of work that proves he can still vididly imagine the futures of cutting-edge technology while also turning traditional sci-fi motifs on their heads.

NOTES

Chapter 1: Understanding William Gibson

1. See Andrew Ross's *Strange Weather* (146) for a discussion of the background and masculinist nature of cyberpunk, and see Scott Bukatman's *Terminal Identity* (144) for his discussion of Ross's claims.

2. Altamont represented the culminating moment of the Rolling Stones' 1969 tour. It resulted in riots and the killing of one audience member by a Hell's Angels biker who had been hired to provide extra security. Chronicled in the classic documentary *Gimme Shelter* (1970), directed by Albert Maysles and David Maysles as well as by Charlotte Zwerin, Altamont is often considered the death knell of the '60s as it demonstrated that the hippie ideal of pacifism was perhaps no more than a pipe dream.

3. *On the Road* represents part of *The Duluoz Legend,* Kerouac's term for his series of semifictionalized autobiographic novels that detail his life and experiences; other major entries include *The Subterraneans* (1958), *The Dharma Bums* (1958), *Visions of Cody* (1960), *Big Sur* (1962), and *Desolation Angels* (1965).

4. The interview appears in *Chaos & Cyberculture* (1994) by Timothy Leary, who himself was a godfather figure for the hippie generation with his motto "Tune in, turn on, drop out" and his advocacy of drug use to expand consciousness. Leary found new inspiration in the invention of computers and the Internet because they opened up new possibilities of consciousness expansion, communication, and experience without the need for drugs.

5. David Cronenberg, whose early body horror films influenced cyberpunk, went on to direct a riveting adaptation of *Crash* (1996) that demonstrated how his body horror aesthetic could be translated to a more realistic milieu.

6. Interestingly, the film was released the same year as David Cronenberg's *Shivers* (aka *The Orgy of the Blood Parasites* and *They Came from Within*), which focuses on a similar apartment building and depicts a parasitic organism that turns victims into insatiable sexual predators.

7. Along with the Velvet Underground, Iggy Pop also helped lay the foundation for punk with his trilogy of albums with the Stooges: *The Stooges* (1969), *Fun House* (1970), and *Raw Power* (1973). Despite releasing only one studio album, the Sex Pistols remain one of the most influential punk bands of all time. Their album *Never Mind the Bollocks, Here's the Sex Pistols* (1977) contains some of the immortal anthems of punk rock, such as "Anarchy in the U.K." and "God Save the Queen," the song that got them banned from performing in England. The Clash represent an equal—if not more important—influence on the punk music scene with their unique mix of historical/

political insight, comedy and satire, catchy hooks, and a grungy, antiestablishment aesthetic that incorporates not only rock stylings but also styles from reggae music. Featuring classics such as "Career Opportunities" and "I'm So Bored with the U.S.A.," the Clash's 1977 self-titled first album was a primal, intelligent, and political attack on the issues of the period. The band continued to experiment with its sound on subsequent classics such as *Give 'Em Enough Rope* (1978), *London Calling* (1979), and *Sandinista!* (1980). In the United States, Patti Smith began to release albums that remain iconic to this day. Strongly influenced by the Beat Generation, Smith represented a more poetic mutation of punk that alternated between hard rocking punk anthems and ballad-style pieces. Her early albums *Horses* (1975) and *Easter* (1976) had a profound impact on punk music and artistic rock more generally. Her spoken word piece "Babelogue," from *Easter,* features the iconic line "I don't fuck much with the past, but I fuck plenty with the future." This slogan could easily be applied to both the punk and the cyberpunk movements, which turned their backs on tradition and embraced the radically new and different. Contemporaneously, the Ramones began releasing satirical and politically charged albums such as *Ramones* (1976), *Leave Home* (1977), *Rocket to Russia* (1977), and *Road to Ruin* (1978), albums filled with sarcastic bite, social criticism, and humorous yet nihilistic expressions of alienation and disillusionment.

8. See Bukatman's *Terminal Identity* and Rapatzikou's *Gothic Motifs* for their discussion of these comics and their relation to cyberpunk. Both authors also discuss lesser cyberpunk-themed comics such as *Iron Man: Crash* (1988) and *Batman: Digital Justice* (1990), both of which bring cyberpunk technology into the world of famous comic book superheroes.

9. James L. Tiptree, Jr., was actually the pen name of Alice Sheldon. Her identity as a woman was not revealed until 1977.

10. The father of cybernetics, Weiner was an American philosopher and mathematician who pioneered thinking about systems and their structures in ways that influenced disciplines as diverse as mathematics, computer science, anthropology, and sociology. Weiner's theories apply equally to machines and biological entities and thus laid the groundwork for the posthuman contention that humans, animals, and machines can all be understood according to the same paradigm. In particular, see Weiner's study *Cybernetics: Or Control and Communication in the Animal and the Machine.*

11. Since O'Barr himself published comic book works that could be considered cyberpunk, such as "Frame 137," this situates the film *The Crow* and Shirley's participation in it firmly within the sphere of cyberpunk's influence. "Frame 137," which first appeared in the anthology comic book series *Dark Horse Presents,* is also collected in Larry McCaffery's *Storming the Reality Studio.* It is a cyberpunk story set in a postapocalyptic world and includes a character that closely resembles the Crow. Proyas himself went on to direct *Dark City* (1998), a noir sci-fi film that features cyberpunk themes of programming human identity and behavior.

12. "Stoked" appears in Larry McCaffery's *Storming the Reality Studio;* "Possessed to Skate" is from Suicidal Tendencies' second album, *Join the Army* (1987).

13. See Gibson's short autobiographical sketch "Rocket Radio" (collected in *Distrust That Particular Flavor*), in which Gibson recounts his meeting with Katsuhiro Otomo.

14. For Habermas's full discussion of modernity, see his book *The Philosophical Discourse of Modernity: Twelve Lectures.*

15. See Daniel Bell's *The Coming of the Post-Industrial Society: A Venture in Social Forecasting* (1974).

16. In many ways, the Frankfurt School gave birth to critical theory as it turned the gaze of philosophy and Marxism to cultural and artistic works as sources of theoretical insight. While its roots can be traced back much farther, Max Horkheimer and Theodor Adorno's *The Dialectic of Enlightenment* (1947) can be considered the inaugural text of critical theory.

17. This quotation comes from Derrida's classic essay "Structure, Sign and Play in the Discourse of the Human Sciences," which appears in the 1968 collection *Writing and Difference* (285). Here, Derrida is quoting from and discussing Claude Lévi-Strauss's classic of structural anthropology, *The Savage Mind* (1962). In the University of Chicago translation of Lévi-Strauss's book, the passage reads "whatever is at hand" (17).

18. See my previous study of science fiction, *Exploring the Limits of the Human through Science Fiction.*

Chapter 2: A Cyborg Apprenticeship

1. Benford's essay is collected in George Slusser and Tom Shippey's anthology *Fiction 2000.*

2. See Fisher's 1988 essay "Of Living Machines and Living-Machines: *Blade Runner* and the Terminal Genre."

3. A golden-age, Gernsbackian science fiction story, *Flash Gordon* appeared as a comic strip in 1934. The long-running comic strip gave rise to a series of film serials that appeared from the '30s through the '50s. The famous comic hero was adapted in the 1980s into a cult-classic film, *Flash Gordon* (1980). The film also featured an equally iconic soundtrack from the classic rock band Queen in the same year.

4. Menzies's film is loosely based on H. G. Wells's *The Shape of Things to Come* (1933) and *The Work, Wealth, and Happiness of Mankind* (1929).

5. For Jung's theory of the collective unconscious, see his classic studies *The Archetypes and the Collective Unconscious* (1934–54) and *Man and His Symbols* (1964).

6. *The Bionic Man* actually refers to *The Six Million Dollar Man* (1974–78), which centered on astronaut Steve Austin, who was transformed into a cyborg. The series led to a spin-off, *The Bionic Woman* (1976–78). *Star Trek: The Original Series,* as fans generally term it now, originally aired from 1966 to 1969 but achieved a real fan base only in reruns, leading to numerous films and spinoff series.

7. Gibson's description of the rockets' "screaming" is clearly meant to evoke the opening line of Thomas Pynchon's postmodern historical epic *Gravity's Rainbow* (1973): "A screaming comes across the sky" (3).

8. *Invasion of the Body Snatchers* was originally a novel by Jack Finney titled *The Body Snatchers* (1954). The novel and the original film have been profoundly influential and led to numerous remakes. Philip Kaufman directed a body horror update of *Invasion of the Body Snatchers* (1978); Abel Ferrara, who adapted Gibson's "New Rose Hotel," shot another remake called simply *Body Snatchers* (1993); and another version, called *The Invasion* (2007), was directed by Oliver Hirschbiegel and starred Nicole Kidman and Daniel Craig. The horror director Tobe Hooper directed a remake of *Invaders from Mars* in 1986. The story line can also be seen in a variety of other texts that feature similar stories, such as Robert Heinlein's *The Puppet Masters* (1951) and John Carpenter's *The Thing* (1982).

9. Gary Westfahl points out that the story also bear similarities to numerous other works: Frederick Pohl's *Gateway* (1976); Stanislaw Lem's *Solaris* (1961), of which Tarkovsky also made a film adaptation in 1972; Arthur C. Clarke's novel *2001: A Space*

Odyssey and Stanley Kubrick's classic film adaptation (both 1968); Damon Knight's "Stranger Station" (1955); and James L. Tiptree, Jr.'s "And I Awoke and Found Me Here on the Cold Hill's Side" (1972) (*WGW* 40–41).

10. Marcel Duchamp remains (in)famous for his "found" pieces such as "Fountain" (1917), a urinal that Duchamp presented as an art "installation."

11. The use of the name "Potemkin" also recalls Sergei Eisenstein's classic silent film *Battleship Potemkin* (1925), which turns the tale of the 1905 ship's mutiny into a tale of Marxist struggle between the classes.

12. A reoccurring character in Hammett's fiction, the Continental Op is most famous from *Red Harvest,* which follows the character as he plays one group against another for his own personal gain. Some consider the novel the paradigm for Akira Kurosawa's samurai classic *Yojimbo* (1961). Sergio Leone went on to remake *Yojimbo* as the classic spaghetti western *A Fistful of Dollars* (1964).

Chapter 3: Beneath the Televisual Sky

1. As Gary Westfahl points out, Gibson borrows the name "Wintermute" from Philip K. Dick's *VALIS* (*WGW* 67).

2. I am indebted to Tatiani G. Rapatzikou, who points out this quotation in her book *Gothic Motifs in the Fiction of William Gibson* (22).

3. Husserl inaugurated the field of phenomenology with a series of long, difficult works, but his *Cartesian Meditations* (1931) provides a concise introduction to his thought and phenomenology in general. Heidegger's most famous explication of phenomenology remains *Being and Time* (1927). Finally, Sartre's *Being and Nothingness* (1943) persists as one of the most profound statements on the nature of existentialism and its relation to being and ethics.

4. A provocative postmodern text that deals with the brain in the jar from a truly cybernetic perspective is Joseph McElroy's novel *Plus* (1977), which is narrated from the point of view of a brain that has been placed in a capsule orbiting Earth and that slowly begins to redevelop its consciousness.

5. The American filmmaker Robert Altman pioneered the multiple converging storylines with ensemble cast films such as *Nashville* (1975) and *Short Cuts* (1993).

6. Undoubtedly one of the Velvet Underground's most famous songs, "Sweet Jane" did not appear until their last album, *Loaded* (1970), which was actually put together and released after the band's breakup.

7. The Corpsegrinder is most likely a reference to the schlocky Ted V. Mikels film *The Corpse Grinders* (1971), in which a cat-food company begins grinding up corpses from a cemetery and inadvertently creates a horde of bloodthirsty felines.

8. For a critical discussion of Survival Research Laboratories, see Scott Bukatman's *Terminal Identity.*

Chapter 4: Nodal Points

1. The three principal early dystopian novels are Yevgeny Zamyatin's *We* (1924), Aldous Huxley's *Brave New World* (1932), and George Orwell's *Nineteen Eighty-Four* (1949). However, as Fredric Jameson points out in *Archaeologies of the Future,* dystopian science fiction works began to predominate over utopian ones after the horrors of World War II. Thus, there was a rise in the number of dystopian novels: Ray Bradbury's *Fahrenheit 451* (1953), Pat Frank's *Alas, Babylon* (1959), Walter M. Miller, Jr.'s *A Canticle for Leibowitz* (1960), Kurt Vonnegut's "Harrison Bergeron" (1961), Anthony

Burgess's *A Clockwork Orange* (1962) and *The Wanting Seed* (1962), William F. Nolan and George Clayton Johnson's *Logan's Run* (1967), and Margaret Atwood's *The Handmaid's Tale* (1985), to name just a handful.

2. "Gunhead" is a reference to Masato Harada's anime mecha film *Gunhed* (1989). The same chapter in *Virtual Light* also references another Japanese cyberpunk film when it mentions "a chain of Japanese gyms named Body Hammer," a clear allusion to Shinya Tsukamoto's *Tetsuo II: Body Hammer* (1992).

3. *The Blob* also received its own body horror remake in 1988.

Chapter 5. Twenty-First-Century Singularities

1. A variety of fictional works have dealt with the 9/11 attacks, but Gibson's was part of the first wave of novels to directly address the attacks' impact. Other important 9/11 novels and stories from the same period include David Foster Wallace's "The Suffering Channel" (2004), Ian McEwan's *Saturday* (2005), Jonathan Safran Foer's *Extremely Loud and Incredibly Close* (2005), and Don DeLillo's *Falling Man* (2007).

2. A standard cliché of any supernatural investigation film, EVP usually involves using a tape recorder to capture any potential paranormal communications. It is believed that such recording devices can capture sounds not audible to human hearing.

Chapter 6: Engaging with Difference

1. The most famous science fiction example of this trend is James Cameron's *Avatar* (2009), which created an entirely new alien world for its audience and broke new ground in 3D-cinema technology.

2. On Christmas Eve 2004, Gibson made the story available without charge on his blog. My quotations derive from this uploaded version, so they feature no page numbers.

3. In Matt Groening's *Futurama* (1999–2013), Santa is a homicidal robot that invades houses via the chimney and slaughters anyone in sight.

4. The cyberpunk television miniseries *Wild Palms* (1993) concerns a future in which television begins to metamorphose thanks to virtual reality. Produced by director Oliver Stone, *Wild Palms* unfolded as a sci-fi drama with increasingly surrealistic subject matter reminiscent not just of cyberpunk but of David Lynch and Mark Frost's genre-shattering series *Twin Peaks* (1990–91). Gibson himself makes a cameo in the first episode of the series and contributed lyrics for a song called "Where the Holograms Go" to *The Wild Palms Reader*, an anthology of various writings and artwork that purport to be from the world of *Wild Palms*.

5. The Quicksilver Messenger Service proves apropos because it is a psychedelic rock jam band, similar to the Grateful Dead, from the mid-1960s that released songs that attempted to take listeners further and further out. Dougal seems to have gone so far out that he literally left his body behind.

6. Shonen Knife is a famous all-female Japanese punk band from the early '80s. Its debut album, *Burning Farm* (1983), exerted a major influence on the punk and alternative music scenes.

7. The original Dark Horse Comics *Aliens* (1988) series, released in the wake of *Aliens*' success, followed a similar plotline that focuses on Hicks and an adult Newt and serves as a sequel to Cameron's film. Written by Mark Verheiden with art by Mark A. Nelson, the original six-issue miniseries is collected in *Alien Omnibus Volume 1* from Dark Horse Comics.

8. Part of the alternative and New Wave musical movements of the 1980s, R.E.M. and New Order profoundly influenced the shape of how music developed in the 1980s and 1990s. "The One I Love" appeared on R.E.M.'s *Document* (1987), and "Bizarre Love Triangle" was on New Order's *Brotherhood* (1986).

9. Dolph Lundren also appears alongside the Belgian martial-arts practitioner and actor Jean-Claude Van Damme in Roland Emmerich's pseudo-cyberpunk film *Universal Soldier* (1992). Van Damme had already appeared in the cheesy cyberpunkish film *Cyborg,* directed by Albert Pyun, in 1989. Both films demonstrate how cyberpunk was appropriated and watered down into a cliché.

10. Henry Rollins was the singer for the highly influential hardcore punk band Black Flag, whose debut album, *Damaged* (1981), remains one of the most influential punk albums of all time.

11. Aside from collaborating with Gibson, Maddox is famous for his short story "Snake Eyes" (1986), which appeared in the *Mirrorshades* cyberpunk anthology, and he supposedly developed the idea of ICE that Gibson introduces in "Burning Chrome."

12. The oxymoronic name the Lone Gunmen refers to the Lone Gunman theory, which claims that Lee Harvey Oswald acted alone and was the sole assassin of John F. Kennedy. This theory has long been contested by conspiracy theorists.

13. The book in its original form is almost impossible to find. For the curious scholar, the best option is *The Agrippa Files* website hosted by UC Santa Barbara. A meticulous archive, the site offers not only complete images of the deluxe edition but also an emulation of the Agrippa program itself. Alan Liu, a professor of English at UC Santa Barbara, has served as the general editor and project leader for the archive.

BIBLIOGRAPHY

Works by William Gibson

NOVELS

Neuromancer. New York: Ace, 1984.
Count Zero. New York: Ace, 1986.
Mona Lisa Overdrive. New York: Bantam, 1988.
The Difference Engine. With Bruce Sterling. New York: Bantam Spectra, 1992.
Virtual Light. New York: Bantam, 1993.
Idoru. New York: Berkley, 1996.
All Tomorrow's Parties. New York: Ace, 1999.
Pattern Recognition. New York: Berkeley, 2003.
Spook Country. New York: G. P. Putnam's Sons, 2007.
Zero History. New York: G. P. Putnam's Sons, 2010.
The Peripheral. New York: G. P. Putnam's Sons, 2014.

COLLECTIONS

Burning Chrome. New York: HarperCollins, 1986.
Distrust That Particular Flavor. New York: G. P. Putnam's Sons, 2012.

SHORT STORIES (COLLECTED AND REPRINTED IN *BURNING CHROME*)

"Fragments of a Hologram Rose." *Unearth* 1.3 (Summer 1977): 72–7.
"The Belonging Kind." With John Shirley. *Shadows* 4. Ed. Charles L. Grant. Garden City: Doubleday, 1981. 49–64.
"Johnny Mnemonic." *Omni* 3.8 (1981): 104–19, 162–4.
"Burning Chrome." *Omni* 4.10 (1982): 72–7, 102–7.
"Red Star, Winter Orbit." With Bruce Sterling. *Omni* 5.10 (1983): 84–90, 112–5.
"New Rose Hotel." *Omni* 6.10 (1984): 46–9, 92–4.
"Dogfight." With Michael Swanwick. *Omni* 7.10 (1985): 44–6, 95–106.
"The Winter Market." *Vancouver Magazine* 18.11 (1985): 62–73, 108–14, 134–6.

SHORT STORIES (UNCOLLECTED)

"Academy Leader." *Cyberspace: First Steps.* Ed. Michael Benedikt. Cambridge: MIT P, 1991. 27–9.
"Cyber-Claus." *Washington Post Book World* 1 Dec. 1991. 14–5.
"Doing Television." *Tesseracts^3.* Ed. Jane Dorsey and Gerry Truscott. Victoria: Porcépic, 1990. 392–4.

"Dougal Discarnate." *Darwin's Bastards*. Ed. Zsuzi Gartner. Vancouver: Douglas & McIntyre, 2010. 231–41.

"Hippie Hat Brain Parasite." *Modern Stories* 1 (Apr. 1983). Rpt. in *Semiotext[e] SF*. Ed. Rudy Rucker, Peter Lamborn Wilson, and Robert Anton Wilson. New York: Semiotext[e], 1989. 108–12.

"Skinner's Room." *Visionary San Francisco*. Ed. Paolo Polledri. Munich: Prestal, 1990. 154–65. Rpt. in *After Yesterday's Crash: The Avant-Pop Anthology*. Ed. Larry McCaffery. New York: Penguin, 1995. 137–48.

"Thirteen Views of a Cardboard City." *New Worlds*. Ed. David Garnett. Clarkston: White Wolf, 1997. 338–49. Rpt. in *Rewired: The Post-Cyberpunk Anthology*. Ed. James Patrick Kelly and John Kessel. San Francisco: Tachyon, 2007. 119–228.

POETRY AND SONG LYRICS

Agrippa: A Book of the Dead. Artwork by Dennis Ashbaugh. New York: Kevin Bogos, 1992.

"Where the Holograms Go." *The Wild Palms Reader*. Ed. Roger Trilling and Stuart Swezey. New York: St. Martin's, 1993. 122.

SCREENPLAYS

Alien3 (1987; unpublished).

Johnny Mnemonic. New York: Ace, 1995.

"Kill Switch" With Tom Maddox. Dir. Rob Bowman. *The X-Files: Season 5*. 20th Century Fox, 1998. DVD.

"First Person Shooter." With Tom Maddox. Dir. Chris Carter. *The X-Files: Season 7*. 20th Century Fox, 2000. DVD.

SELECTED ESSAYS (COLLECTED IN *DISTRUST THAT PARTICULAR FLAVOR*)

"Disneyland with the Death Penalty." *Wired* 1.4 (1993): 51–114.

"My Obsession." *Wired* 7.1 (1999): 102–5, 156–58.

"Rocket Radio." *Rolling Stone* 15 June 1989: 84–87.

SELECTED INTERVIEWS (UNCOLLECTED)

Leonard, Andrew. "Nodal Point: Interview with William Gibson." *Salon.com*. 13 Feb. 2003. Web. 25 Mar. 2012.

Wallace-Wells, David. "The Art of Fiction No. 211: William Gibson." *Paris Review* 197 (Summer 2011): 104–49.

WEB SOURCES

"Source Code" (Blog). *William Gibson: The Official Website*. Author's Website, n.d. Web. 13 Nov. 2014.

Liu, Alan, ed. *The Agrippa Files*. U of California, Santa Barbara English Department, n.d. Web. 13 Nov. 2014.

Other Sources

Aguierre, Peio. "Semiotic Ghosts: Science Fiction and Historicism." *Afterfall: A Journal of Art, Context, and Enquiry* 28 (Autumn/Winter 2011): 124–34.

Asimov, Isaac. *Asimov on Science Fiction*. New York: Avon, 1982.

———. "The Bicentennial Man." *Robot Visions*. New York: Roc/Penguin, 1990. 245–90.
———. *The Caves of Steel*. New York: Bantam, 1953.
———. *I, Robot*. New York: Bantam, 1950.
———. *The Naked Sun*. New York: Bantam, 1957.
———. "Segregationist." *Robot Visions*. New York: Roc/Penguin, 1990. 312–18.
Atwood, Margaret. *The Handmaid's Tale*. New York: Anchor, 1986.
Bacigalupi, Paolo. *The Windup Girl*. San Francisco: Night Shade, 2009.
Baez, Joan. "Silver Dagger." *Joan Baez*. Vanguard Records, 1960. CD.
Ballard, J. G. *Concrete Island*. New York: Picador, 1973.
———. *Crash*. New York: Picador, 1973.
———. *High Rise*. London: HarperPerennial, 1975.
Balsamo, Anne. "Feminism for the Incurably Informed." *Postmodern Literary Theory: An Anthology*. Ed. Niall Lucy. Oxford: Blackwell, 2000.
Baudrillard, Jean. *Simulacra and Simulation*. Trans. Sheila Faria Glaser. Ann Arbor: U of Michigan P, 1981.
Baudrillard, Jean.*The Spirit of Terrorism and Other Essays*. Trans. Chris Turner. London: Verso, 2002.
Baudrillard, Jean.*Symbolic Exchange and Death*. Trans. Iain Hamilton Grant. London: Sage, 1976.
Bear, Greg. *Blood Music*. New York: Ace, 1985.
Bell, Daniel. *The Coming of the Post-Industrial Society: A Venture in Social Forecasting*. New York: Basic, 1973.
Bergson, Henri. *Matter and Memory*. Trans. N. M. Paul and W. S. Palmer. New York: Zone, 1896.
———. *Time and Free Will: An Essay on the Immediate Data of Consciousness*. Trans. F.L. Pogson. Mineola: Dover, 1913.
Berlant, Lauren. "Intuitionists: History and the Affective Event." *American Literary History* 20.4 (2008): 845–60.
Bester, Alfred. *The Demolished Man*. New York: Vintage, 1951.
———. *The Stars My Destination*. New York: Vintage, 1956.
Bigelow, Kathryn, dir. *Strange Days*. 20th Century Fox, 1995. DVD.
Black Flag. *Damaged*. Sst Records, 1981. CD.
Blake, Victoria, ed. *Cyberpunk: Stories of Hardware, Software, Wetware, Revolution, and Evolution*. Underland, 2013.
Bradbury, Ray. *Fahrenheit 451*. New York: Simon & Schuster, 1951.
Bredehoft, Thomas A. "The Gibson Continuum: Cyberspace and William Gibson's Mervyn Kihn Stories." *Science Fiction Studies* 22.2 (1995): 252–63.
Briggs, Robert. "The Future of Prediction: Speculating on William Gibson's Meta-science-fiction." *Textual Practice* 27.4 (2013): 671–93.
Brunner, John. *The Shockwave Rider*. New York: Del Rey, 1975.
Burgess, Anthony. *A Clockwork Orange*. New York: Norton, 1962.
———. *The Wanting Seed*. New York: Norton, 1962.
Burroughs, William S. *Blade Runner (a movie)*. Berkeley: Blue Wind, 1979.
———. *Naked Lunch*. New York: Grove, 1959.
———. *Nova Express*. New York: Grove, 1964.
———. *The Soft Machine*. New York: Grove, 1961.
———. *The Ticket That Exploded*. New York: Grove, 1962.

———. *The Wild Boys: A Book of the Dead*. New York: Grove, 1971.
Cadigan, Pat. *Mindplayers*. Toronto: Bantam, 1987.
———. *Synners*. New York: Bantam, 1991.
Calvino, Italo. *Invisible Cities*. Trans. William Weaver. San Diego: Harvest, 1972.
Cameron, James, dir. *Aliens*. 20th Century Fox, 1986. DVD.
———. *Avatar*. 20th Century Fox, 2009. Blu-Ray.
———. *The Terminator*. 20th Century Fox, 1984. DVD.
Camus, Albert. *The Myth of Sisyphus and Other Essays*. Trans. Justin O'Brien. New York: Vintage, 1955.
Carpenter, John, dir. *Escape from New York*. 20th Century Fox, 1981. DVD.
———. *The Thing*. Universal Pictures, 1982. DVD.
Chaykin, Howard. *American Flagg! Volume 1*. Berkeley: Image, 2009.
Cheang, Shu Lea. *I.K.U.* Eclectic, 2000. DVD.
Clarke, Arthur C. *2001: A Space Odyssey*. New York: Roc, 1968.
Clash, the. *The Clash*. Sony, 1977. CD.
———. *Give 'Em Enough Rope*. Sony, 1984. CD.
———. *London Calling*. Sony, 1980. CD.
———. *Sandinista!* Sony, 1981. CD.
Concannon, Kevin. "The Contemporary Space of the Border: Gloria Anzaldua's *Borderlands* and William Gibson's *Neuromancer*." *Textual Practice* 12.3 (1998): 429–42.
Cox, Alex, dir. *Repo Man*. Criterion Collection, 1984. Blu-Ray.
Cramer, Kathryn. "Hard Science Fiction." *The Cambridge Companion to Science Fiction*. Ed. Edward James and Farah Menlesohn. Cambridge: Cambridge UP, 2003. 186–96.
Cronenberg, David, dir. *The Brood*. MGM, 1979. DVD.
———. *Rabid*. Somerville House, 1976. DVD.
———. *Scanners*. Criterion, 1981. DVD.
———. *Shivers*. Image, 1975. DVD.
———. *Videodrome*. Criterion, 1983. DVD.
Csicsery-Ronay, Jr., Istvan. "Antimancer: Cybernetics and Art in Gibson's *Count Zero*." *Science Fiction Studies* 22.1 (1995): 63–86.
———. "The Sentimental Futurist: Cybernetics and Art in William Gibson's *Neuromancer*." *Critique* 33.3 (1992): 221–40.
Czarniawska, Barbara, and Eva Gustavsson. "The (D)evolution of the Cyberwoman?" *Organization* 15.5 (2008): 665–83.
Davidson, Cynthia. "Riviera's Golem, Haraway's Cyborg: Reading *Neuromancer* as Baudrillard's Simulation of Crisis." *Science Fiction Studies* 23.2 (1996): 188–98.
Debord, Guy. *The Society of the Spectacle*. Trans. Donald Nicholson Smith. New York: Zone Books, 1967.
De Certeau, Michel. *The Practice of Everyday Life*. Berkeley: U of California P, 1984.
Delany, Paul, ed. "'Hardly the Center of the World': Vancouver in William Gibson's 'The Winter Market.'" *Vancouver: Representing the Postmodern City*. Vancouver: Arsenal Pulp P, 1994. 179–192.
Delany, Samuel R. "Is Cyberpunk a Good or a Bad Thing?" *Mississippi Review* 16.2–3 (1988): 28–35.
Deleuze, Gilles. *Bergsonism*. Trans. Hugh Tomlinson and Barbara Habberjam. New York: Zone, 1966.
Deleuze, Gilles. *Foucault*. Trans. Seán Hand. Minneapolis: U of Minnesota P, 1986.

———. *Nietzsche and Philosophy*. Trans. Hugh Tomlinson. New York: Columbia UP, 1962.
———. "Postscript on Control Societies." *Negotiations, 1972–1990*. Trans. Martin Joughin. New York: Columbia UP, 1990. 177–82.
———. *Pure Immanence: Essays on A Life*. Trans. Anne Boyman. New York: Zone, 2001.
———. "What Is the Creative Act?" *Two Regimes of Madness: Texts and Interviews 1975–1995*. Ed. David Lapoujade. Trans. Ames Hodges and Mike Taormina. New York: Semiotext(e), 206. 312–24.
Deleuze, Gilles, and Félix Guattari. *Anti-Oedipus: Capitalism and Schizophrenia*. Trans. Robert Hurley, Mark Seem, and Helen R. Lane. Minneapolis: U of Minnesota P, 1972.
———. *A Thousand Plateaus: Capitalism and Schizophrenia*. Trans. Brian Massumi. Minneapolis: U of Minnesota P, 1980.
DeLillo, Don. *Falling Man*. New York: Scribner, 2007.
Dellinger, Paul. "William Gibson." *Guide to Literary Masters and Their Works*. Hackensack: Salem P, 2007. Web. 3 Nov. 2014.
Derrida, Jacques. *Dissemination*. Trans. Barbara Johnson. Chicago: U of Chicago P, 1972.
———. *Writing and Difference*. Trans. Alan Bass. Chicago: U of Chicago P, 1967.
Dick, Philip K. *Do Androids Dream of Electric Sheep?* New York: Del Rey, 1968.
———. *The Man in the High Castle*. New York: Vintage, 1962.
———. *VALIS*. New York: Vintage, 1981.
Doctorow, Cory. *Down and Out in the Magic Kingdom*. New York: Tor, 2003.
Dos Passos, John. *1919*. Boston: Mariner, 1932.
———. *The 42nd Parallel*. Boston: Mariner, 1930.
———. *The Big Money*. Boston: Mariner, 1933.
Easterbrook, Neil. "The Arc of Our Destruction: Reversal and Erasure in Cyberpunk." *Science Fiction Studies* 19.3 (1992): 378–94.
Ellison, Harlan. *I Have No Mouth & I Must Scream*. New York: Edgeworks Abbey, 1967.
Emmerich, Roland, dir. *Universal Soldier*. Lions Gates, 1992. DVD.
Fabijancic, Tony. "The Sadness Is in You: Memory in the Boxes of Joseph Cornell, William Gibson, and E. L. Doctorow." *Word & Image* 28.3 (2012): 233–42.
Fair, Benjamin. "Stepping Razor in Orbit: Postmodern Identity and Political Alternatives in William Gibson's *Neuromancer*." *Critique* 46.2 (2005): 92–103.
Farnell, Ross. "Posthuman Topologies: William Gibson's 'Architexture' in *Virtual Light* and *Idoru*." *Science Fiction Studies* 25.3 (1998): 459–80.
Feller, Thomas R. "William Gibson." *Magill's Survey of World Literature*. Revised Ed. Hackensack: Salem P, 2009. Web. 03 Nov. 2014.
Ferrara, Abel, dir. *Body Snatchers*. Warner Home Video, 1993. DVD.
———. *New Rose Hotel*. Santa Monica: Lions Gate, 1998. DVD.
Fincher, David, dir. *Alien*^{3}. 20th Century Fox, 1992. DVD.
Finney, Jack. *The Body Snatchers*. New York: Scribner, 1954.
Fisher, William. "Of Living Machines and Living-Machines: *Blade Runner* and the Terminal Genre." *New Literary History* 20.1 (1988): 187–98.
Foer, Jonathan Safran. *Extremely Loud and Incredibly Close*. Boston: Mariner, 2005.
Foucault, Michel. *Discipline and Punish: The Birth of the Prison*. Trans. Alan Sheridan. New York: Vintage, 1975.

———. *The Order of Things: An Archaeology of the Human Sciences*. New York: Vintage, 1966.
Frank, Pat. *Alas, Babylon*. New York: HarperPerennial, 1959.
Frentz, Thomas S. "Transcending Embodiment: Communication in the Posthuman Condition." *Southern Communication Journal* 79.1 (2014): 59–72.
Fukui, Shozin, dir. *964 Pinocchio*. Unearthed Films, 1991. DVD.
———. *Rubber's Lover*. Unearthed Films, 1996. DVD.
Futurama. Fox/Comedy Central, 1999-2013.
Geraci, Robert M. "Robots and the Sacred in Science and Science Fiction: Technological Implications of Artificial Intelligence." *Zygon* 42.4 (2007): 961–980.
Gernsback, Hugo. *Ralph 124C 41+: A Romance of the Year 2660*. Lincoln: U of Nebraska P, 1911.
Gillis, Stacy. "The (Post)Feminist Politics of Cyberpunk." *Gothic Studies* 9.2 (2007): 7–19.
Ginsberg, Allen. *Howl and Other Poems*. San Francisco: City Lights, 1956.
Golding, William. *The Lord of the Flies*. New York: Perigee, 1954.
Grace, Dominick M. "From *Videodrome* to *Virtual Light:* David Cronenberg and William Gibson." *Extrapolation* 44.3 (2003): 344–55.
Grant, Glenn. "Transcendence through *Detournement* in William Gibson's *Neuromancer*." *Science Fiction Studies* 17.1 (1990): 41–9.
Griffith, Mike. "Death of the Digital Messiah: Increased Complexity in Virtual Narratives." *Critical Insights: Technology and Humanity* (2012): 240–55.
Grimstad, Paul C. "Algorithm—Genre—*linguisterie:* Creative Distortion in *Count Zero* and *Nova Express*." *Journal of Modern Literature* 27.4 (2004): 82–92.
Guitiérrez-Jones, Carl. "Stealing Kinship: *Neuromancer* and Artificial Intelligence." *Science Fiction Studies* 41.1 (2014): 69–92.
Habermas, Jürgen. "Modernity versus Postmodernity." *New German Critique* 22 (1981): 3–14.
———. *The Philosophical Discourse of Modernity: Twelve Lectures*. Trans. Frederick G. Lawrence. Cambridge: MIT P, 1985.
Hammett, Dashiel. *Red Harvest*. New York: Vintage Crime/Black Lizard, 1929.
Hantke, Steffen. "Surgical Strikes and Prosthetic Warriors: The Soldier's Body in Contemporary Science Fiction." *Science Fiction Studies* 25.3 (1998): 495–509.
Harada, Masato, dir. *Gunhed*. Section 23, 1989. DVD.
Hardt, Michael, and Antonio Negri. *Empire*. Cambridge: Harvard UP, 2000.
———. *Multitude: War and Democracy in the Age of Empire*. New York: Penguin, 2004.
Hartmann, Doreen. "Space Construction as Cultural Practice: Reading William Gibson's *Neuromancer* with Respect to Postmodern Concepts of Space." *Spatial Practices: An Interdisciplinary Series in Cultural History* 9 (April 2009): 275–99.
Haslam, Jason. "Memory's Guilted Cage: Delany's *Dhalgren* and Gibson's *Pattern Recognition*." *English Studies in Canada* 32.1 (2006): 77–104.
Hayles, N. Katherine. "Computing the Human." *Theory, Culture, and Society* 22.1 (2005): 132–51.
———. *How We Became Posthuman: Virtual Bodies in Cybernetics, Literature, and Informatics*. Chicago: U of Chicago P, 1999.
Hayles, N. Katherine N. "Traumas of Code." *Critical Inquiry* 33.1 (2006): 136–57.
Heidegger, Martin. *Being and Time*. Trans. John Macquarrie and Edward Robinson. San Francisco: Harper & Row, 1927.

Heinlein, Robert. *The Puppet Masters*. New York: Del Rey, 1951.

Henthorne, Tom. *William Gibson: A Literary Companion*. Jefferson: McFarland, 2011.

Heuser, Sabine. "(En)gendering Artificial Intelligence in Cyberspace." *Yearbook of English Studies* 37.2 (2007): 129–45.

Hicks, Heather. "'Whatever it is That's She's Since Become': Writing Bodies of Text and Bodies of Women in James Tiptree, Jr.'s 'The Girl Who Was Plugged In' and William Gibson's 'The Winter Market.'" *Contemporary Literature* 37.1 (1996): 62–93.

Hirschbiegel, Oliver, dir. *The Invasion*. Warner, 2007. DVD.

Hodges, Mike, dir. *Flash Gordon*. Universal, 1980. DVD.

Hollinger, Veronica. "Cybernetic Deconstructions: Cyberpunk and Postmodernism." *Mosaic* 23 (Spring 1990): 29–44.

———. "Stories about the Future: From Patterns to Expectations in *Pattern Recognition*." *Science Fiction Studies* 33.3 (Fall 2006): 452–72.

Hooper, Tobe, dir. *Invaders from Mars*. MGM, 1986. DVD.

Horkheimer, Max, and Theodor W. Adorno. *Dialectic of Enlightenment: Philosophical Fragments*. Ed. Gunzelin Schmid Noerr. Trans. Edmund Jephcott. Stanford: Stanford UP, 1944.

Husserl, Edmund. *Cartesian Meditations: An Introduction to Phenomenology*. Trans. Dorion Cairns. Dordrecht: Kluwer Academic Publishers, 1931.

Hutcheon, Linda. *The Politics of Postmodernism*. London: Routledge, 1989.

Huxley, Aldous. *Brave New World*. New York: Perennial Classics, 1932.

Ilis, Florina. "The Science Fiction Phenomenon and the Faces of Time." Trans. Ágnes Korondi. *Philobiblon* 15 (2010): 143–60.

Jameson, Fredric. *Archaeologies of the Future: The Desire Called Utopia and Other Science Fictions*. London: Verso, 2005.

———. "Fear and Loathing in Globalization." *New Left Review* 23 (2003): 105–14. Rpt. in *Archaeologies of the Future: The Desire Called Utopia and Other Science Fictions*. London: Verso, 2005. 384–92.

———. *Postmodernism, or, the Cultural Logic of Late Capitalism*. Durham: Duke UP, 1991.

Jeunet, Jean-Pierre, dir. *Alien: Resurrection*. 20th Century Fox, 1997. DVD.

Jeunet, Jean-Pierre, and Marc Caro, dirs. *The City of Lost Children*. Sony, 1995. DVD.

Jodorowsky, Alejandro, and Moebius. *The Incal*. Paris: Humanoids, 2011.

Johnston, John. "*The Intuitionist* and *Pattern Recognition*: A Response to Lauren Berlant." *American Literary History* 20.4 (2008): 861–9.

Jones, Christine Kenyo. "SF and Romantic Biofictions: Aldiss, Gibson, Sterling, Powers." *Science Fiction Studies* 24.1 (1997): 47–56.

Jones, Gwyneth. "*Virtual Light*: A Shocking Dose of Comfort and Joy from William Gibson (Review)." *Deconstructing the Starships: Essays and Reviews*. Liverpool: Liverpool UP, 1999. 156–60.

Jonze, Spike, dir. *Her.* Warner, 2013. DVD.

Jung, Carl. *The Archetypes and the Collective Unconscious*. 2nd ed. Ed. and trans. Gerhard Adler and R. F. C. Hull. New York: Bollingen, 1959.

———. *Man and His Symbols*. New York: Anchor, 1964.

Kafka, Franz. "In the Penal Colony." *The Complete Stories*. Ed. Nahum N. Glatzer. New York: Shocken, 1919. 140–67.

———. "The Metamorphosis." *The Complete Stories*. Ed. Nahum N. Glatzer. New York: Shocken, 1915. 89–139.

———. *The Trial*. Trans. Willa Muir, Edwin Muir, and E. M. Butler. New York: Schocken, 1925.

Kant, Immanuel. *Critique of Pure Reason*. Trans. and ed. Paul Guyer and Allen W. Wood. Cambridge: Cambridge UP, 1781.

Kaufman, Philip, dir. *Invasion of the Body Snatchers*. 20th Century Fox, 1978. DVD.

Kelly, James Patrick, and John Kessel, ed. *Rewired: The Post-Cyberpunk Anthology*. San Francisco: Tachyon, 2007.

Kerouac, Jack. *Big Sur*. New York: Penguin, 1962.

———. *The Dharma Bums*. New York: Penguin, 1958.

———. *Desolation Angels*. New York: Riverhead, 1965.

———. *On the Road*. New York: Penguin, 1959.

———. *The Subterraneans*. New York: Penguin, 1958.

———. *Visions of Cody*. New York: Penguin, 1972.

Kessel, John. "The Humanist Manifesto." *Science Fiction Eye* 1.1 (1987): 52–6.

Kishiro, Yukito. *Battle Angel Alita*. San Francisco: Viz, 1990-1995.

Klein, Herbert. "From Romanticism to Virtual Reality: Charles Babbage, William Gibson, and the Construction of Cyberspace." *Interdisciplinary Humanities* 24.1 (2007): 36–50.

Knight, Damon. "Stranger Station." *In Deep*. New York: Berkley Medallion, 1956.

Konstantinou, Lee. "The Brand as Cognitive Map in William Gibson's *Pattern Recognition*." *Boundary 2* 36.2 (2009): 67–97.

Kroker, Arthur, and David Cook. *The Postmodern Scence: Excremental Culture and Hyper-Aesthetics*. New York: St. Martin's, 1986.

Kroker, Arthur, and Marilouise Kroker, ed. "Theses on the Disappearing Body in the Hyper-Modern Condition." *Body Invaders: Panic Sex in America*. Montreal: New World Perspectives, 1987.

Kubrick, Stanley, dir. *2001: A Space Odyssey*. Warner, 1968. DVD.

———. *A Clockwork Orange*. Warner, 1972. DVD.

Kurosawa, Akira, dir. *Yojimbo*. Criterion Collection, 1961. DVD.

Lacan, Jacques. *The Seminar of Jacques Lacan Book I: Freud's Papers on Technique 1953–1954*. Ed. Jacques-Alain Miller. Trans. John Forrester. New York and London: Norton, 1975.

———. *The Seminar of Jacques Lacan Book II: The Ego in Freud's Theory and in the Technique of Psychoanalysis, 1954–1955*. Ed. Jacques-Alain Miller. Trans. Sylvania Tomaselli. New York and London: Norton, 1988.

Lang, Fritz, dir. *Metropolis*. Kino, 1927. DVD.

Latham, Rob. "Cyberpunk = Gibson = *Neuromancer* (Review)." *Science Fiction Studies* 20.2 (1993): 266–72.

Leandro, Tim, dir. *Tomorrow Calling*. Film4, 1993. Film.

Le Guin, Ursula K. *The Dispossessed*. New York : HarperPerennial, 1974.

———. Ursula K. *The Lathe of Heaven*. New York: Scribner, 1971.

———. Ursula K. *The Left Hand of Darkness*. New York: Ace, 1969.

———. Ursula K. *A Wizard of Earthsea*. New York: Bantam, 1968.

Lem, Stanislaw. Solaris. San Diego: Harvest, 1961.

Leone, Sergio, dir. *Fistful of Dollars*. *The Sergio Leone Anthology*. MGM, 1964. DVD.

Lethem, Jonathan. *Gun, with Occasional Music*. Orlando: Harvest, 1994.
Levinas, Emmanuel. *Totality and Infinity: An Essay on Exteriority*. Trans. Alphonso Lingis. Pittsburgh: Duquesne UP, 1961.
Lévi-Strauss, Claude. *The Savage Mind*. Chicago: U of Chicago P, 1962.
Leyner, Mark. *My Cousin, My Gastroenterologist*. New York: Harmony, 1990.
Lindberg, Kathryne V. "Prosthetic Mnemonics and Prophylactic Politics: William Gibson among the Subjectivity Mechanisms." *Boundary 2* 23.2 (1996): 47–83.
Link, Alex. "Global War, Global Capital, and the Work of Art in William Gibson's *Pattern Recognition*." *Contemporary Literature* 49.2 (2008): 209–31.
Lisberger, Steven, dir. *Tron*. Beuna Vista/Disney, 1982. DVD.
Longo, Robert, dir. *Johnny Mnemonic*. Sony, 1995. DVD.
Lucas, George, dir. *Star Wars, Episode IV: A New Hope*. 20th Century Fox, 1977. DVD.
Lyotard, François. *The Postmodern Condition: A Report on Knowledge*. Trans. Geoff Bennington and Brian Massumi. Minneapolis: U of Minnesota P, 1979.
Marx, John. "The Feminization of Globalization." *Cultural Critique* 63 (Spring 2006): 1–32.
McAvan, Em. "Paranoia in *Spook Country:* William Gibson and the Technological Sublime of the War on Terror." *Journal of Postcolonial Writing* 46.3–4 (2010): 405–13.
McCaffery, Larry, ed. *After Yesterday's Crash: The Avant-Pop Anthology*. New York: Penguin, 1995.
———. *Storming the Reality Studio: A Casebook of Cyberpunk and Postmodern Fiction*. Durham: Duke UP, 1991.
McElroy, Joseph. *Plus*. New York: Alfred A. Knopf, 1976.
McEwan, Ian. *Saturday*. New York: Anchor, 2005.
McHale, Brian. "Elements of a Poetics of Cyberpunk." *Critique* 33.3 (1992): 149–175.
———. *Postmodernist Fiction*. London: Routledge, 1987.
McLuhan, Marshall, and Quentin Fiore. *The Medium Is the Massage: An Inventory of Effects*. Corte Madera: Gingko, 1967.
Mead, David G. "Technological Transfiguration in William Gibson's Sprawl Novels: *Neuromancer*, *Count Zero*, and *Mona Lisa Overdrive*." *Extrapolation* 32.4 (1991): 350–60.
Mehan, Uppinder. "Postcolonial Science, Cyberpunk, and *The Calcutta Chromosome*." *Intertexts* 16.2 (2012): 1–12.
Menzies, William Cameron, dir. *Invaders from Mars*. Image Entertainment, 1953. DVD.
———. *Things to Come*. Legend, 1936. DVD.
Miéville, China. *Perdido Street Station*. New York: Ballantine, 2000.
Miike, Takashi, dir. *Full Metal Yakuza*. Arts Magix, 1997. DVD.
Mikels, Ted. V., dir. *The Corpse Grinders*. Image, 1971. DVD.
Miller, Jr., Walter M. *A Canticle for Leibowitz*. New York: HarperCollins, 1959.
Miyazaki, Hayao, dir. *Castle in the Sky*. Disney, 1986. DVD.
———. dir. *Howl's Moving Castle*. Disney, 2004. DVD.
Moreno, Pepe. *Batman: Digital Justice*. Burbank: DC, 1995.
Murphy, Geoff, dir. *Freejack*. Warner, 1992. DVD.
Murphy, Graham. "Post/Humanity and the Interstitial: A Glorification of Possibility in Gibson's Bridge Sequence." *Science Fiction Studies* 30.1 (2003): 72–90.
———. "Stray Penetration and Heteronormative Systems Crash: Queering Gibson." *Queer Universes: Sexualities in Science Fiction*. Ed. Wendy Gay Pearson, Veronica Hollinger, and Joan Gordon. Liverpool: Liverpool UP, 2010. 121–38.

Myers, Tony. "The Postmodern Imaginary in William Gibson's *Neuromancer*." *Modern Fiction Studies* 47.4 (2001): 887–909.

Nabokov, Vladimir. *Ada, or Ardor: A Family Chronicle*. New York: Vintage, 1969.

Nayar, Pramod K. "Wetware Fiction: Cyberpunk and the Ideologies of Posthuman Bodies." *The ICFAI Journal of English Studies* 3.2 (2008): 31–40.

Nazare, Joe. "Marlowe in Mirrorshades: The Cyberpunk (Re-)Vision of Chandler." *Studies in the Novel* 35.3 (2003): 383–404.

New Order. *Brotherhood*. Rhino, 1986. CD.

Nietzsche, Friedrich. *Thus Spoke Zarathustra: A Book for None and All*. Trans. Walter Kaufmann. New York: Penguin, 1883–92.

Nishimura, Yoshihiro, dir. *Tokyo Gore Police*. Tokyo Shock, 2008. DVD.

Nolan, William F., and George Clayton Johnson. *Logan's Run*. New York: Bantam, 1967.

O'Barr, James. The *Crow*. New York: Gallery Books, 1989.

Olivier, Bert. "Literature after Ranciére: Ishiguro's *When We Were Orphans* and Gibson's *Neuromancer*." *Journal of Literary Studies* 29.3 (2013): 23–45.

Olsen, Lance. "The Shadow of Spirit in William Gibson's Matrix Trilogy." *Extrapolation* 32.3 (1991): 278–89.

———. "Virtual Termites: A Hypotextual Technomutant Explo(it)ration of William Gibson and the Electronic Beyond(s)." *Style* 29.2 (1995): 287–313.

Orwell, George. *Nineteen Eighty-Four*. New York: Penguin, 1949.

Oshii, Mamoru, dir. *Ghost in the Shell*. Manga, 1995. DVD.

Otomo, Katsuhiro. *Akira*. 6 vols. Trans. Yoko Umezawa, Jo Duffy, and Dark Horse Comics. Milwaukee: Dark Horse Comics, 1985–86.

Otomo, Katsuhiro, dir. *Akira*. Funimation, 1988. DVD.

———. *Steamboy*. Sony, 2004. DVD.

Pal, George, dir. *The War of the Worlds*. Paramount, 1953. DVD.

Palmer, Christopher. "*Mona Lisa Overdrive* and the Prosthetic." *Science Fiction Studies* 31.2 (2004): 227–43.

———. "*Pattern Recognition*: 'None of What We Do Here is Ever Really Private." *Science Fiction Studies* 33.3 (2006): 473–82.

Pardzik, Ralph. "The Posthuman Future of Man: Anthropocentrism and the Other of Technology in Anglo-American Science Fiction." *Utopian Studies* 23.1 (2012): 142–61.

Paroush, David. "Cybernauts in Cyberspace: William Gibson's *Neuromancer*." *Aliens: The Anthropology of Science Fiction*. Ed. George C. Slusser and Eric Rabkin. Carbondale: Southern Illinois UP, 1987. 168–78.

———. "Prigogine, Chaos, and Contemporary Science Fiction." *Science Fiction Studies* 18.3 (1991): 367–86.

———. *The Soft Machine: Cybernetic Fiction*. New York: Methuen, 1985.

Paulk, Charles. "Post-National Cool: William Gibson's Japan." *Science Fiction Studies* 38.3 (2011): 478–500.

Plato. *Phaedrus*. *Plato: The Complete Dialogues Including the Letters*. Ed. Edith Hamilton and Huntington Cairns. Princeton: Princeton UP, 1961. 475–525.

Pohl, Frederick. *Gateway*. New York: Ballantine, 1976.

Proyas, Alex, dir. *The Crow*. Miramax/Lionsgate, 1994. DVD.

———. *Dark City*. New Line, 1998. DVD.

Punday, Daniel. "The Narrative Construction of Cyberspace: Reading *Neuromancer*, Reading Cyberspace Debates." *College English* 63.2 (2000): 194–213.

Pynchon, Thomas. *The Crying of Lot 49*. New York: HarperPerennial, 1965.

———. *Gravity's Rainbow*. New York: Penguin, 1973.

Pyun, Albert, dir. *Cyborg*. MGM, 1989. DVD.

Ramones, the. *Leave Home*. Rhino, 1977. CD.

———. *Ramones*. Rhino, 1976. CD.

———. *Road to Ruin*. Rhino, 1978. CD.

———. *Rocket to Russia*. Rhino, 19

Rapatzikou, Tatiani G. "Authorial Identity in the Era of Electronic Technologies." *Authorship in Context: From the Theoretical to the Material*. Eds. Kyriaki Hadjiafxendi and Polina Mackay. New York: Palgrave Macmillan, 2007. 145–62.

Renegar, Valerie R., and George N. Dionisopoulos. "The Dream of a Cyberpunk Future? Entelechy, Dialectical Tension, and the Comic Corrective in William Gibson's *Neuromancer*." *Southern Communication Journal* 76.4 (2011): 323–41.

Ross, Andrew. "Getting Out of the Gernsback Continuum." *Critical Inquiry* 17 (Winter 1991): 411–33.

Rucker, Rudy. *The Ware Tetralogy*. Gaithersburg: Prime, 2010.

Saenz, Mike. *Iron Man: Crash*. New York: Marvel/Epic, 1991.

Sartre, Jean-Paul. *Being and Nothingness: A Phenomenological Essay on Ontology*. Trans. Hazel E. Barnes. New York: Washington Square P, 1943.

———. *Existentialism Is a Humanism*. Trans. Carol Macomber. New Haven: Yale UP, 2007.

Schroeder, Randy. "Determinacy, Indeterminacy, and the Romantic in William Gibson." *Science Fiction Studies* 21.2 (1994): 155–63.

Schroeder, Randy. "Neu-Criticizing William Gibson." *Extrapolation* 35.4 (1994): 330–41.

Schmitt, Ronald. "Mythology and Technology: The Novels of William Gibson." *Extrapolation* 34.1 (1993): 64–78.

Scott, Ridley, dir. *Alien*. 20th Century Fox, 1979. DVD.

———. *Prometheus*. 20th Century Fox, 2012. DVD.

Sex Pistols, the. *Never Mind the Bollocks, Here's the Sex Pistols*. Warner Bros., 1977. CD.

Shiner, Lewis. *Frontera*. Burton: Subterranean, 1984.

Shirley, John. *A Song Called Youth*. Gaithersburg: Prime, 2012.

Shirley, John. "Wolves of the Plateau." *Storming the Reality Studio: A Casebook of Cyberpunk and Postmodern Fiction*. Ed. Larry McCaffrey. Durham: Duke UP, 1991. 139–53.

Shirow, Masamune. *Ghost in the Shell*. Trans. Frederick Schodt and Toren Smith. Milwaukee: Dark Horse Comics, 1989-1990.

Shonen Knife. *Burning Farm*. Oglio, 1983. CD.

Siegel, Don, dir. *Invasion of the Body Snatchers*. Olive Films, 1956. DVD.

Slotkin, Joel Elliot. "Haunted Infocosms and Prosthetic Gods: Gibsonian Cyberpsace and Renaissance Arts of Memory." *The Journal of Popular Culture* 45.4 (2012): 862–82. Smith, Patti. *Easter*. Arista, 1978. CD.

———. *Horses*. Arista, 1975. CD.

Sonic Youth. *Daydream Nation*. Geffen Records, 1988. CD.

Spencer, Nicolas. "Rethinking Ambivalence: Technopolitics and the Luddites in William Gibson's and Bruce Sterling's *The Difference Engine*." *Contemporary Literature* 40.3 (1999): 403–29.

Sponsler, Claire. "Cyberpunk and the Dilemmas of Postmodern Narrative: The Example of William Gibson." *Contemporary Literature* 33.4 (1992): 625–644.

Stanley, Richard, dir. *Hardware*. Severin/ADA, 1990. DVD.

Stephenson, Neal. *Cryptonomicon*. New York: Harper/Perennial, 1999.

———. *The Diamond Age: Or, a Young Lady's Illustrated Primer*. New York: Bantam, 1995.

———. *Snow Crash*. New York: Bantam, 1992.

Sterling, Bruce. *The Artificial Kid*. San Francisco: Hardwired, 1980.

———. *Involution Ocean*. New York: Jove/HBJ, 1977.

———. *Islands in the Net*. New York: Ace, 1988.

———. Preface. *Burning Chrome*. New York: Harp erCollins, 1986. xi-xiv.

———. *Schismatrix Plus*. New York: Ace, 1996.

Sterling, Bruce, ed. *Mirrorshades: The Cyberpunk Anthology*. New York: Ace Books, 1986.

Stevens, Tyler. "'Sinister Fruitiness': *Neuromancer,* Internet Sexuality, and the Turing Test." *Studies in the Novel* 28.3 (1996): 414–33.

Stooges, the. *Fun House*. Elektra, 1970. CD.

———. *Raw Power*. Sony Legacy, 1973. CD.

———. *The Stooges*. Elektra/Ada, 1969. CD.

Strombeck, Andrew. "The Network and the Archive: The Specter of Imperial Management in William Gibson's *Neuromancer*." *Science Fiction Studies* 37.2 (2010): 275–91.

Stross, Charles. *Accelerando*. New York: Ace, 2005.

———. *Saturn's Children*. New York: Ace, 2008.

———. *Singularity Sky*. New York: Ace, 2003.

Strugatsky, Boris, and Arkady Strugatsky. *Roadside Picnic*. London: Victor Gollancz, 1971.

Suicidal Tendencies. *Join the Army*. Caroline, 1987. CD.

Sussman, Herbert. "Cyberpunk Meets Charles Babbage: *The Difference Engine* as Alternative Victorian History." *Victorian Studies* 38.1 (1994): 1–23.

Swanwick, Michael. *Vacuum Flowers*. New York: Ace, 1987.

Tandt, Christophe Den. "Cyberpunk as Naturalist Science Fiction." *Studies in American Naturalism* 8.1 (2013): 93–108.

Tarkovsky, Andrei, dir. *Solaris*. Criterion, 1972. DVD.

———. *Stalker*. Kino, 1979. DVD.

Tatsumi, Takauki. "Comparative Metafiction: Somewhere Between Ideology and Rhetoric." *Critique* 39.1 (1997): 2–17.

Tiptree, Jr., James L. "And I Awoke and Found Me Here on the Cold Hill's Side." *Her Smoke Rose Up Forever*. San Francisco: Tachyon, 1973. 33–41.

———. "The Girl Who Was Plugged In." *Her Smoke Rose Up Forever*. San Francisco: Tachyon, 1973. 43–78.

Tobeck, Janine. "Discretionary Subjects: Decision and Participation in William Gibson's Fiction." *Modern Fiction Studies* 56.2 (2010): 378–400.

Toffler, Alvin. *Future Shock*. New York: Bantam, 1970.

Tomberg, Jaak. "On the 'Double Vision' of Realism and SF Estrangement in William Gibson's *Bigend Trilogy*." *Science Fiction Studies* 40.2 (2013): 263–285.

Trumbull, Douglas, dir. *Silent Running*. Universal, 1972. DVD.

———, *Brainstorm*. Warner, 1983. DVD.

Tsukamoto, Shinya, dir. *Tetsuo: The Bullet Man*. MPI, 2010. DVD.
———. dir. *Tetsuo: The Iron Man*. Tartan Asian Extreme, 1989. DVD.
———. dir. *Tetsuo II: Body Hammer*. Manga, 1992. DVD.
U2. *Zooropa*. Island, 1993. CD.
Velvet Underground, the. *Loaded*. Warner, 1970. CD.
———, *The Velvet Underground & Nico*. Polydor, 1967. CD.
Verheiden, Mark, and Mark A. Nelson. *Aliens Omnibus Volume 1*. Milwaukee: Dark Horse Books, 2007.
Verhoeven, Paul, dir. *Robocop*. Orion, 1987. DVD.
Virilio, Paul. *Ground Zero*. Trans. Chris Turner. London: Verso, 2002.
———, *The Vision Machine*. Trans. Julie Rose. Bloomington: Indiana UP, 1988.
Vonnegut, Kurt. "Harrison Bergeron." *Welcome to the Monkey House*. New York: Delta, 1968. 7–14.
Wackowski, Andy, and Lana Wachowski, dirs. *The Matrix*. Warner, 2001. DVD.
———. dirs. *The Matrix Reloaded*. Warner, 2003. DVD.
———. dirs. *The Matrix Revolutions*. Warner, 2003. DVD.
Wahl, Wendy. "Bodies and Technologies: Dora, *Neuromancer*, and Strategies of Resistance." *Postmodern Culture* 3.2 (1992): 1–9.
Wallace, David Foster. "The Suffering Channel." *Oblivion*. New York: Black Bay, 2004. 238–329.
Wegner, Leonard. "Recognizing the Patterns." *New Literary History: A Journal of Theory and Interpretation* 38.1 (Winter 2007): 183–200.
Weiner, Norbert. *Cybernetics: Or Control and Communication in the Animal and the Machine*. 2nd ed. Cambridge: MIT P, 1948.
Wells, H. G. *The Shape of Things to Come*. New York: Penguin, 2006.
———, *The Work, Wealth and Happiness of Mankind*. London: William Heinemann, 1932.
Westfahl, Gary. "'The Gernsback Continuum': William Gibson in the Context of Science Fiction." *Fiction 2000: Cyberpunk and the Future of Narrative*. Ed. George Slusser and Tom Shippey. Athens: U of Georgia P, 1993. 88–108.
When, Jin. "Race and Redemption: Impure Spiritualities in Pynchon's *Vineland* and Gibson's *Pattern Recognition*." *Critique* 54.3 (2013): 238–53.
Wild Palms. MGM, 1993. DVD.
Worthington, Marjorie. "Bodies tThat Natter: Virtual Translations and Transmissions of the Physical." *Critique: Studies in Contemporary Fiction* 43.2 (2002): 192–208.
Yamaguchi, Yūdai, and Jun'ichi Yamamoto, dirs. *Meatball Machine*. Danger After Dark, 2005. DVD.
Yeaworth, Jr., Irvin S., dir. The Blob. Criterion Collection, 1958. DVD
Yoke, Carl B., and Carol L. Robinson, eds. *The Cultural Influences of William Gibson, the Father of Cyberpunk Science Fiction: Critical and Interpretative Essays*. Lewiston: Mellen, 2007.
Yu, Timothy. "Oriental Cities, Postmodern Futures: *Naked Lunch, Blade Runner,* and *Neuromancer*." *MELUS* 33.4 (2008): 45–71.
Zamyatin, Yevgeny. *We*. 1924. Trans. Clarence Brown. New York: Penguin, 1993.
Žižek, Slavoj. *Welcome to the Desert of the Real: Five Essays on September 11 and Related Dates*. London: Verso, 2002.
Zwaan, Victoria de. "Rethinking the Slipstream: Kathy Acker Reads *Neuromancer*." *Science Fiction Studies* 24.3 (1997): 459–70.

INDEX

All unattributed titles are by Erdrich.